LUCKY DEVIL

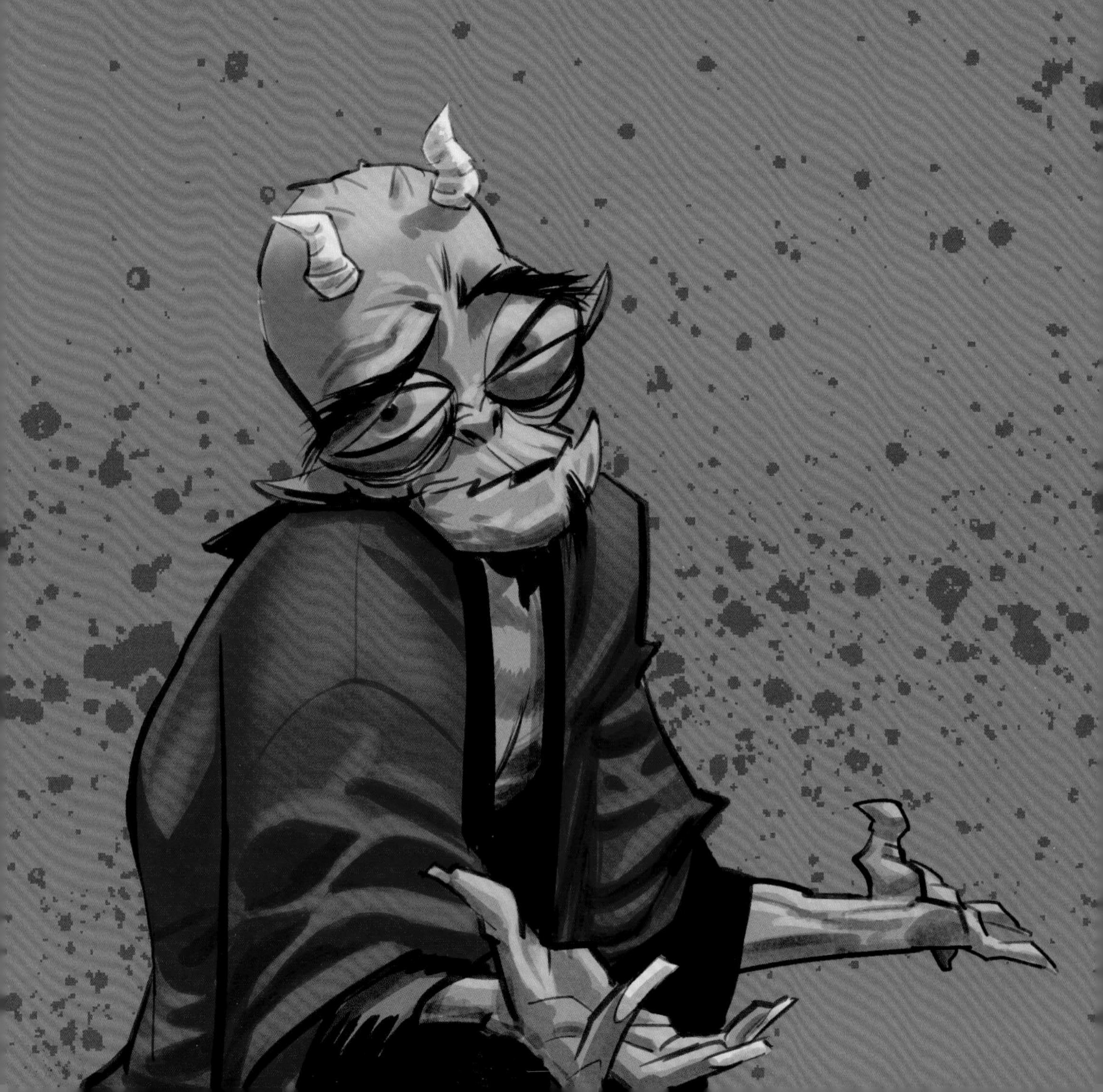

LUCKY DEVIL ™

SCRIPT
CULLEN BUNN

ART
FRAN GALÁN

LETTERS
EL TORRES

COVER
FRAN GALÁN

LUCKY DEVIL CREATED BY
CULLEN BUNN AND FRAN GALÁN

DARK HORSE BOOKS

PRESIDENT & PUBLISHER
MIKE RICHARDSON

EDITOR
DANIEL CHABON

ASSISTANT EDITORS
CHUCK HOWITT AND **KONNER KNUDSEN**

DESIGNER
MAY HIJIKURO

DIGITAL ART TECHNICIAN
ALLYSON HALLER

NEIL HANKERSON Executive Vice President • TOM WEDDLE Chief Financial Officer • DALE LaFOUNTAIN Chief Information Officer • TIM WIESCH Vice President of Licensing • MATT PARKINSON Vice President of Marketing • VANESSA TODD-HOLMES Vice President of Production and Scheduling • MARK BERNARDI Vice President of Book Trade and Digital Sales • RANDY LAHRMAN Vice President of Product Development • KEN LIZZI General Counsel • DAVE MARSHALL Editor in Chief • DAVEY ESTRADA Editorial Director • CHRIS WARNER Senior Books Editor • CARY GRAZZINI Director of Specialty Projects • LIA RIBACCHI Art Director • MATT DRYER Director of Digital Art and Prepress • MICHAEL GOMBOS Senior Director of Licensed Publications • KARI YADRO Director of Custom Programs • KARI TORSON Director of International Licensing

Collects issues #1–#4 of the Dark Horse Comics series *Lucky Devil*.

Published by Dark Horse Books
A division of Dark Horse Comics LLC
10956 SE Main Street, Milwaukie, OR 97222

DarkHorse.com | To find a comics shop in your area, visit comicshoplocator.com

First edition: February 2022
Ebook ISBN 978-1-50672-200-9 | Trade Paperback ISBN 978-1-50672-199-6

10 9 8 7 6 5 4 3 2 1
Printed in China

Library of Congress Cataloging-in-Publication Data

Names: Bunn, Cullen, author. | Galán, Fran, artist. | El Torres, 1972- letterer.
Title: Lucky devil / script, Cullen Bunn ; art, Fran Galán ; letters, El Torres.
Description: First edition. | Milwaukie, OR : Dark Horse Books, 2022. | "Lucky Devil created by Cullen Bunn and Fran Galán" | Summary: "A down-on-his-luck schlub is possessed by a malevolent demon. Just when he thinks things can't get worse, the exorcism goes wrong and he finds that somehow he's retained all of the entity's supernatural gifts"-- Provided by publisher.
Identifiers: LCCN 2021041715 (print) | LCCN 2021041716 (ebook) | ISBN 9781506721996 (trade paperback) | ISBN 9781506722009 (ebook)
Subjects: LCGFT: Horror comics.
Classification: LCC PN6728.L796 B66 2022 (print) | LCC PN6728.L796 (ebook) | DDC 741.5/973--dc23
LC record available at https://lccn.loc.gov/2021041715
LC ebook record available at https://lccn.loc.gov/2021041716

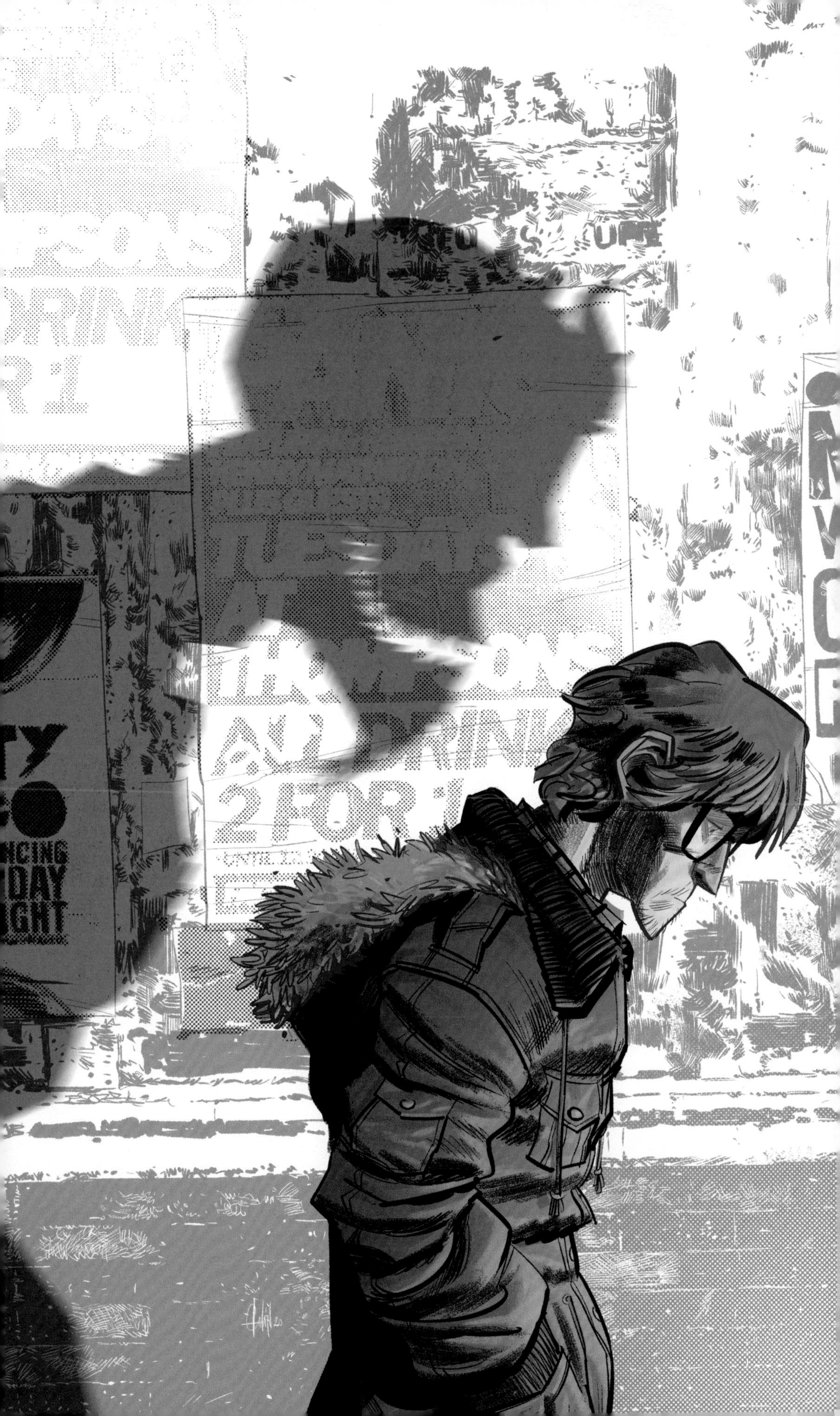
NCING
IDAY
IGHT

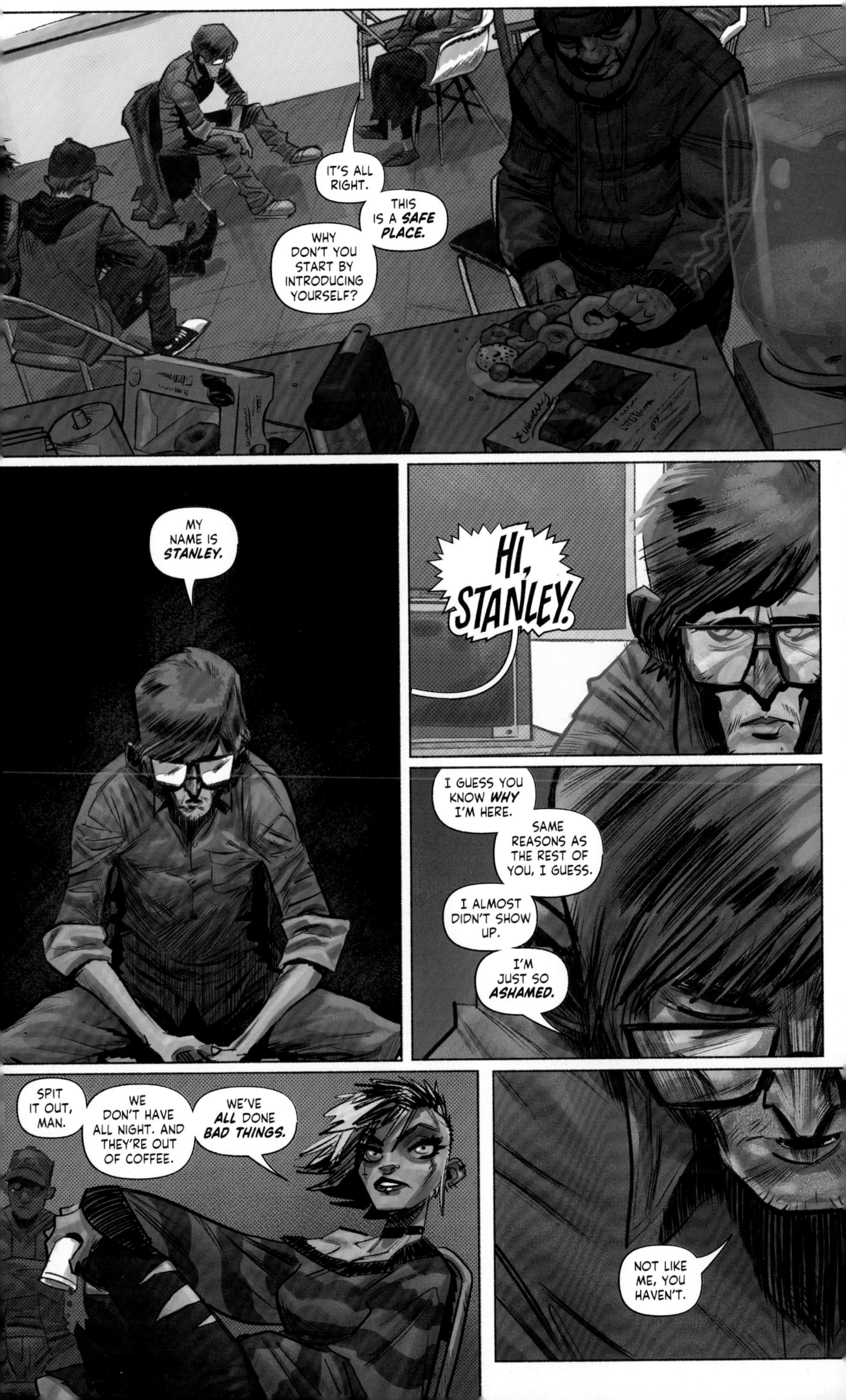
IT'S ALL RIGHT.
THIS IS A SAFE PLACE.
WHY DON'T YOU START BY INTRODUCING YOURSELF?
MY NAME IS STANLEY.
HI, STANLEY.
I GUESS YOU KNOW WHY I'M HERE.
SAME REASONS AS THE REST OF YOU, I GUESS.
I ALMOST DIDN'T SHOW UP.
I'M JUST SO ASHAMED.
SPIT IT OUT, MAN.
WE DON'T HAVE ALL NIGHT. AND THEY'RE OUT OF COFFEE.
WE'VE ALL DONE BAD THINGS.
NOT LIKE ME, YOU HAVEN'T.

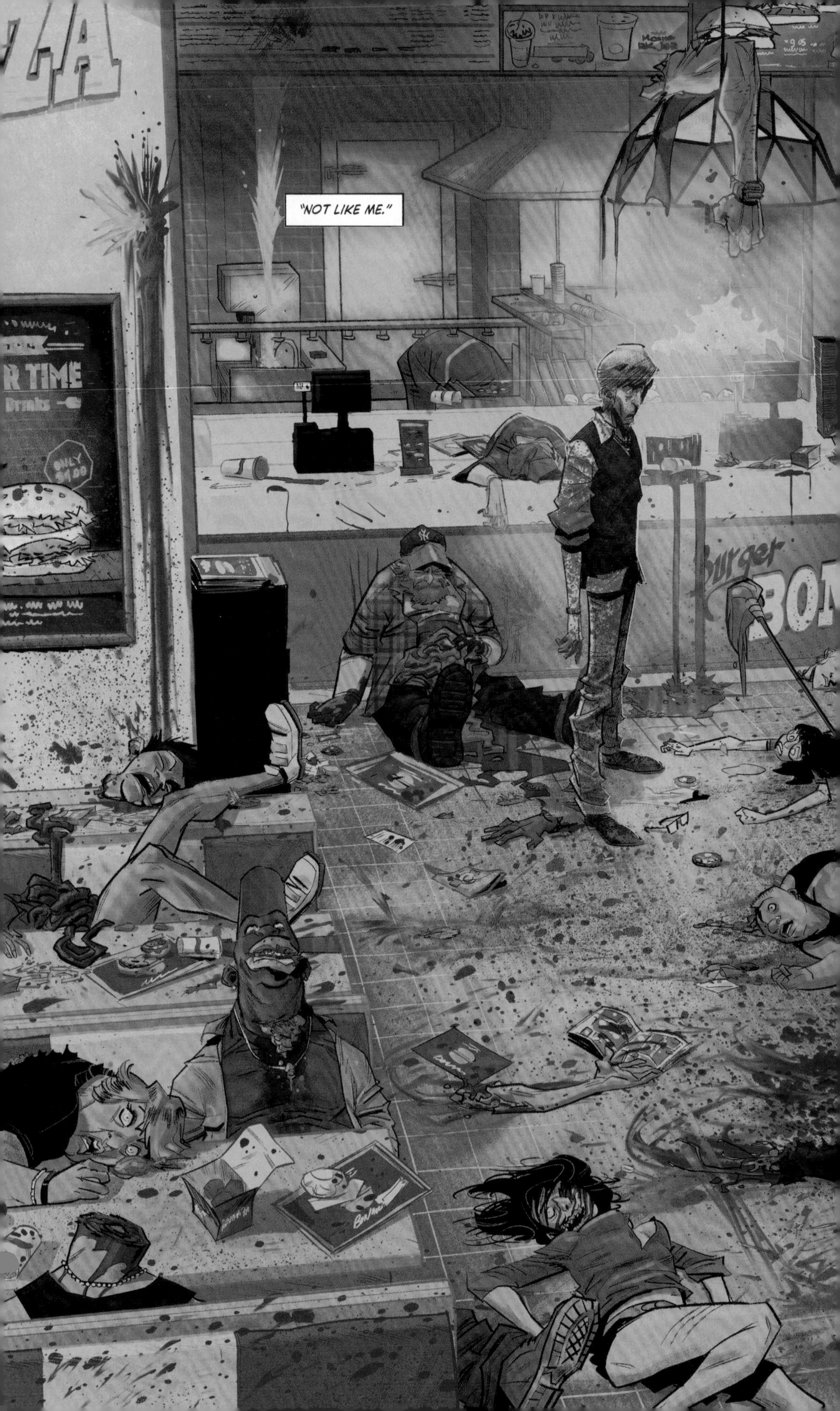
"NOT LIKE ME."
R TIME
Drinks
ONLY $1.00
Burger
BOM

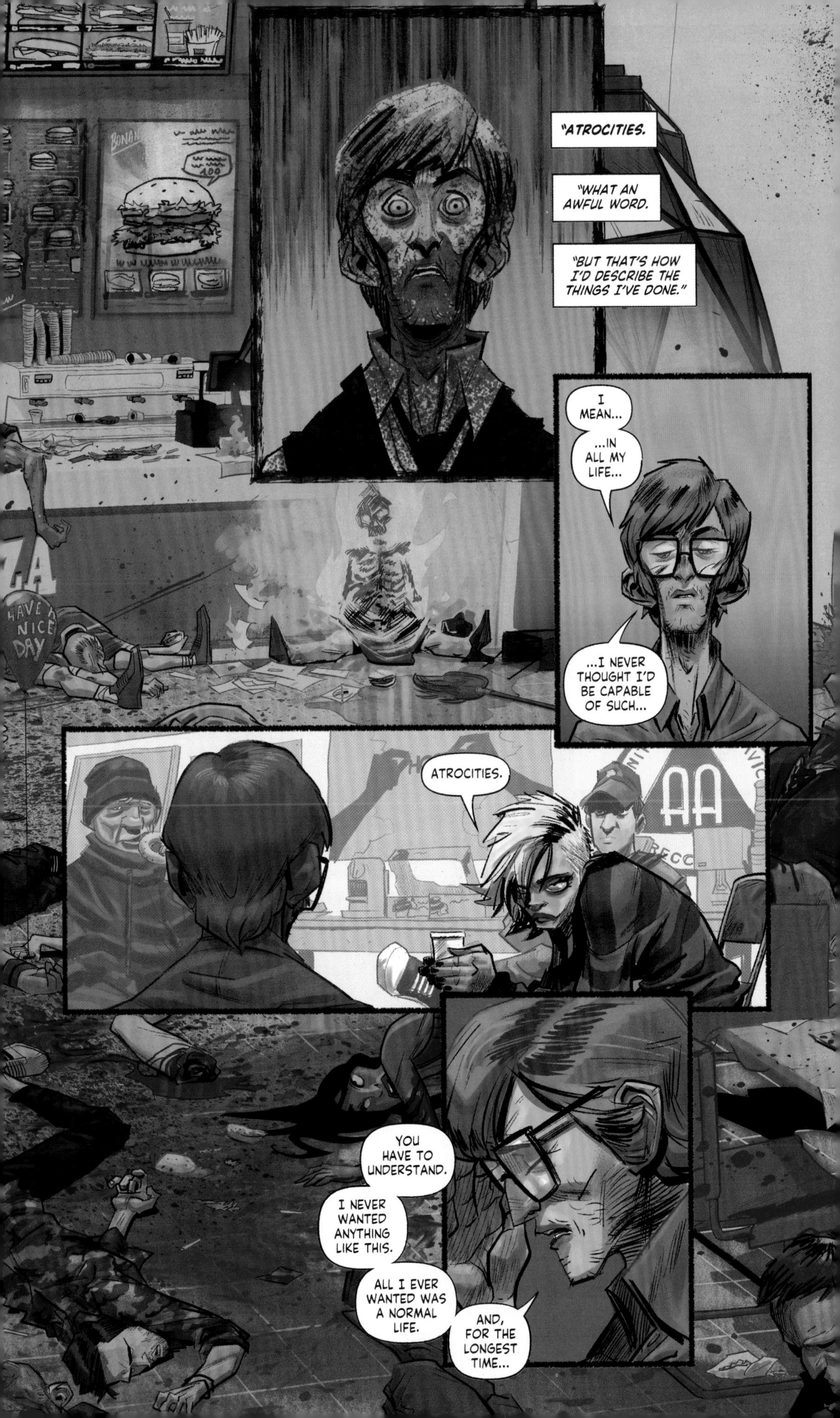

"ATROCITIES.
"WHAT AN AWFUL WORD.
"BUT THAT'S HOW I'D DESCRIBE THE THINGS I'VE DONE."
I MEAN...
...IN ALL MY LIFE...
...I NEVER THOUGHT I'D BE CAPABLE OF SUCH...
ATROCITIES.
HAVE A NICE DAY
YOU HAVE TO UNDERSTAND.
I NEVER WANTED ANYTHING LIKE THIS.
ALL I EVER WANTED WAS A NORMAL LIFE.
AND, FOR THE LONGEST TIME...

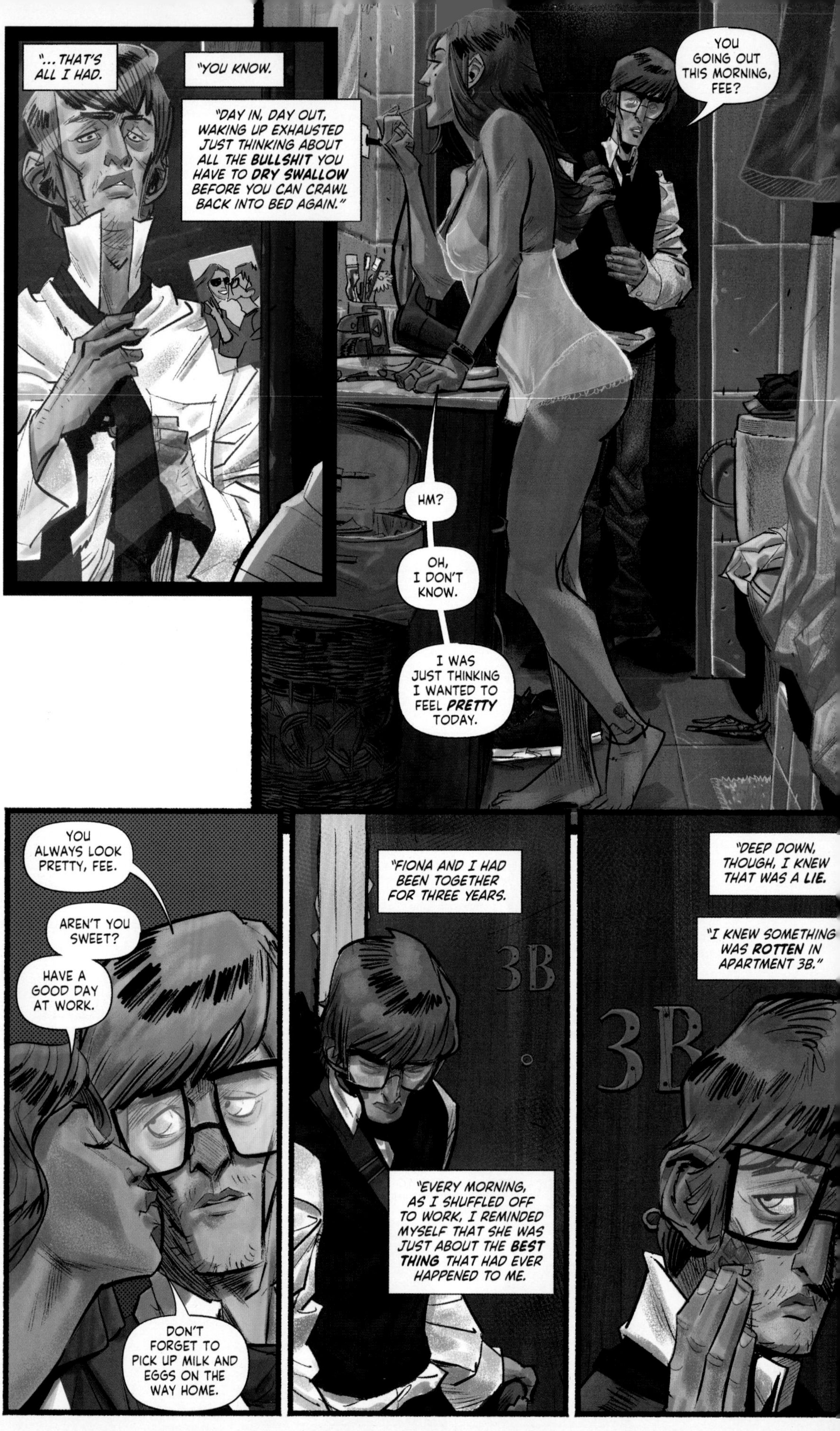
"...THAT'S ALL I HAD.
"YOU KNOW.
"DAY IN, DAY OUT, WAKING UP EXHAUSTED JUST THINKING ABOUT ALL THE **BULLSHIT** YOU HAVE TO **DRY SWALLOW** BEFORE YOU CAN CRAWL BACK INTO BED AGAIN."
YOU GOING OUT THIS MORNING, FEE?
HM?
OH, I DON'T KNOW.
I WAS JUST THINKING I WANTED TO FEEL **PRETTY** TODAY.
YOU ALWAYS LOOK PRETTY, FEE.
AREN'T YOU SWEET?
HAVE A GOOD DAY AT WORK.
DON'T FORGET TO PICK UP MILK AND EGGS ON THE WAY HOME.
"FIONA AND I HAD BEEN TOGETHER FOR THREE YEARS.
3B
"EVERY MORNING, AS I SHUFFLED OFF TO WORK, I REMINDED MYSELF THAT SHE WAS JUST ABOUT THE **BEST THING** THAT HAD EVER HAPPENED TO ME.
"DEEP DOWN, THOUGH, I KNEW THAT WAS A **LIE**.
"I KNEW SOMETHING WAS **ROTTEN** IN APARTMENT 3B."
3B

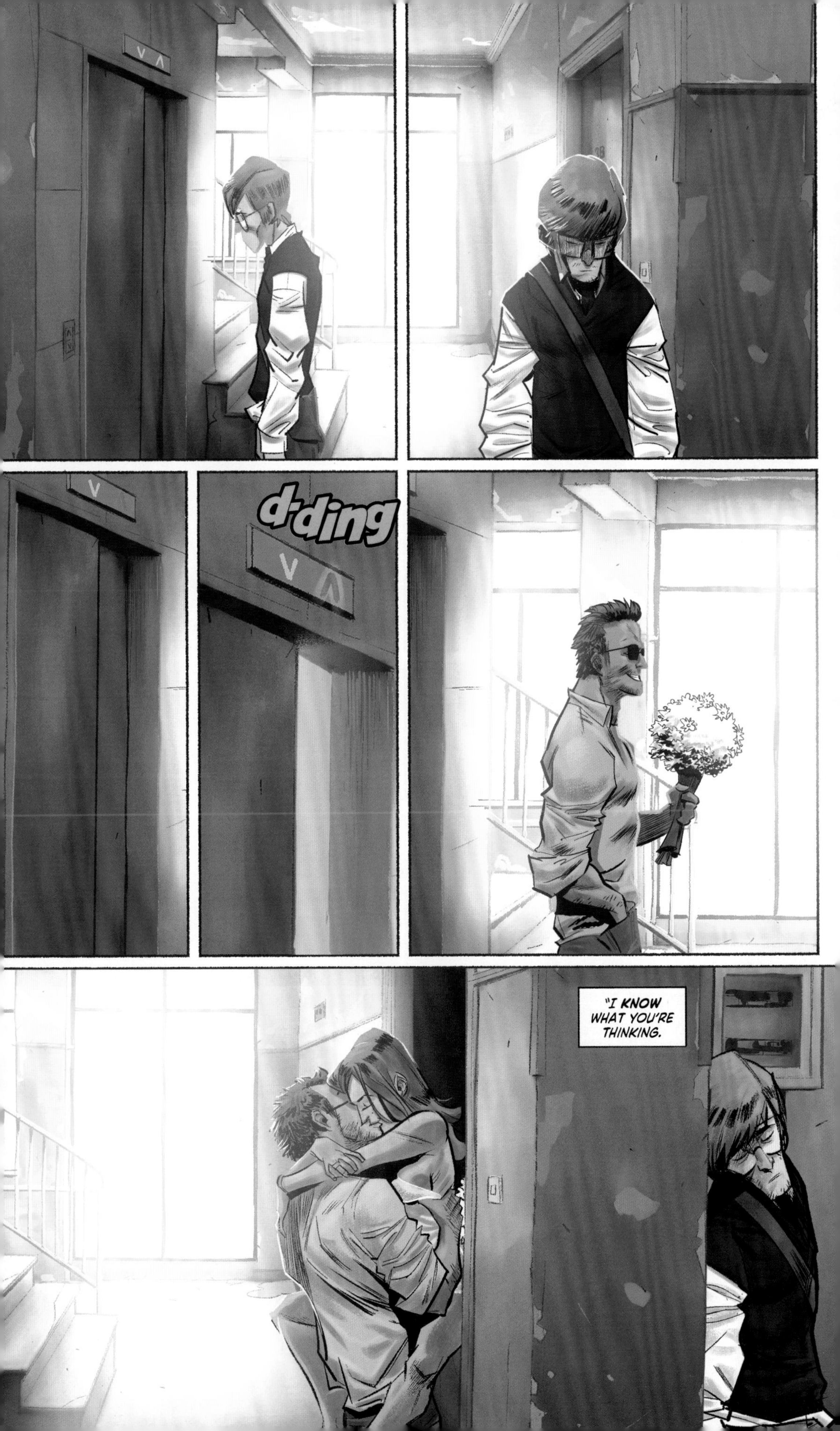
d-ding
"I KNOW WHAT YOU'RE THINKING.

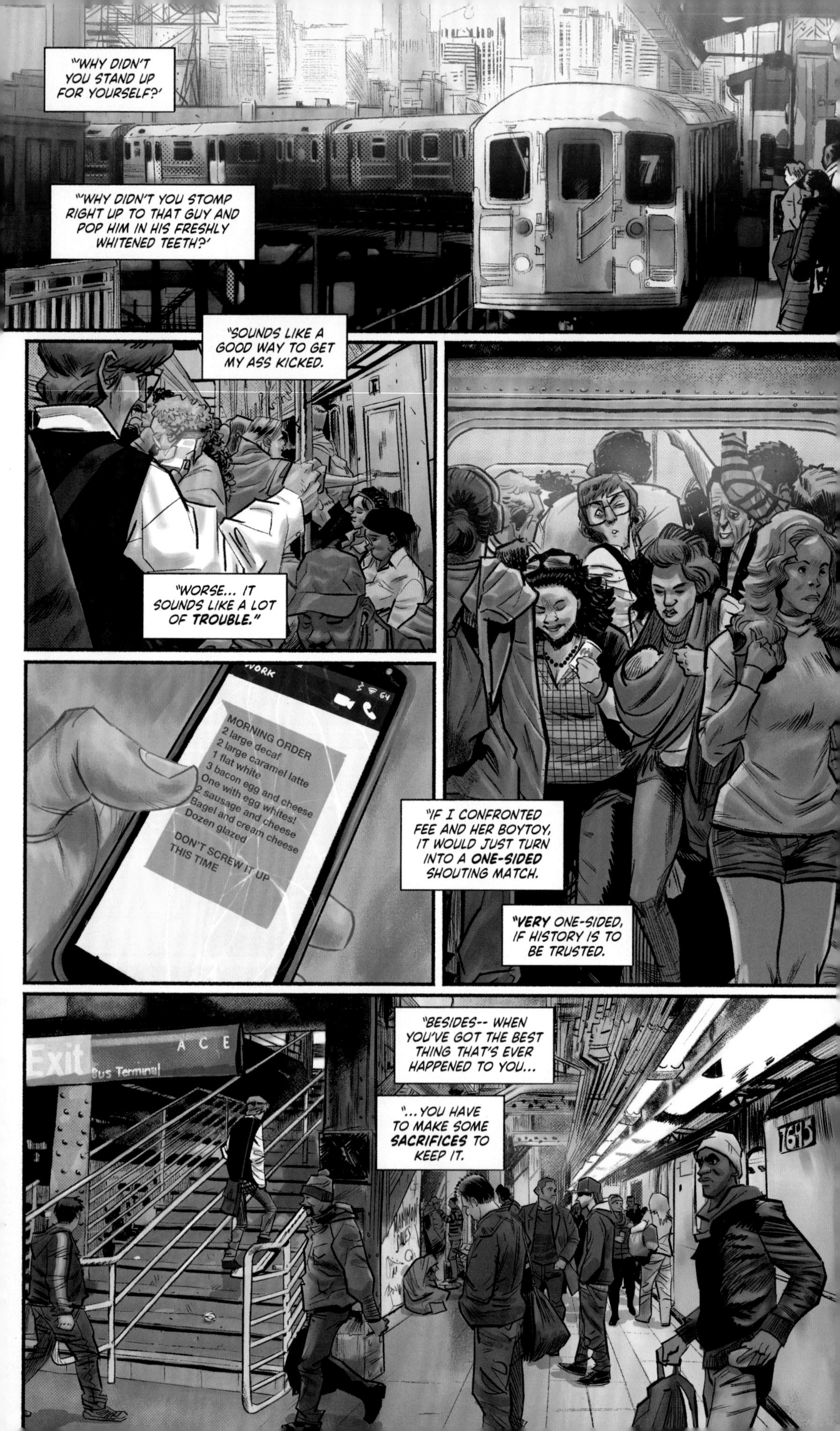
"WHY DIDN'T YOU STAND UP FOR YOURSELF?'
"WHY DIDN'T YOU STOMP RIGHT UP TO THAT GUY AND POP HIM IN HIS FRESHLY WHITENED TEETH?'
7
"SOUNDS LIKE A GOOD WAY TO GET MY ASS KICKED.
"WORSE... IT SOUNDS LIKE A LOT OF **TROUBLE.**"
MORNING ORDER
2 large decaf
2 large caramel latte
1 flat white
3 bacon egg and cheese
One with egg whites!
2 sausage and cheese
Bagel and cream cheese
Dozen glazed
DON'T SCREW IT UP THIS TIME
"IF I CONFRONTED FEE AND HER BOYTOY, IT WOULD JUST TURN INTO A **ONE-SIDED** SHOUTING MATCH.
"**VERY** ONE-SIDED, IF HISTORY IS TO BE TRUSTED.
Exit
A C E
Bus Terminal
"BESIDES-- WHEN YOU'VE GOT THE BEST THING THAT'S EVER HAPPENED TO YOU...
"...YOU HAVE TO MAKE SOME **SACRIFICES** TO KEEP IT.
1645

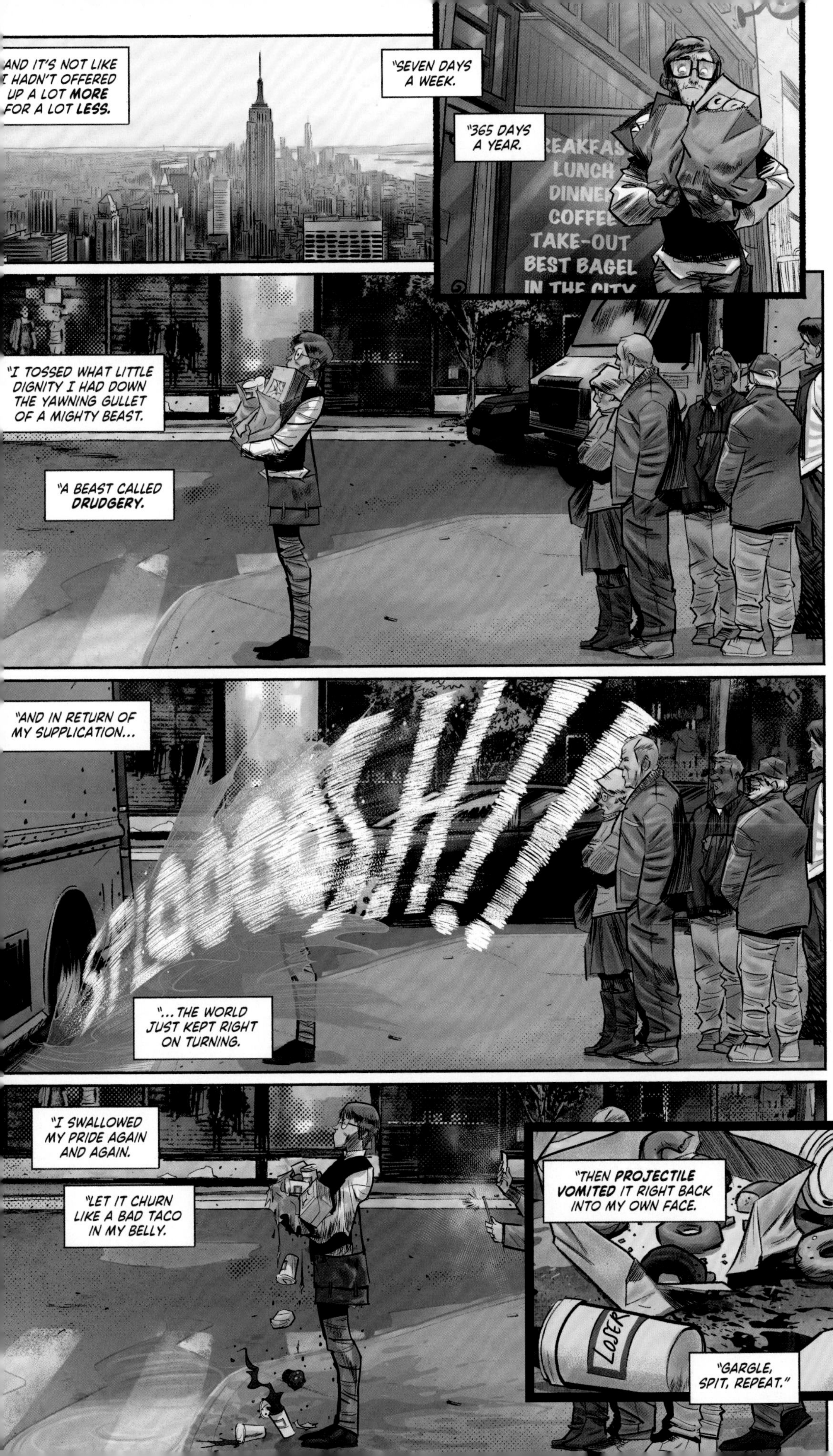
AND IT'S NOT LIKE I HADN'T OFFERED UP A LOT MORE FOR A LOT LESS.
"SEVEN DAYS A WEEK.
"365 DAYS A YEAR.
REAKFAS
LUNCH
DINNE
COFFEE
TAKE-OUT
BEST BAGEL
"I TOSSED WHAT LITTLE DIGNITY I HAD DOWN THE YAWNING GULLET OF A MIGHTY BEAST.
"A BEAST CALLED DRUDGERY.
"AND IN RETURN OF MY SUPPLICATION...
"...THE WORLD JUST KEPT RIGHT ON TURNING.
"I SWALLOWED MY PRIDE AGAIN AND AGAIN.
"LET IT CHURN LIKE A BAD TACO IN MY BELLY.
"THEN PROJECTILE VOMITED IT RIGHT BACK INTO MY OWN FACE.
LOSER
"GARGLE, SPIT, REPEAT."

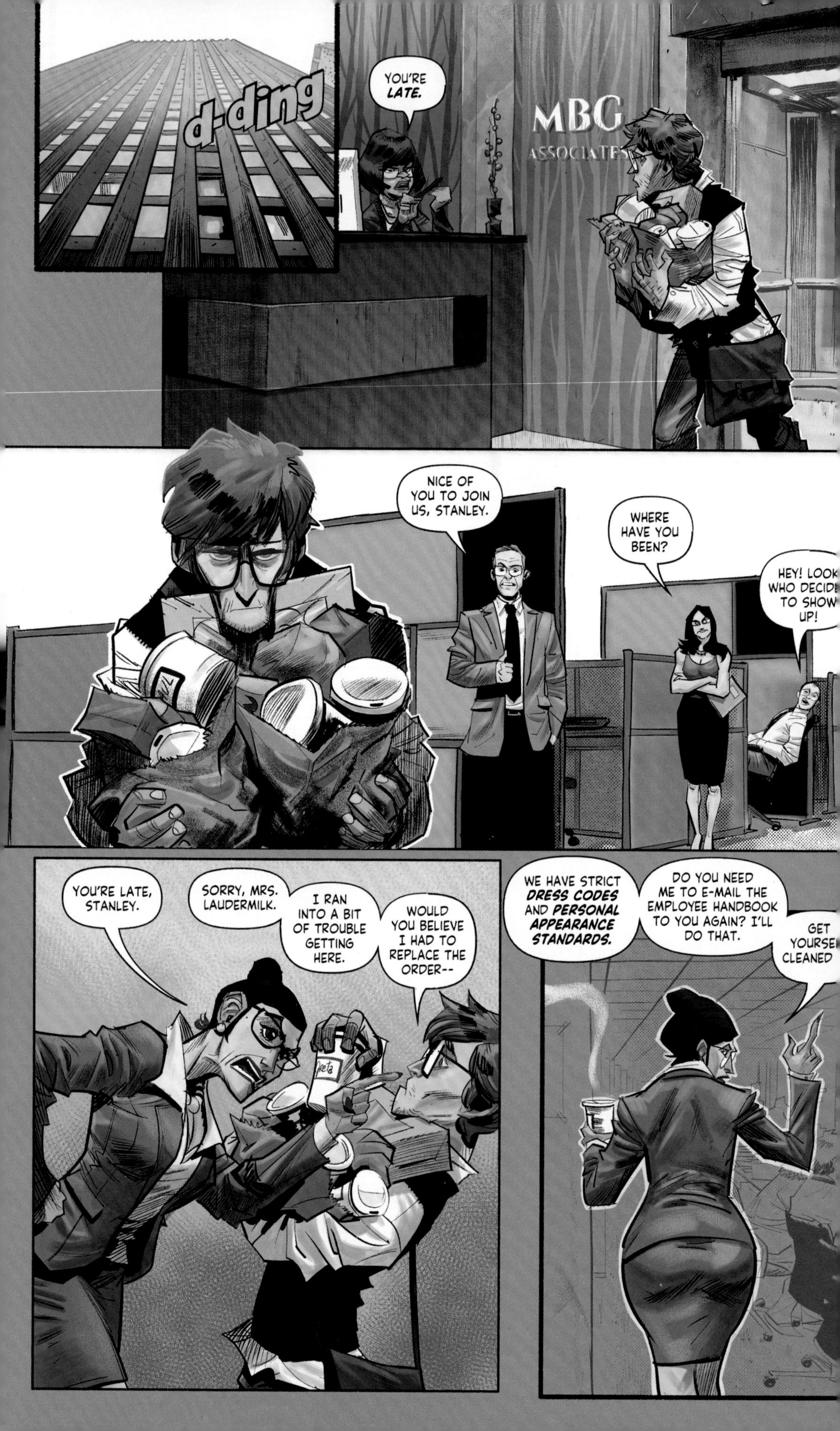
d-ding
YOU'RE LATE.
MBG ASSOCIATES
NICE OF YOU TO JOIN US, STANLEY.
WHERE HAVE YOU BEEN?
HEY! LOOK WHO DECIDE TO SHOW UP!
YOU'RE LATE, STANLEY.
SORRY, MRS. LAUDERMILK.
I RAN INTO A BIT OF TROUBLE GETTING HERE.
WOULD YOU BELIEVE I HAD TO REPLACE THE ORDER--
WE HAVE STRICT DRESS CODES AND PERSONAL APPEARANCE STANDARDS.
DO YOU NEED ME TO E-MAIL THE EMPLOYEE HANDBOOK TO YOU AGAIN? I'LL DO THAT.
GET YOURSE CLEANED

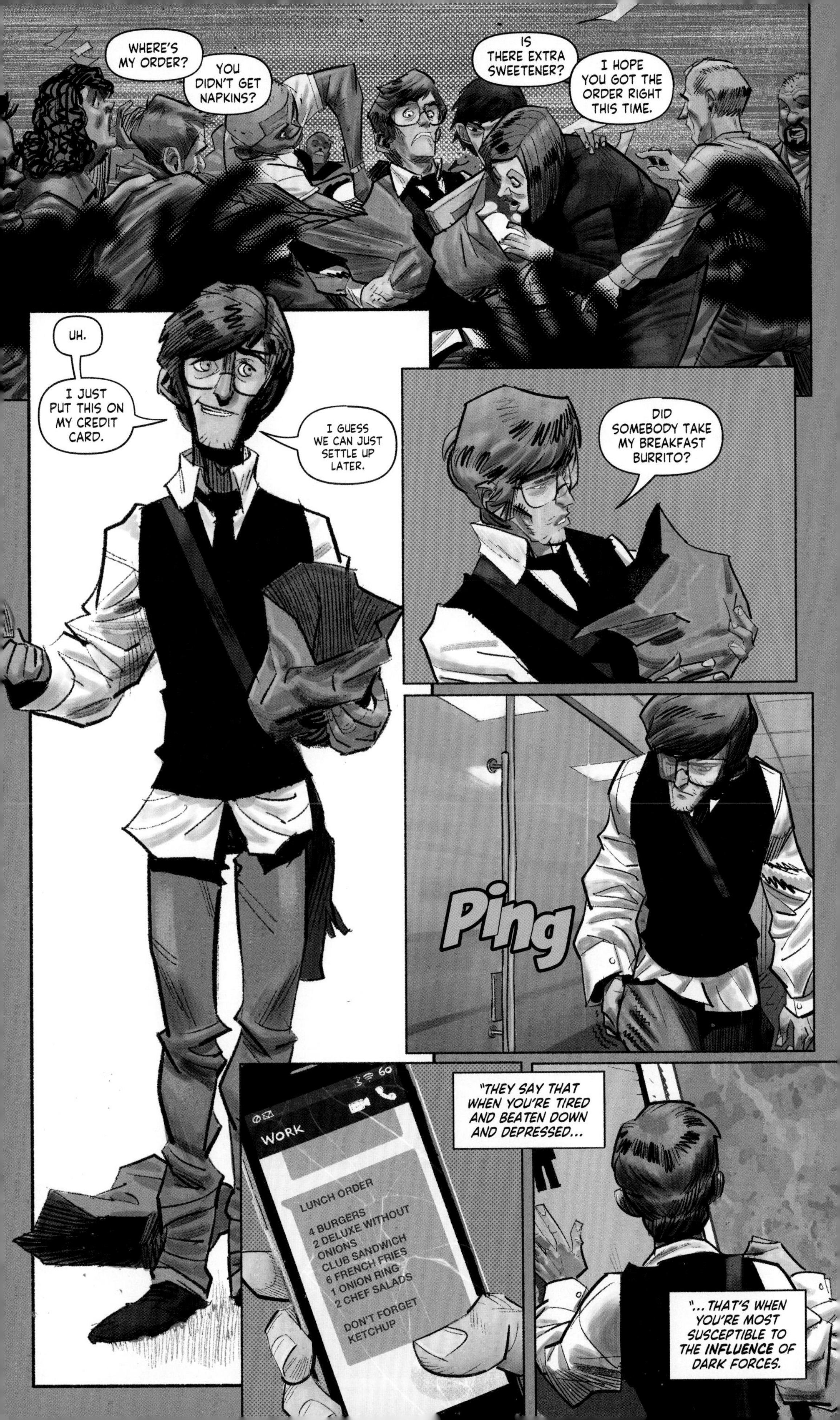
WHERE'S MY ORDER?
YOU DIDN'T GET NAPKINS?
IS THERE EXTRA SWEETENER?
I HOPE YOU GOT THE ORDER RIGHT THIS TIME.
UH.
I JUST PUT THIS ON MY CREDIT CARD.
I GUESS WE CAN JUST SETTLE UP LATER.
DID SOMEBODY TAKE MY BREAKFAST BURRITO?
Ping
60
WORK
LUNCH ORDER
4 BURGERS
2 DELUXE WITHOUT ONIONS
CLUB SANDWICH
6 FRENCH FRIES
1 ONION RING
2 CHEF SALADS
DON'T FORGET KETCHUP
"THEY SAY THAT WHEN YOU'RE TIRED AND BEATEN DOWN AND DEPRESSED...
"...THAT'S WHEN YOU'RE MOST SUSCEPTIBLE TO THE INFLUENCE OF DARK FORCES.

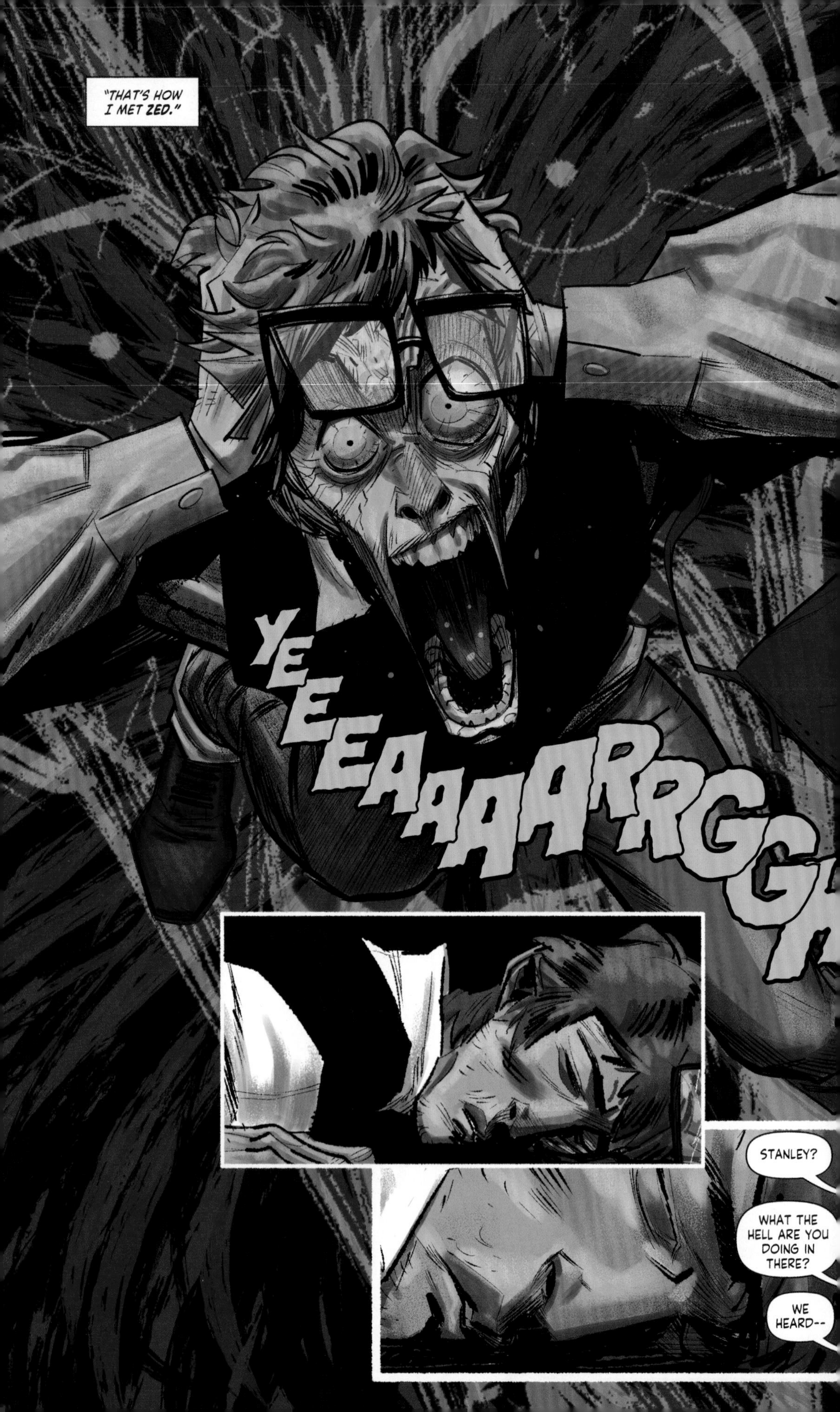
"THAT'S HOW I MET ZED."
YEEEAAAAARRGGH
STANLEY?
WHAT THE HELL ARE YOU DOING IN THERE?
WE HEARD--

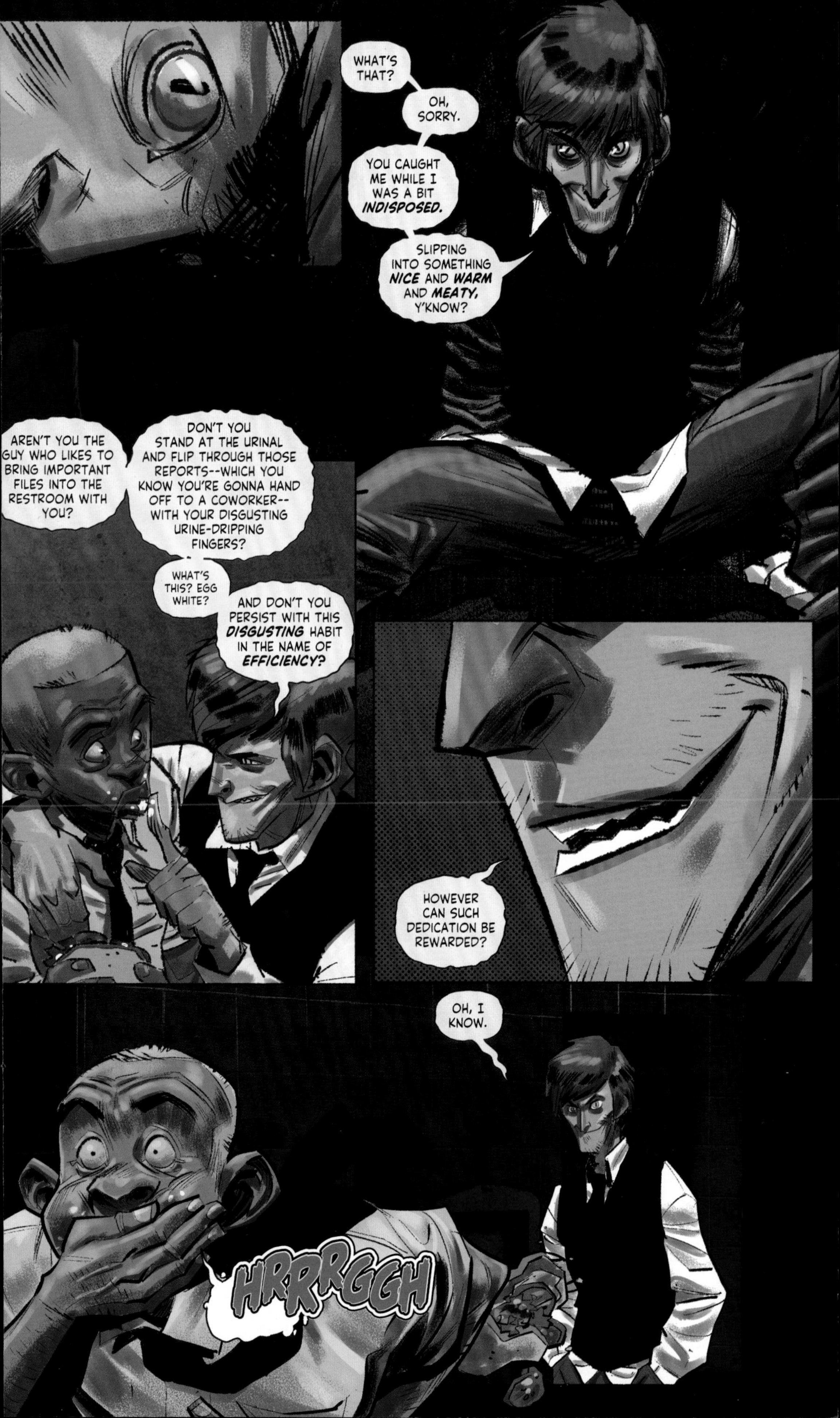
WHAT'S THAT?
OH, SORRY.
YOU CAUGHT ME WHILE I WAS A BIT *INDISPOSED.*
SLIPPING INTO SOMETHING ***NICE*** AND ***WARM*** AND ***MEATY,*** Y'KNOW?
AREN'T YOU THE GUY WHO LIKES TO BRING IMPORTANT FILES INTO THE RESTROOM WITH YOU?
DON'T YOU STAND AT THE URINAL AND FLIP THROUGH THOSE REPORTS--WHICH YOU KNOW YOU'RE GONNA HAND OFF TO A COWORKER--WITH YOUR DISGUSTING URINE-DRIPPING FINGERS?
WHAT'S THIS? EGG WHITE?
AND DON'T YOU PERSIST WITH THIS ***DISGUSTING*** HABIT IN THE NAME OF ***EFFICIENCY?***
HOWEVER CAN SUCH DEDICATION BE REWARDED?
OH, I KNOW.
HRRRGGH

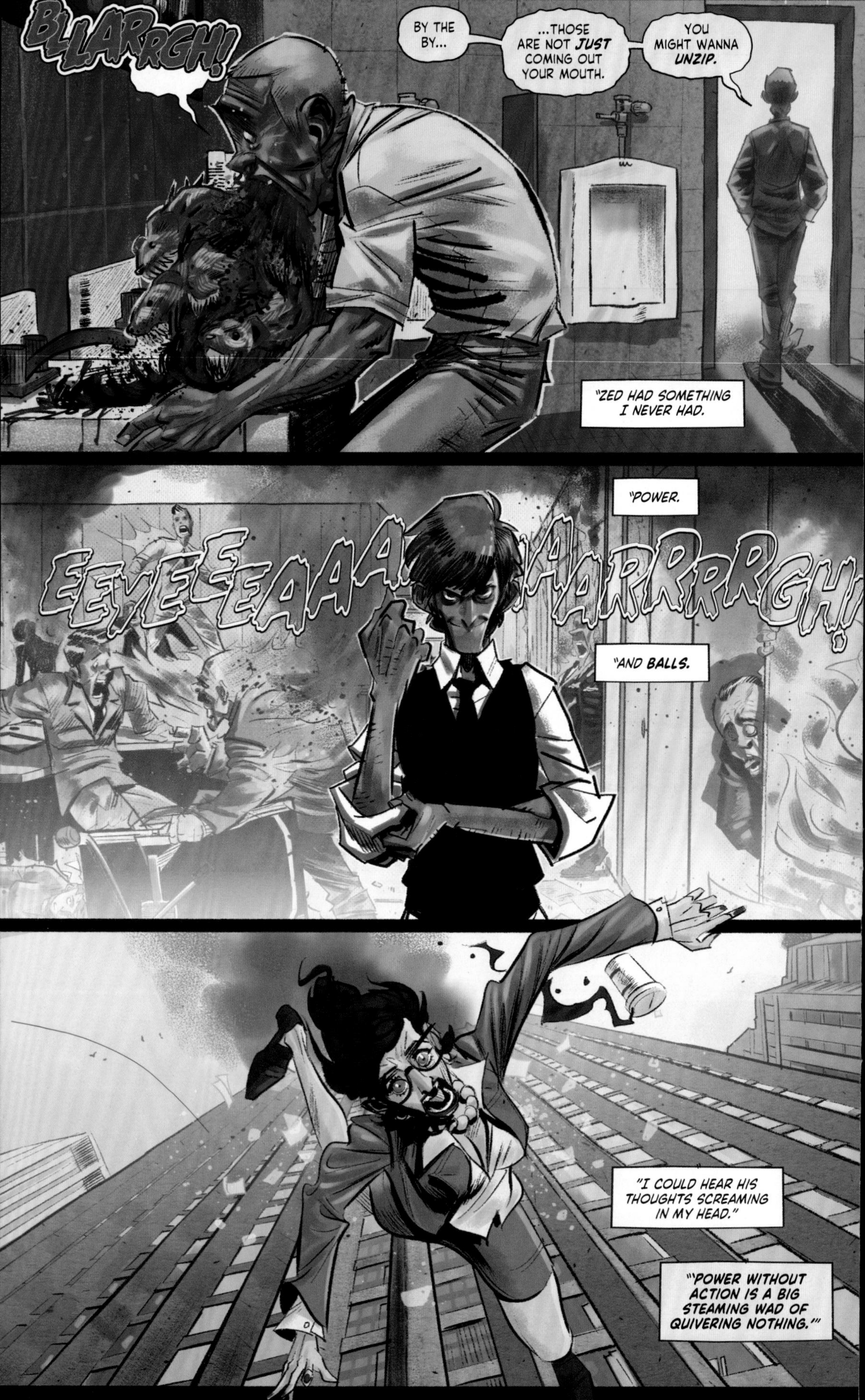
BLLARRGH!
BY THE BY...
...THOSE ARE NOT JUST COMING OUT YOUR MOUTH.
YOU MIGHT WANNA UNZIP.
"ZED HAD SOMETHING I NEVER HAD.
"POWER.
EEYEEEAAA
AARRRRGH!
"AND BALLS.
"I COULD HEAR HIS THOUGHTS SCREAMING IN MY HEAD."
"'POWER WITHOUT ACTION IS A BIG STEAMING WAD OF QUIVERING NOTHING.'"

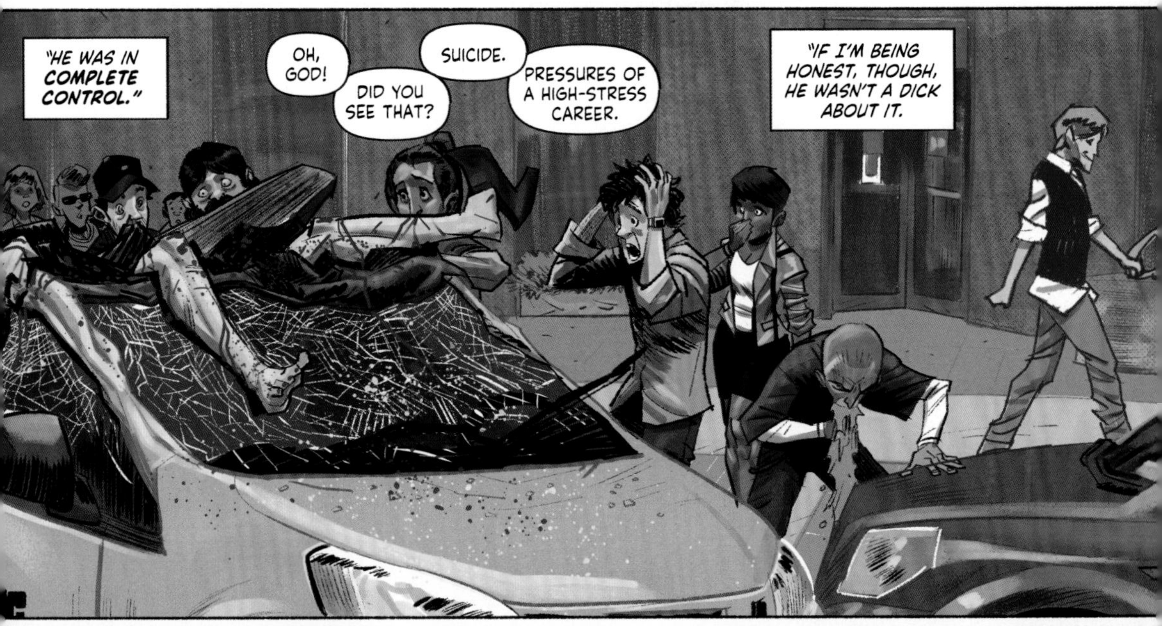

"HE WAS IN **COMPLETE CONTROL.**"
OH, GOD!
DID YOU SEE THAT?
SUICIDE.
PRESSURES OF A HIGH-STRESS CAREER.
"IF I'M BEING HONEST, THOUGH, HE WASN'T A DICK ABOUT IT.

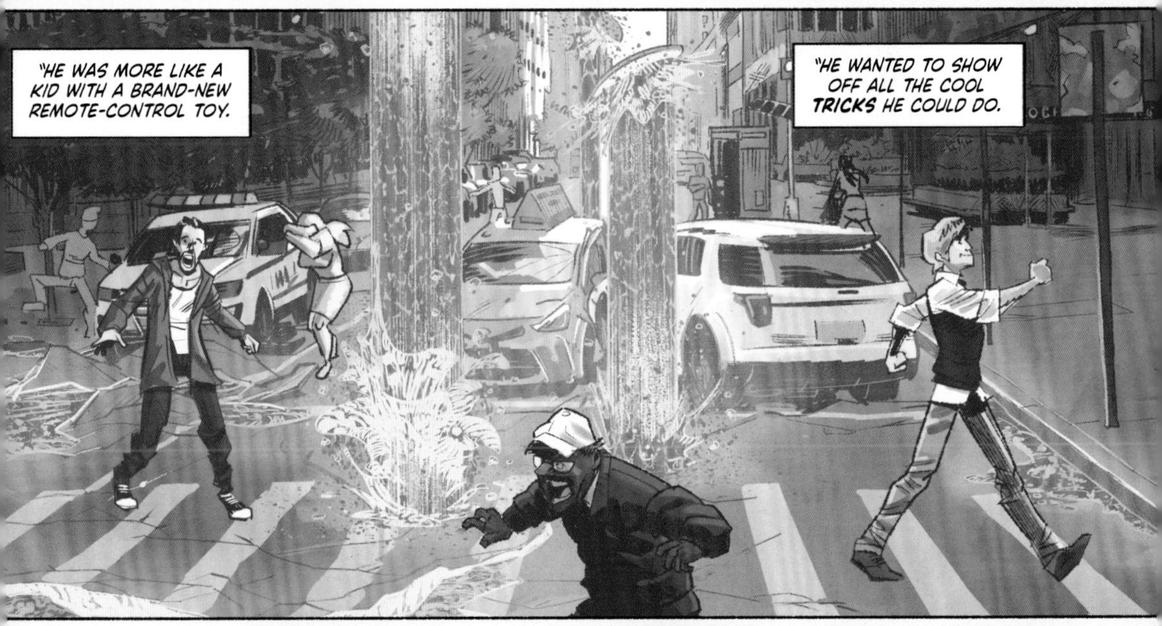

"HE WAS MORE LIKE A KID WITH A BRAND-NEW REMOTE-CONTROL TOY.
"HE WANTED TO SHOW OFF ALL THE COOL **TRICKS** HE COULD DO.

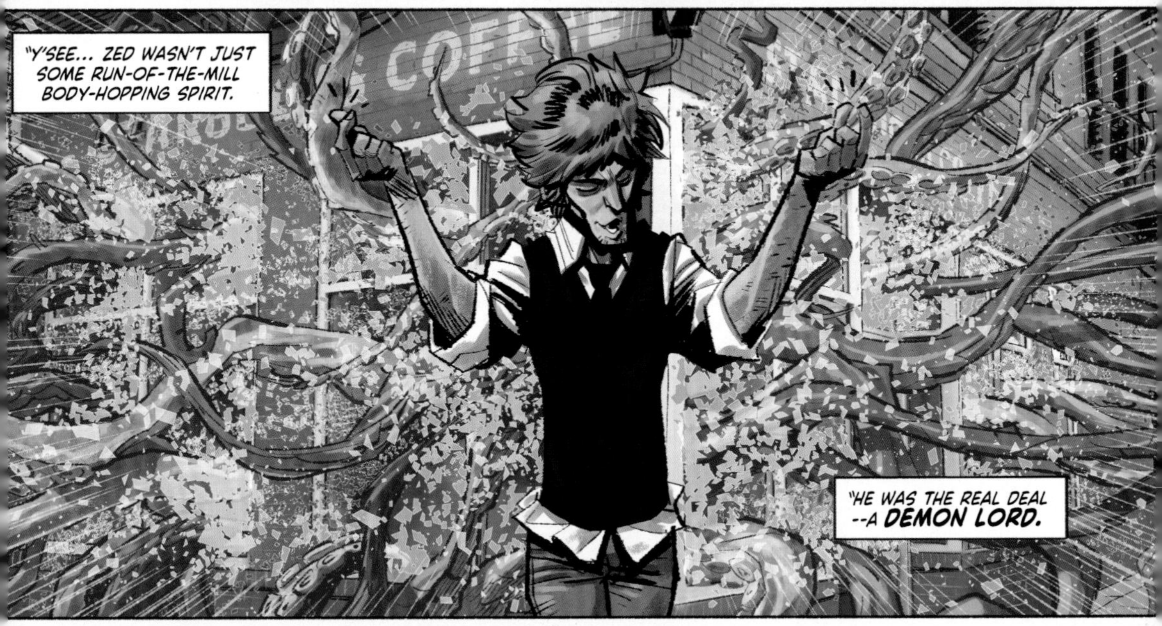

"Y'SEE... ZED WASN'T JUST SOME RUN-OF-THE-MILL BODY-HOPPING SPIRIT.
"HE WAS THE REAL DEAL --A **DEMON LORD.**

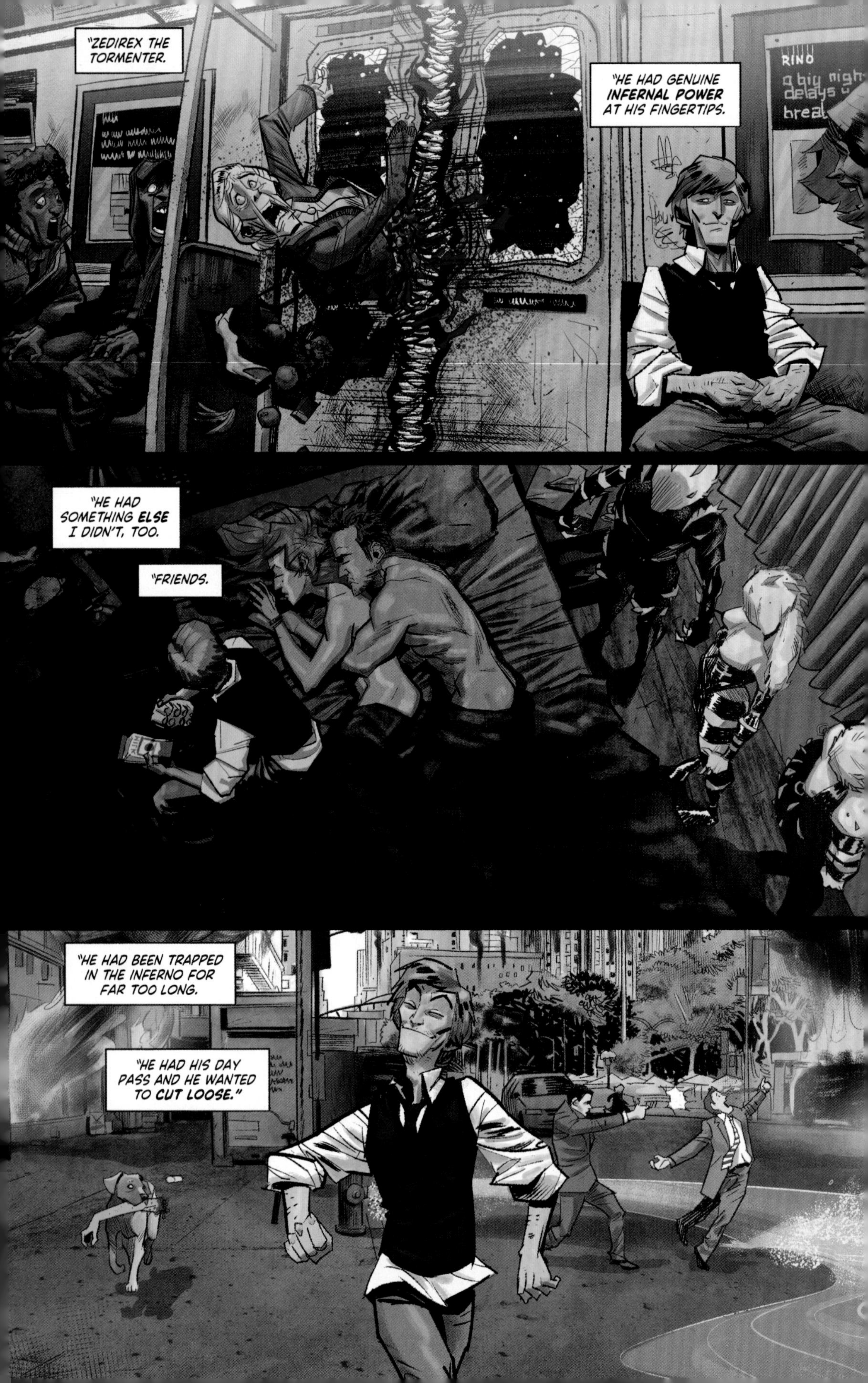
"ZEDIREX THE TORMENTER.
"HE HAD GENUINE INFERNAL POWER AT HIS FINGERTIPS.
RINO
"HE HAD SOMETHING ELSE I DIDN'T, TOO.
"FRIENDS.
"HE HAD BEEN TRAPPED IN THE INFERNO FOR FAR TOO LONG.
"HE HAD HIS DAY PASS AND HE WANTED TO CUT LOOSE."

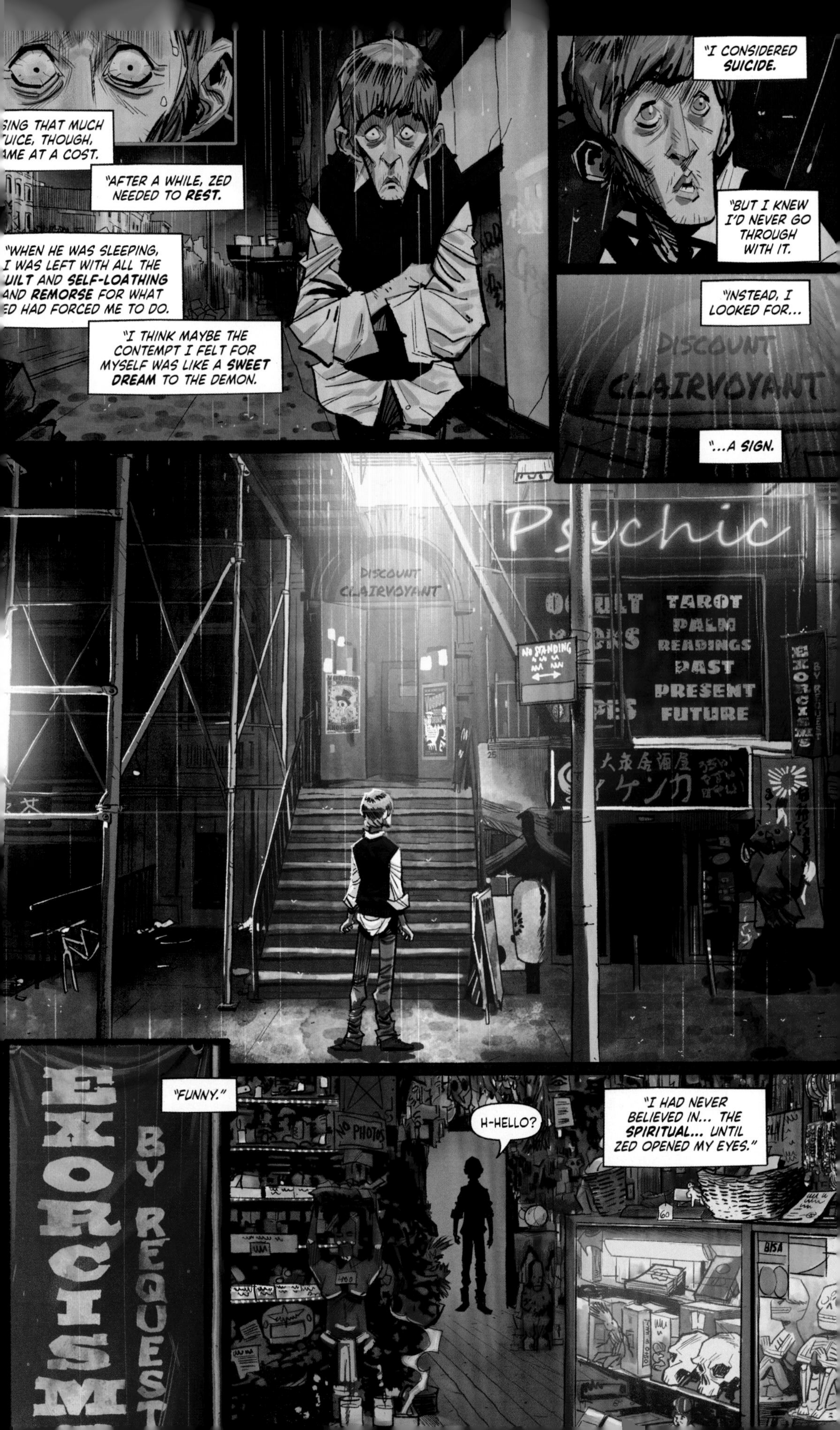

SING THAT MUCH
JUICE, THOUGH,
AME AT A COST.
"AFTER A WHILE, ZED NEEDED TO REST.
"WHEN HE WAS SLEEPING, I WAS LEFT WITH ALL THE UILT AND SELF-LOATHING AND REMORSE FOR WHAT ED HAD FORCED ME TO DO.
"I THINK MAYBE THE CONTEMPT I FELT FOR MYSELF WAS LIKE A SWEET DREAM TO THE DEMON.
"I CONSIDERED SUICIDE.
"BUT I KNEW I'D NEVER GO THROUGH WITH IT.
"INSTEAD, I LOOKED FOR...
DISCOUNT CLAIRVOYANT
"...A SIGN.
Psychic
DISCOUNT CLAIRVOYANT
TAROT
PALM
READINGS
PAST
PRESENT
FUTURE
NO STANDING
EXORCISMS BY REQUEST
"FUNNY."
H-HELLO?
"I HAD NEVER BELIEVED IN... THE SPIRITUAL... UNTIL ZED OPENED MY EYES."

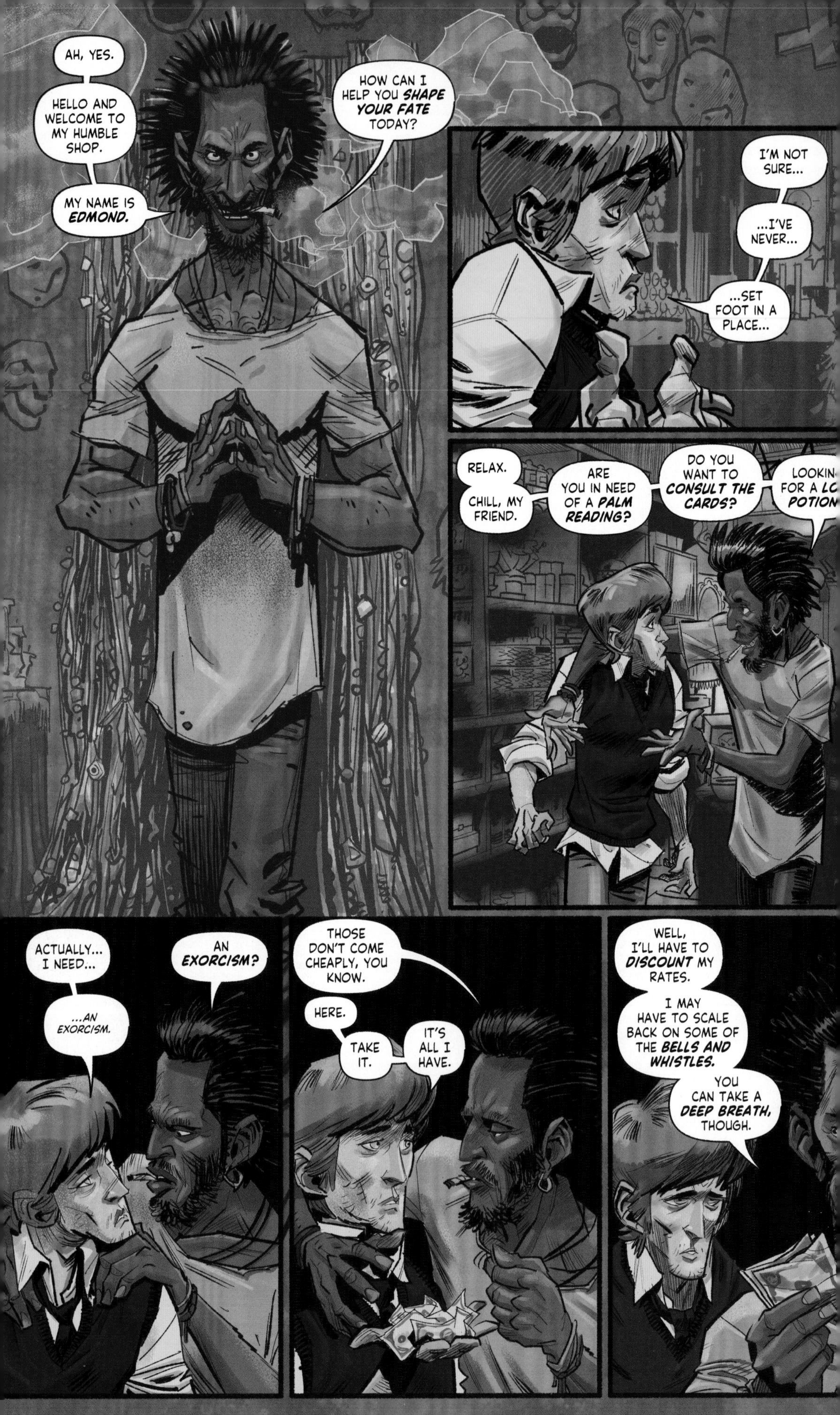
AH, YES.
HELLO AND WELCOME TO MY HUMBLE SHOP.
MY NAME IS *EDMOND.*
HOW CAN I HELP YOU *SHAPE YOUR FATE* TODAY?
I'M NOT SURE...
...I'VE NEVER...
...SET FOOT IN A PLACE...
RELAX.
CHILL, MY FRIEND.
ARE YOU IN NEED OF A *PALM READING?*
DO YOU WANT TO *CONSULT THE CARDS?*
LOOKIN FOR A LO POTION
ACTUALLY... I NEED...
...AN EXORCISM.
AN *EXORCISM?*
THOSE DON'T COME CHEAPLY, YOU KNOW.
HERE.
TAKE IT.
IT'S ALL I HAVE.
WELL, I'LL HAVE TO *DISCOUNT* MY RATES.
I MAY HAVE TO SCALE BACK ON SOME OF THE *BELLS AND WHISTLES.*
YOU CAN TAKE A *DEEP BREATH,* THOUGH.

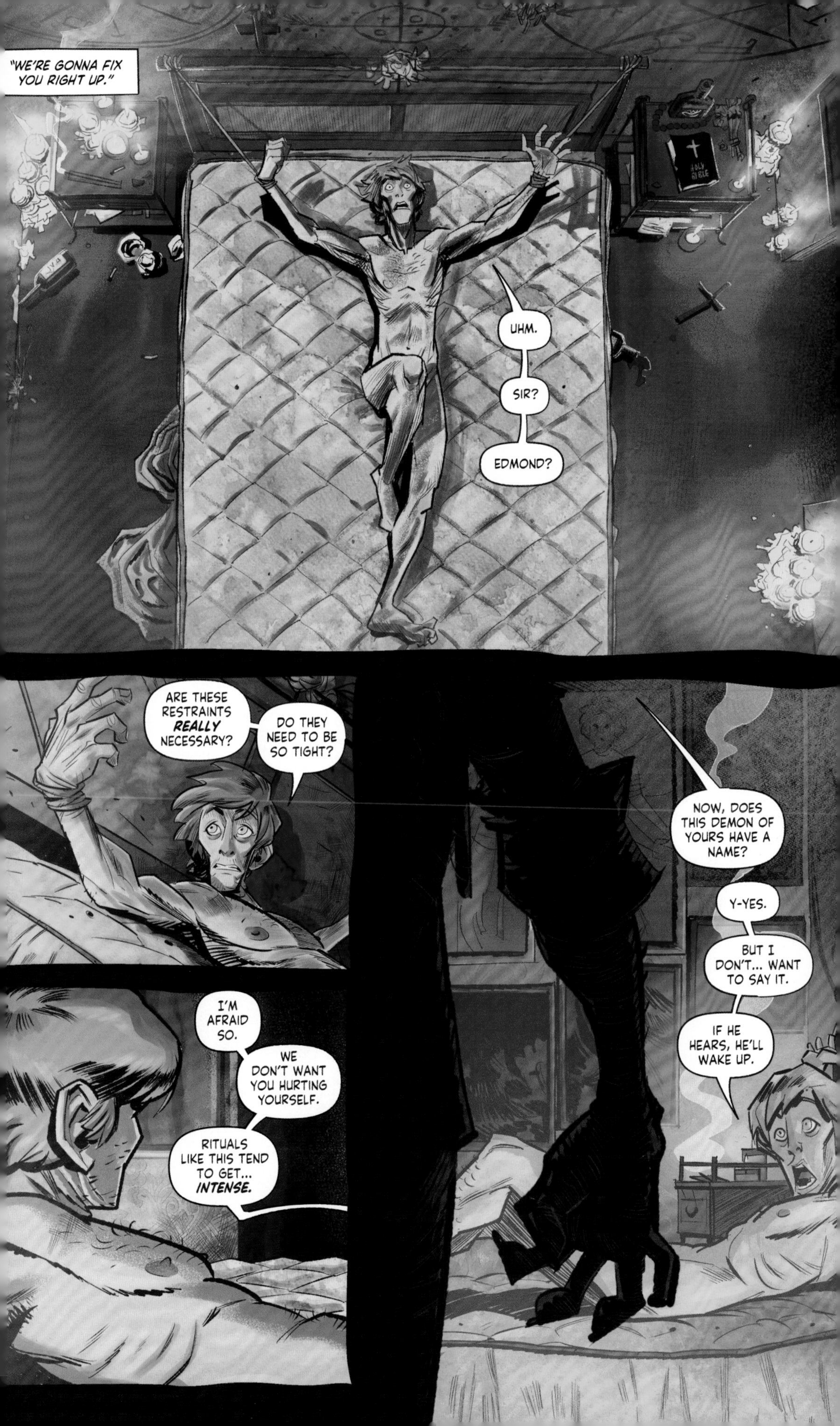
"WE'RE GONNA FIX YOU RIGHT UP."
UHM.
SIR?
EDMOND?
ARE THESE RESTRAINTS **REALLY** NECESSARY?
DO THEY NEED TO BE SO TIGHT?
I'M AFRAID SO.
WE DON'T WANT YOU HURTING YOURSELF.
RITUALS LIKE THIS TEND TO GET... ***INTENSE.***
NOW, DOES THIS DEMON OF YOURS HAVE A NAME?
Y-YES.
BUT I DON'T... WANT TO SAY IT.
IF HE HEARS, HE'LL WAKE UP.

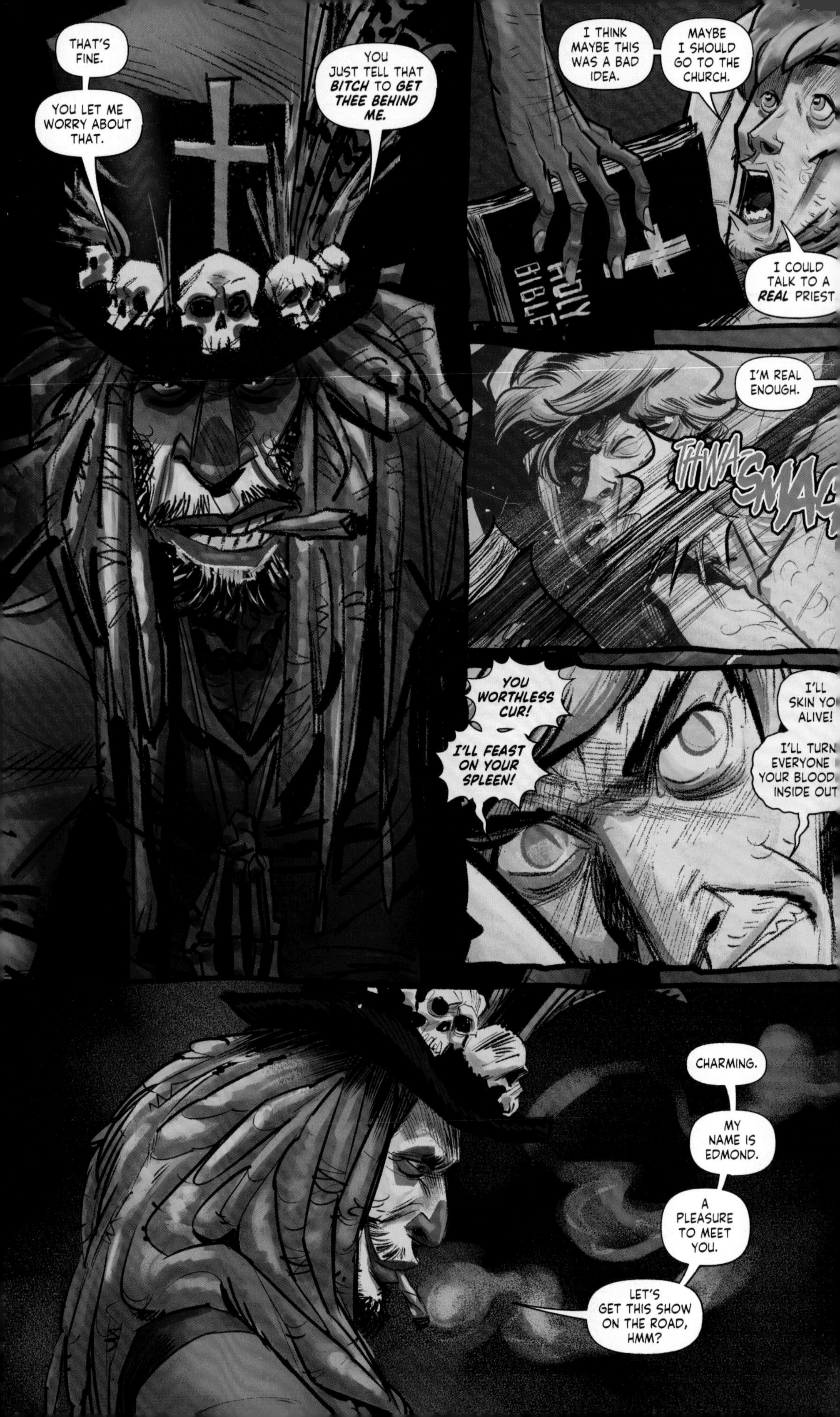
THAT'S FINE.
YOU LET ME WORRY ABOUT THAT.
YOU JUST TELL THAT *BITCH* TO *GET THEE BEHIND ME.*
I THINK MAYBE THIS WAS A BAD IDEA.
MAYBE I SHOULD GO TO THE CHURCH.
HOLY BIBLE
I COULD TALK TO A *REAL* PRIEST
I'M REAL ENOUGH.
THWASMAC
YOU WORTHLESS CUR!
I'LL FEAST ON YOUR SPLEEN!
I'LL SKIN YO ALIVE!
I'LL TURN EVERYONE YOUR BLOOD INSIDE OUT
CHARMING.
MY NAME IS EDMOND.
A PLEASURE TO MEET YOU.
LET'S GET THIS SHOW ON THE ROAD, HMM?

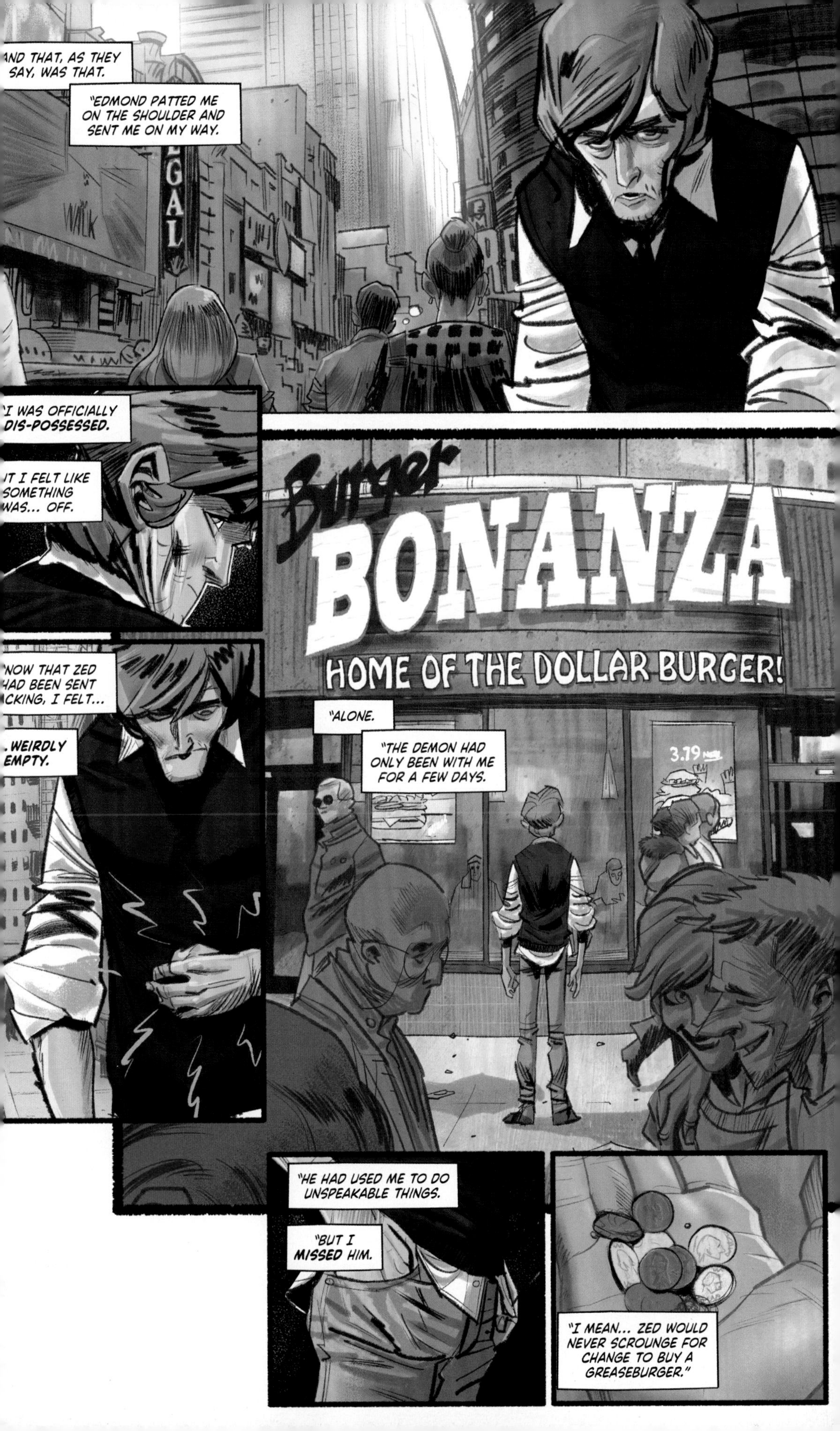

AND THAT, AS THEY SAY, WAS THAT.
"EDMOND PATTED ME ON THE SHOULDER AND SENT ME ON MY WAY.
REGAL
WALK
"I WAS OFFICIALLY DIS-POSSESSED.
IT I FELT LIKE SOMETHING WAS... OFF.
Burger BONANZA
HOME OF THE DOLLAR BURGER!
"NOW THAT ZED HAD BEEN SENT CKING, I FELT...
. WEIRDLY EMPTY.
"ALONE.
"THE DEMON HAD ONLY BEEN WITH ME FOR A FEW DAYS.
3.79
"HE HAD USED ME TO DO UNSPEAKABLE THINGS.
"BUT I MISSED HIM.
"I MEAN... ZED WOULD NEVER SCROUNGE FOR CHANGE TO BUY A GREASEBURGER."

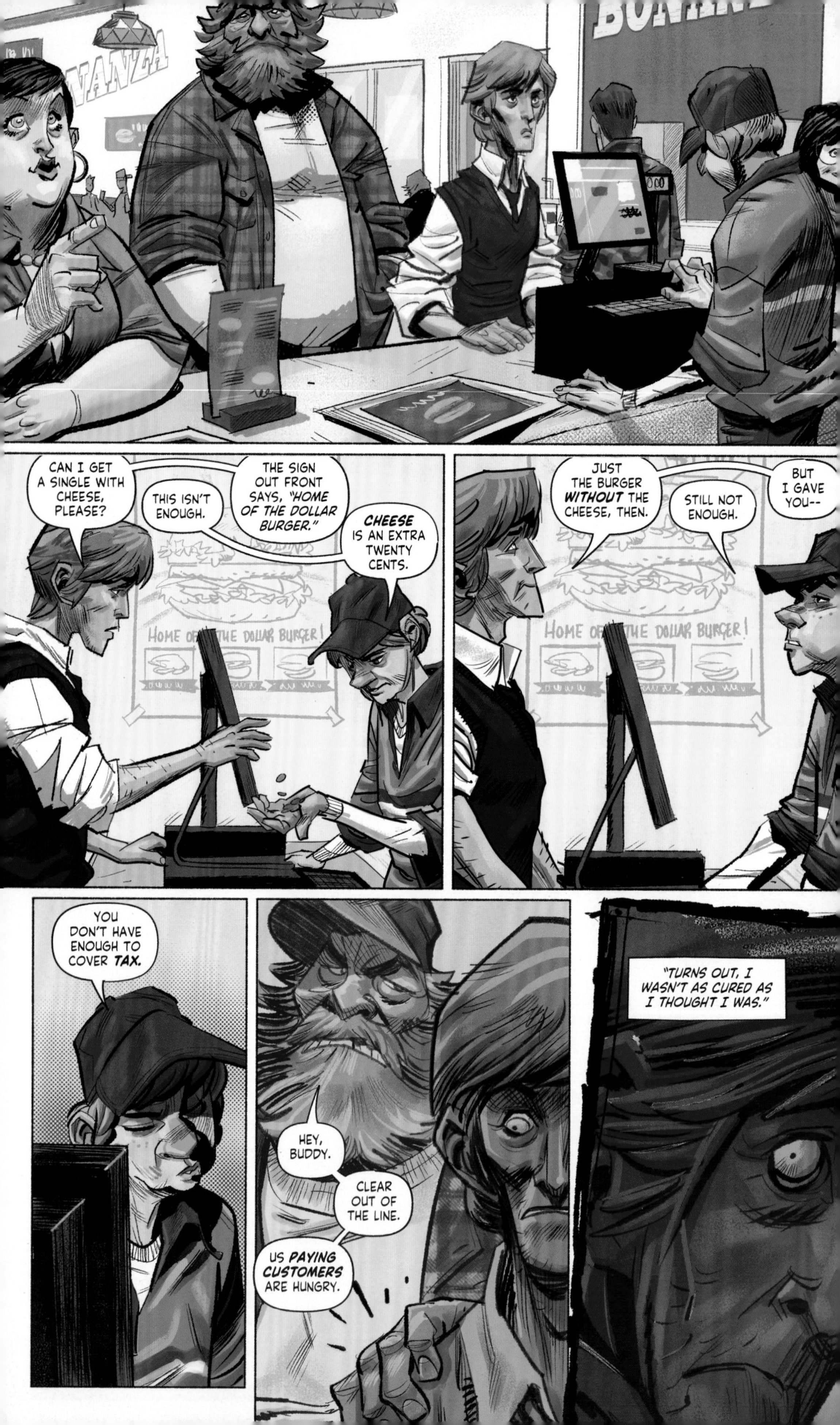
CAN I GET A SINGLE WITH CHEESE, PLEASE?
THIS ISN'T ENOUGH.
THE SIGN OUT FRONT SAYS, "HOME OF THE DOLLAR BURGER."
CHEESE IS AN EXTRA TWENTY CENTS.
HOME OF THE DOLLAR BURGER!
JUST THE BURGER WITHOUT THE CHEESE, THEN.
STILL NOT ENOUGH.
BUT I GAVE YOU--
HOME OF THE DOLLAR BURGER!
YOU DON'T HAVE ENOUGH TO COVER TAX.
HEY, BUDDY.
CLEAR OUT OF THE LINE.
US PAYING CUSTOMERS ARE HUNGRY.
"TURNS OUT, I WASN'T AS CURED AS I THOUGHT I WAS."

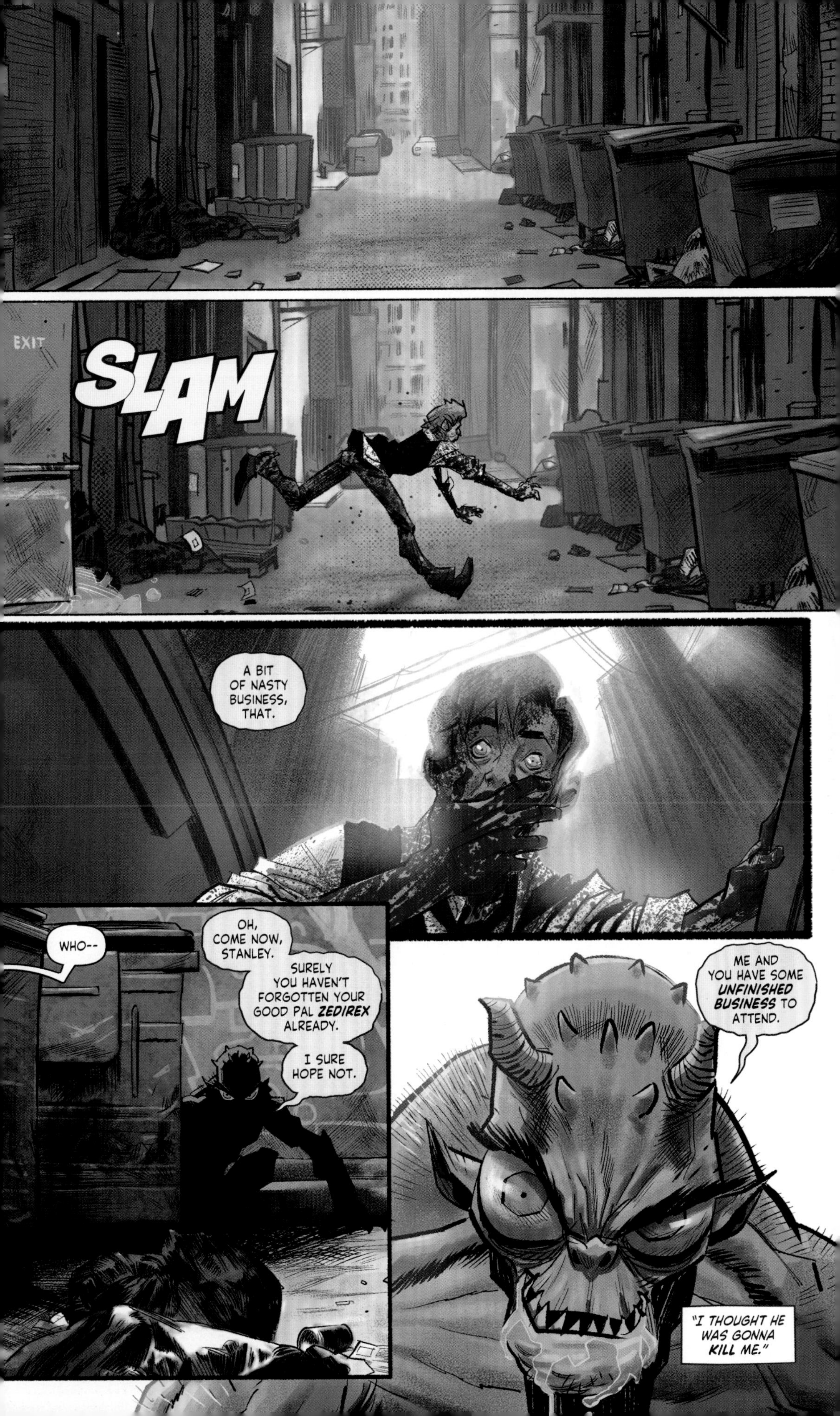
EXIT
SLAM
A BIT OF NASTY BUSINESS, THAT.
WHO--
OH, COME NOW, STANLEY.
SURELY YOU HAVEN'T FORGOTTEN YOUR GOOD PAL **ZEDIREX** ALREADY.
I SURE HOPE NOT.
ME AND YOU HAVE SOME ***UNFINISHED BUSINESS*** TO ATTEND.
*"I THOUGHT HE WAS GONNA **KILL** ME."*

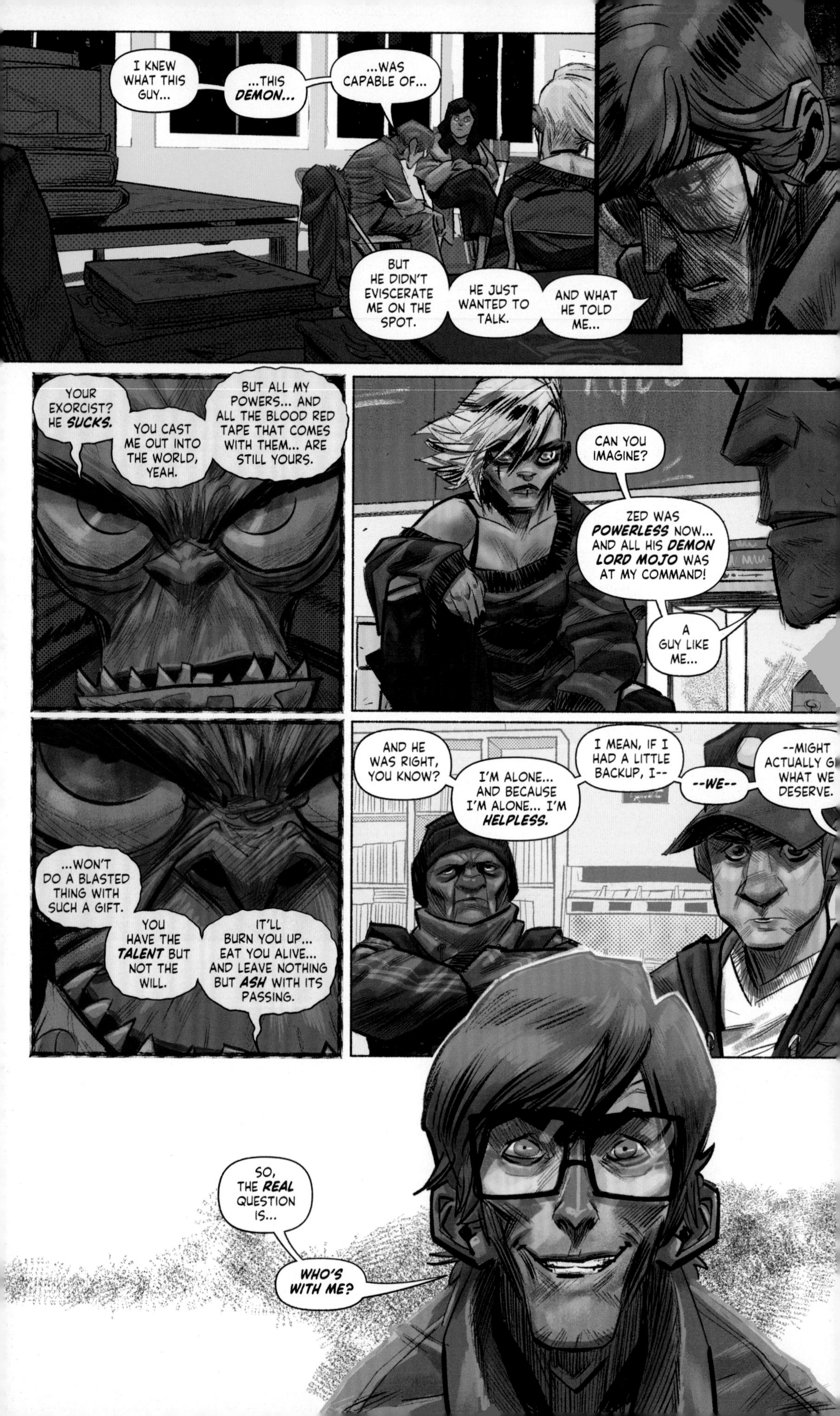
I KNEW WHAT THIS GUY...
...THIS DEMON...
...WAS CAPABLE OF...
BUT HE DIDN'T EVISCERATE ME ON THE SPOT.
HE JUST WANTED TO TALK.
AND WHAT HE TOLD ME...
YOUR EXORCIST? HE SUCKS.
YOU CAST ME OUT INTO THE WORLD, YEAH.
BUT ALL MY POWERS... AND ALL THE BLOOD RED TAPE THAT COMES WITH THEM... ARE STILL YOURS.
CAN YOU IMAGINE?
ZED WAS POWERLESS NOW... AND ALL HIS DEMON LORD MOJO WAS AT MY COMMAND!
A GUY LIKE ME...
...WON'T DO A BLASTED THING WITH SUCH A GIFT.
YOU HAVE THE TALENT BUT NOT THE WILL.
IT'LL BURN YOU UP... EAT YOU ALIVE... AND LEAVE NOTHING BUT ASH WITH ITS PASSING.
AND HE WAS RIGHT, YOU KNOW?
I'M ALONE... AND BECAUSE I'M ALONE... I'M HELPLESS.
I MEAN, IF I HAD A LITTLE BACKUP, I--
--WE--
--MIGHT ACTUALLY G WHAT WE DESERVE.
SO, THE REAL QUESTION IS...
WHO'S WITH ME?

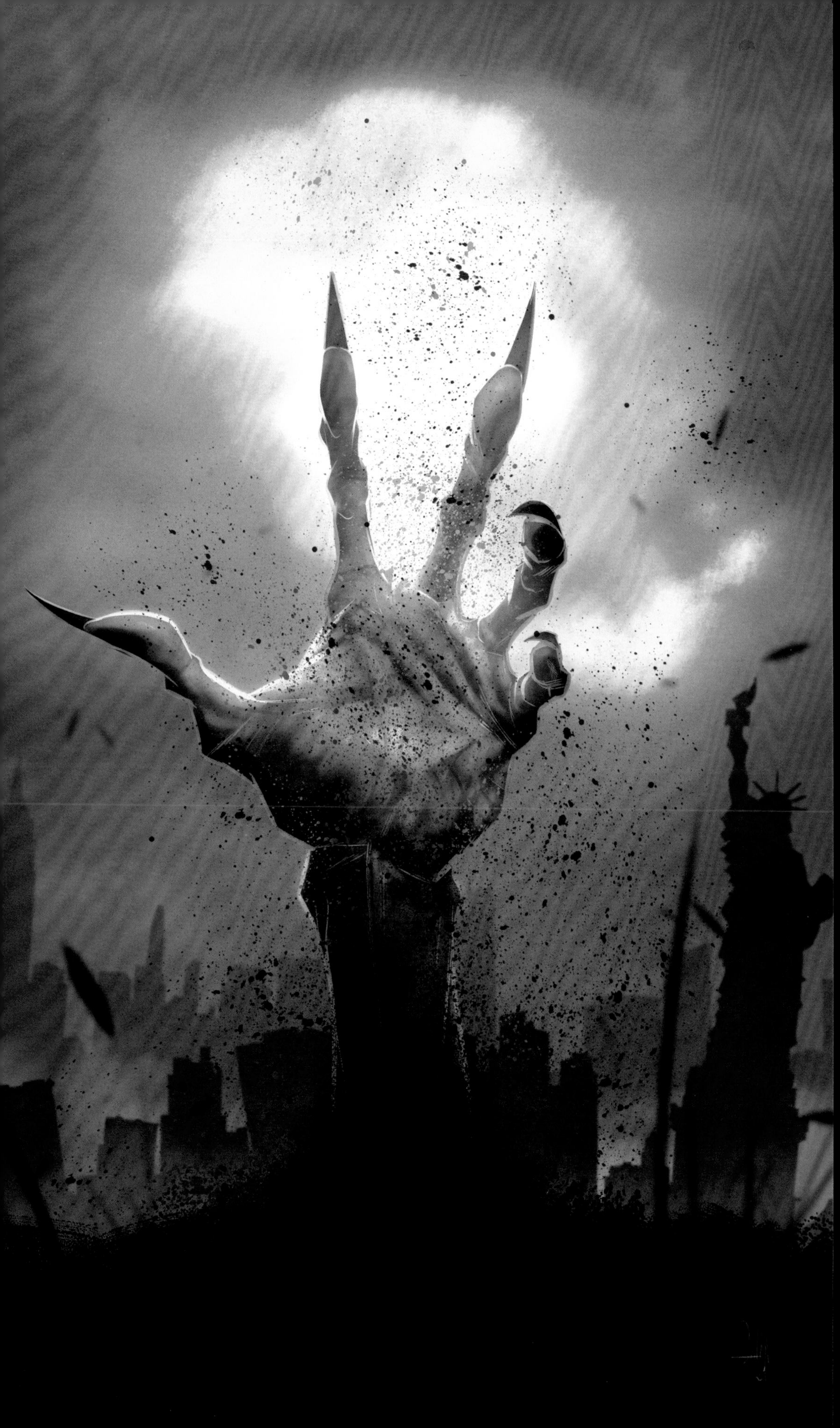

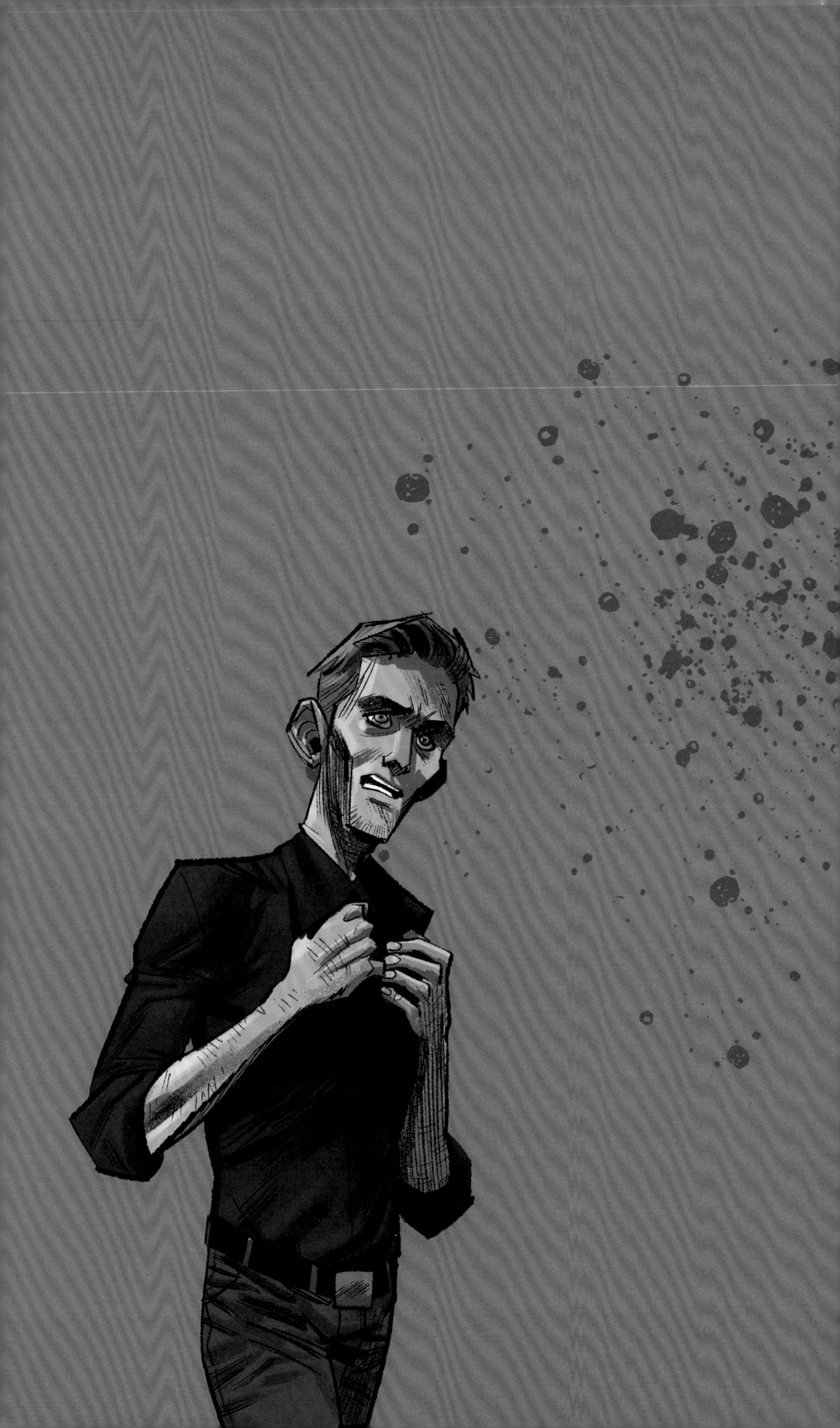

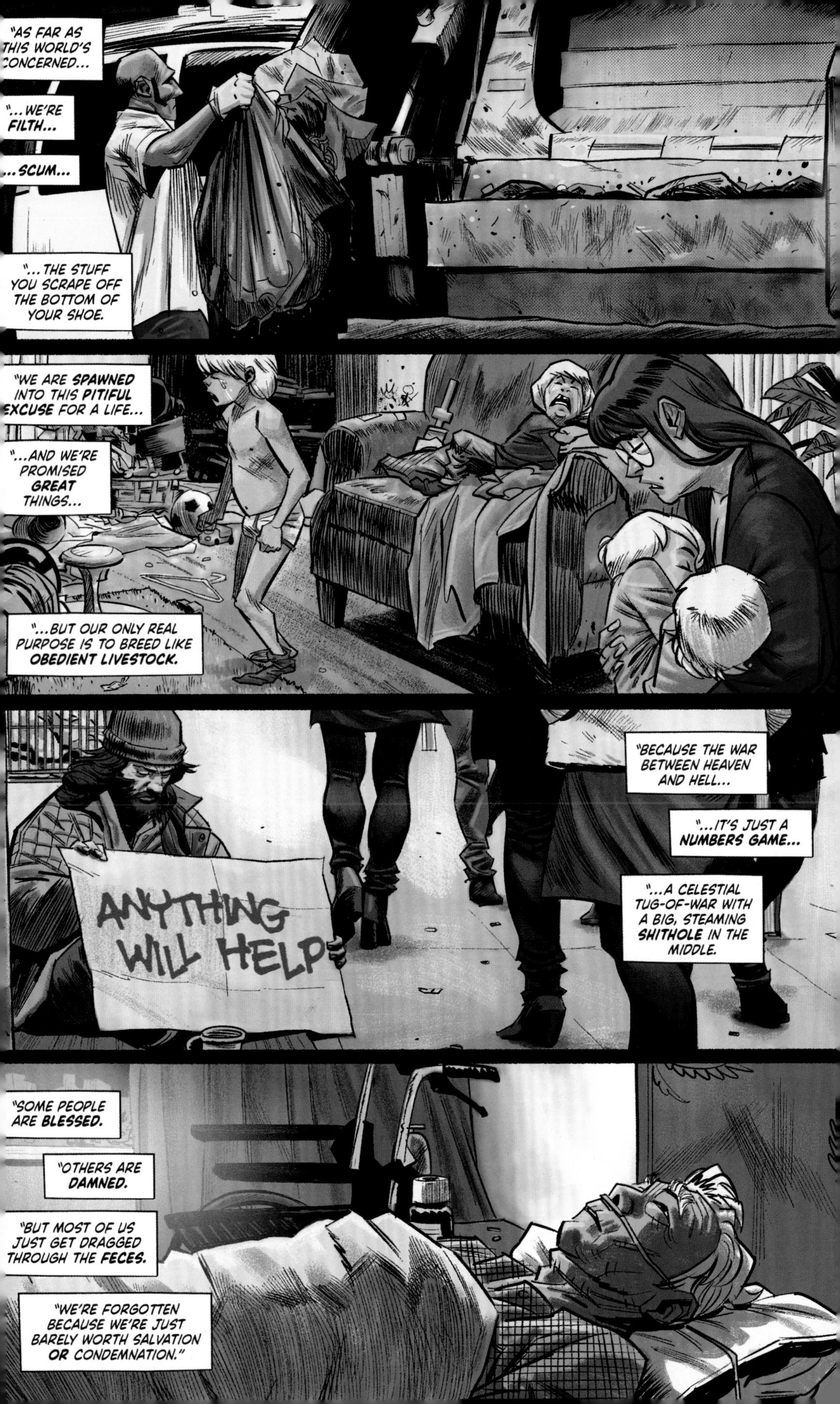
"AS FAR AS THIS WORLD'S CONCERNED...
"...WE'RE FILTH...
...SCUM...
"...THE STUFF YOU SCRAPE OFF THE BOTTOM OF YOUR SHOE.
"WE ARE SPAWNED INTO THIS PITIFUL EXCUSE FOR A LIFE...
"...AND WE'RE PROMISED GREAT THINGS...
"...BUT OUR ONLY REAL PURPOSE IS TO BREED LIKE OBEDIENT LIVESTOCK.
ANYTHING WILL HELP
"BECAUSE THE WAR BETWEEN HEAVEN AND HELL...
"...IT'S JUST A NUMBERS GAME...
"...A CELESTIAL TUG-OF-WAR WITH A BIG, STEAMING SHITHOLE IN THE MIDDLE.
"SOME PEOPLE ARE BLESSED.
"OTHERS ARE DAMNED.
"BUT MOST OF US JUST GET DRAGGED THROUGH THE FECES.
"WE'RE FORGOTTEN BECAUSE WE'RE JUST BARELY WORTH SALVATION OR CONDEMNATION."

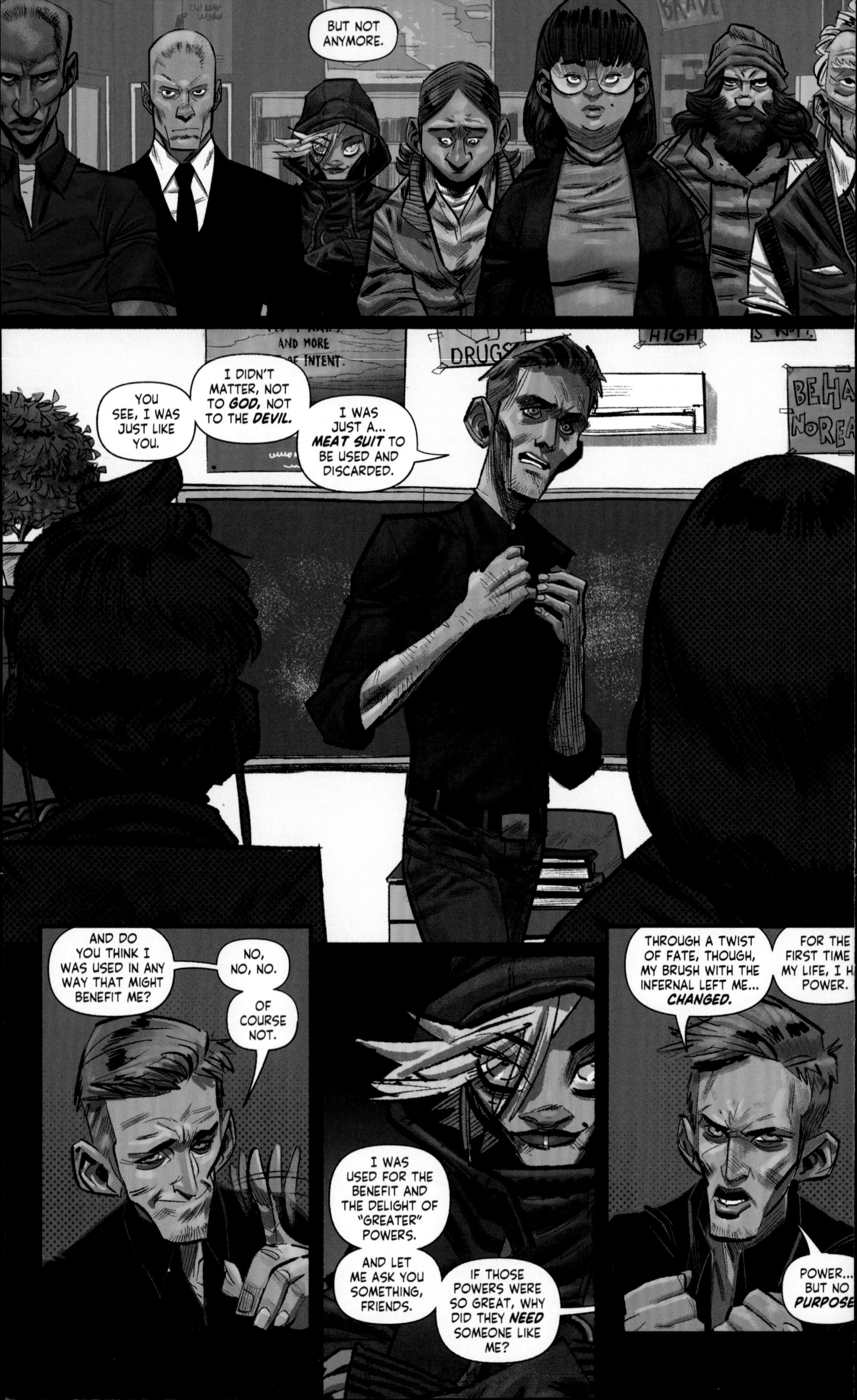
BUT NOT ANYMORE.
AND MORE
INTENT.
DRUGS
HIGH
YOU SEE, I WAS JUST LIKE YOU.
I DIDN'T MATTER, NOT TO GOD, NOT TO THE DEVIL.
I WAS JUST A... MEAT SUIT TO BE USED AND DISCARDED.
AND DO YOU THINK I WAS USED IN ANY WAY THAT MIGHT BENEFIT ME?
NO, NO, NO.
OF COURSE NOT.
I WAS USED FOR THE BENEFIT AND THE DELIGHT OF "GREATER" POWERS.
AND LET ME ASK YOU SOMETHING, FRIENDS.
IF THOSE POWERS WERE SO GREAT, WHY DID THEY NEED SOMEONE LIKE ME?
THROUGH A TWIST OF FATE, THOUGH, MY BRUSH WITH THE INFERNAL LEFT ME... CHANGED.
FOR THE FIRST TIME MY LIFE, I H POWER.
POWER... BUT NO PURPOSE

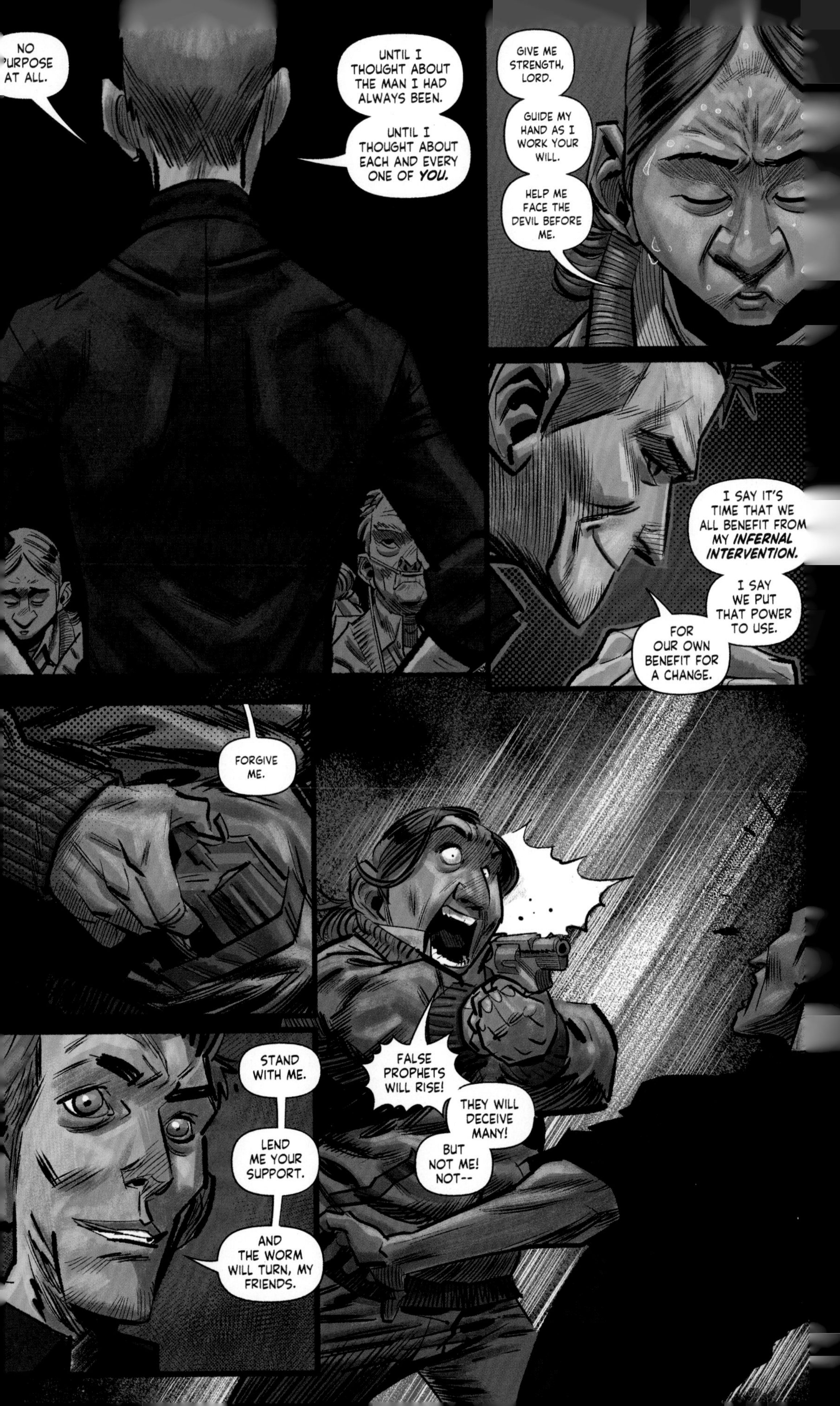

NO PURPOSE AT ALL.
UNTIL I THOUGHT ABOUT THE MAN I HAD ALWAYS BEEN.
UNTIL I THOUGHT ABOUT EACH AND EVERY ONE OF YOU.
GIVE ME STRENGTH, LORD.
GUIDE MY HAND AS I WORK YOUR WILL.
HELP ME FACE THE DEVIL BEFORE ME.
I SAY IT'S TIME THAT WE ALL BENEFIT FROM MY INFERNAL INTERVENTION.
I SAY WE PUT THAT POWER TO USE.
FOR OUR OWN BENEFIT FOR A CHANGE.
FORGIVE ME.
STAND WITH ME.
LEND ME YOUR SUPPORT.
AND THE WORM WILL TURN, MY FRIENDS.
FALSE PROPHETS WILL RISE!
THEY WILL DECEIVE MANY!
BUT NOT ME! NOT--

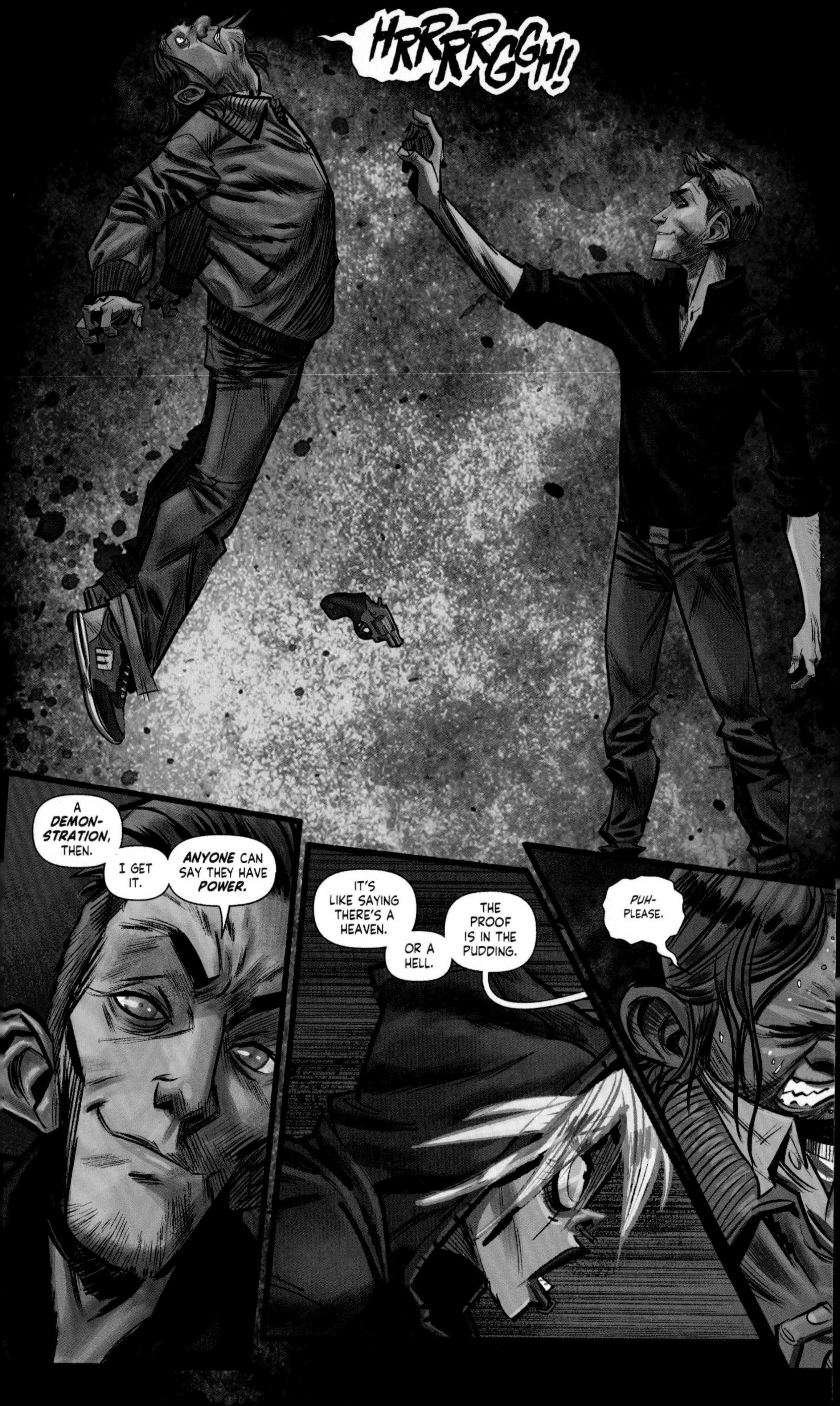
HRRRRGGH!
A DEMON-STRATION, THEN.
I GET IT.
ANYONE CAN SAY THEY HAVE POWER.
IT'S LIKE SAYING THERE'S A HEAVEN.
OR A HELL.
THE PROOF IS IN THE PUDDING.
PUH-PLEASE.

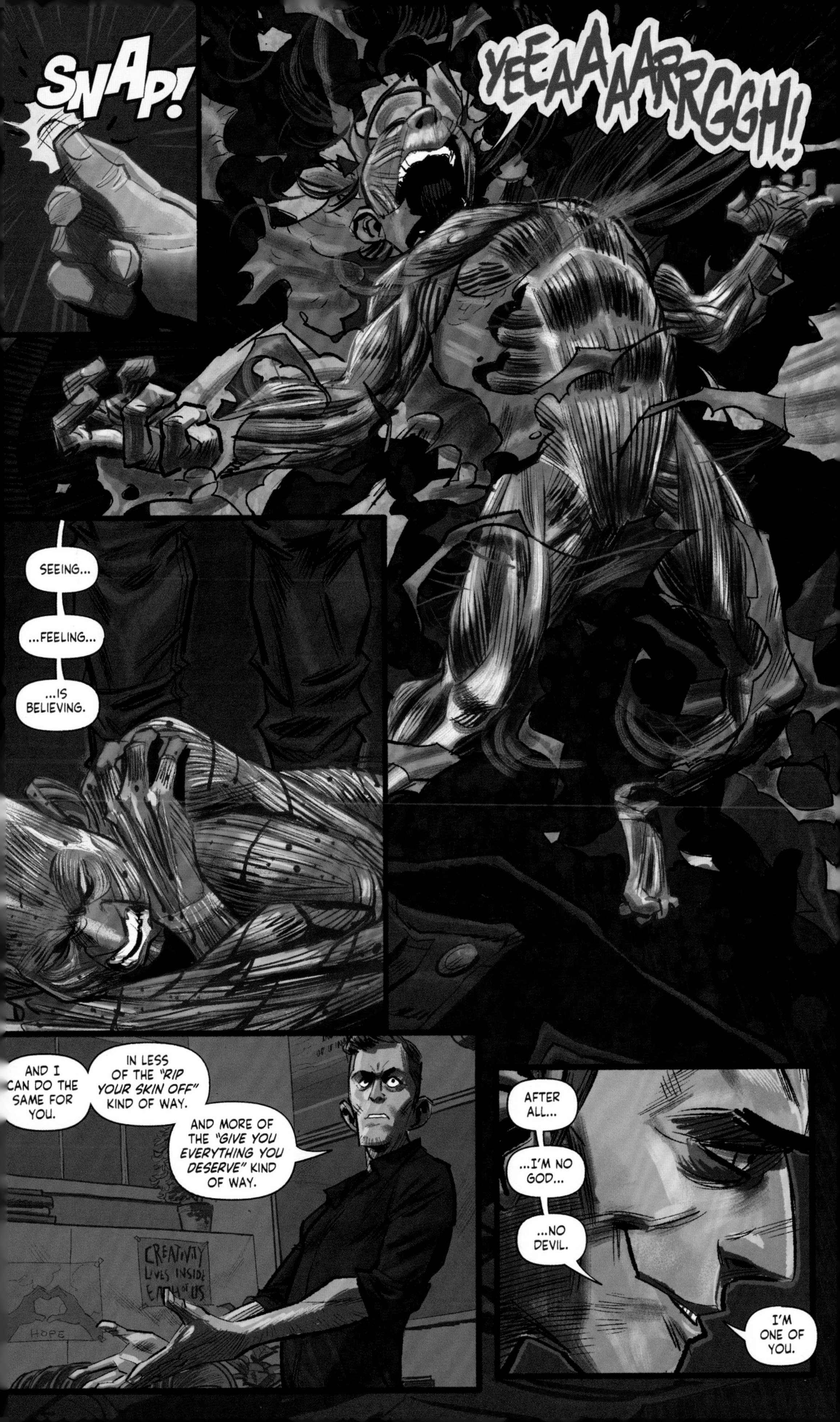
SNAP!
YEEAAAARRGGH!
SEEING...
...FEELING...
...IS BELIEVING.
AND I CAN DO THE SAME FOR YOU.
IN LESS OF THE "RIP YOUR SKIN OFF" KIND OF WAY.
AND MORE OF THE "GIVE YOU EVERYTHING YOU DESERVE" KIND OF WAY.
CREATIVITY LIVES INSIDE EACH OF US
HOPE
AFTER ALL...
...I'M NO GOD...
...NO DEVIL.
I'M ONE OF YOU.

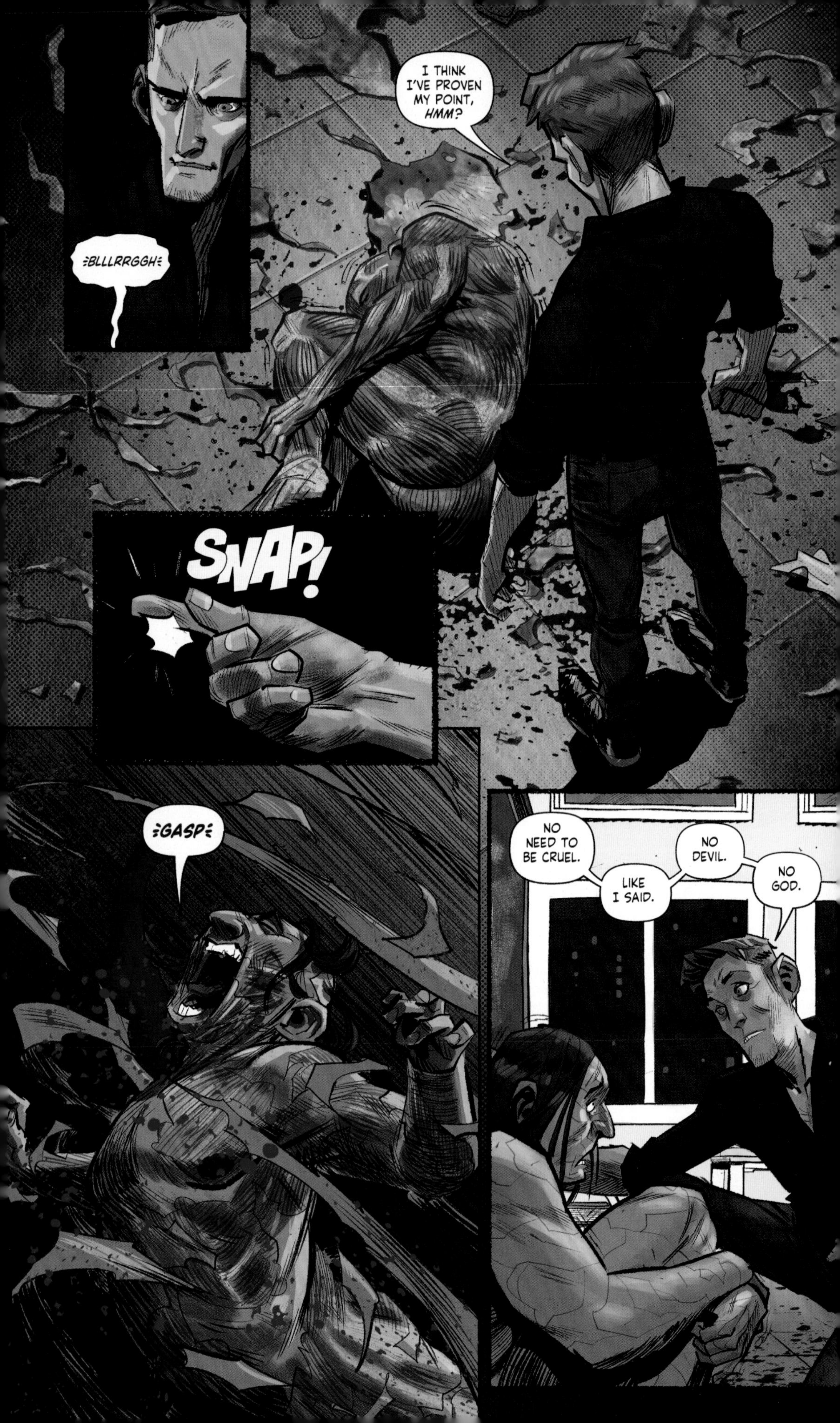
BLLLRRGGH
I THINK I'VE PROVEN MY POINT, *HMM?*
SNAP!
GASP
NO NEED TO BE CRUEL.
LIKE I SAID.
NO DEVIL.
NO GOD.

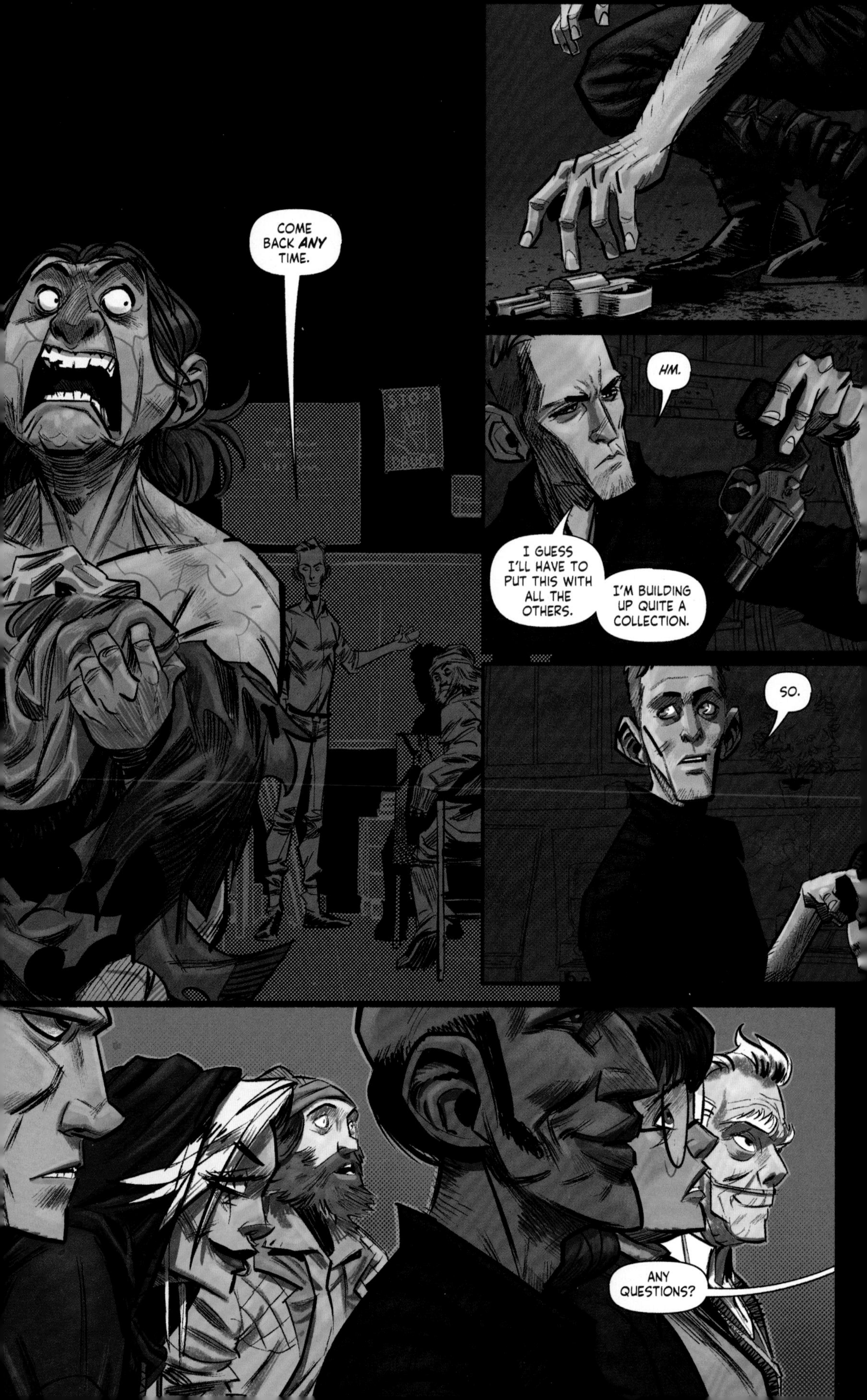
COME BACK ANY TIME.
HM.
I GUESS I'LL HAVE TO PUT THIS WITH ALL THE OTHERS.
I'M BUILDING UP QUITE A COLLECTION.
SO.
ANY QUESTIONS?

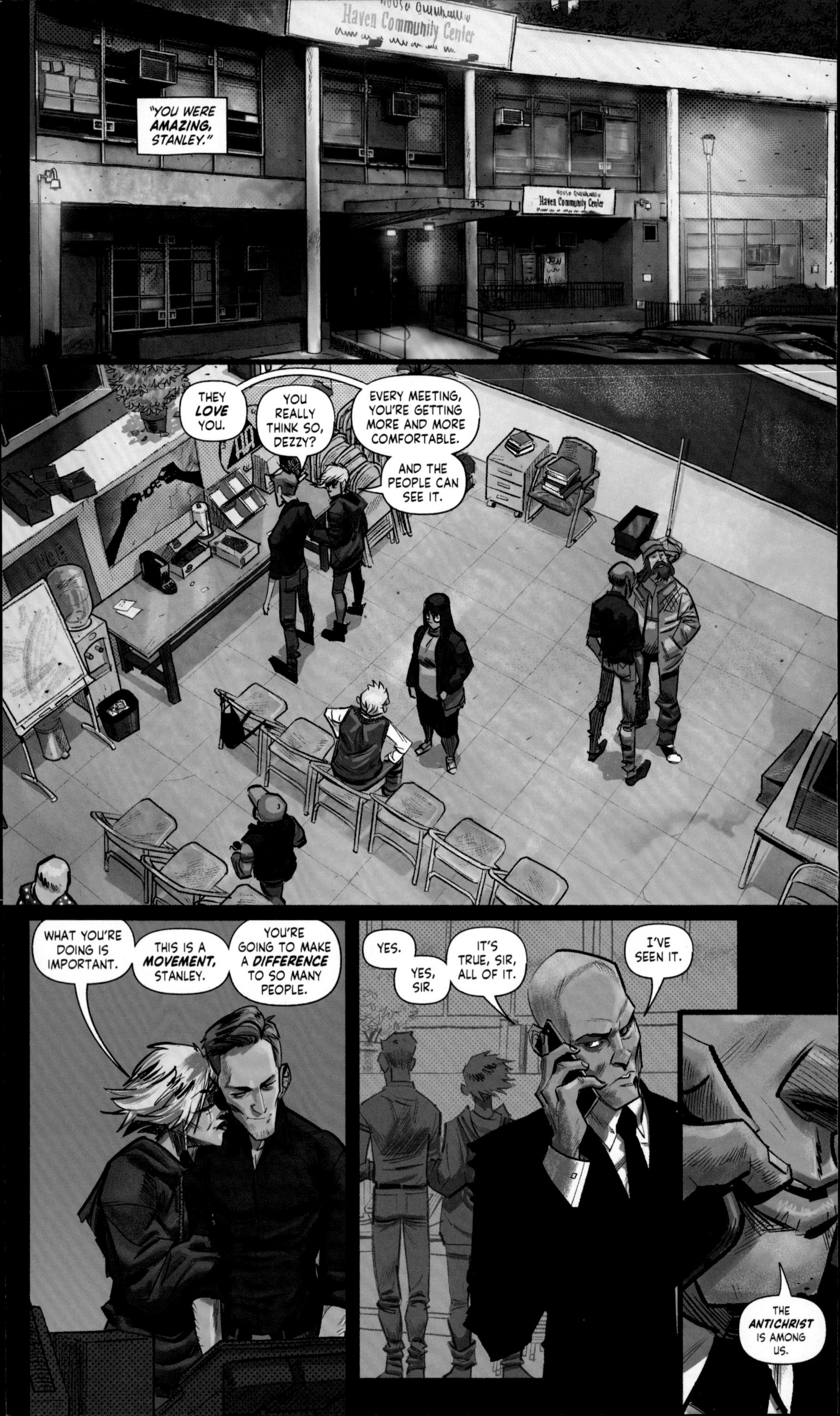
Haven Community Center
"YOU WERE AMAZING, STANLEY."
375
Haven Community Center
THEY LOVE YOU.
YOU REALLY THINK SO, DEZZY?
EVERY MEETING, YOU'RE GETTING MORE AND MORE COMFORTABLE.
AND THE PEOPLE CAN SEE IT.
HOPE
WHAT YOU'RE DOING IS IMPORTANT.
THIS IS A MOVEMENT, STANLEY.
YOU'RE GOING TO MAKE A DIFFERENCE TO SO MANY PEOPLE.
YES.
YES, SIR.
IT'S TRUE, SIR, ALL OF IT.
I'VE SEEN IT.
THE ANTICHRIST IS AMONG US.

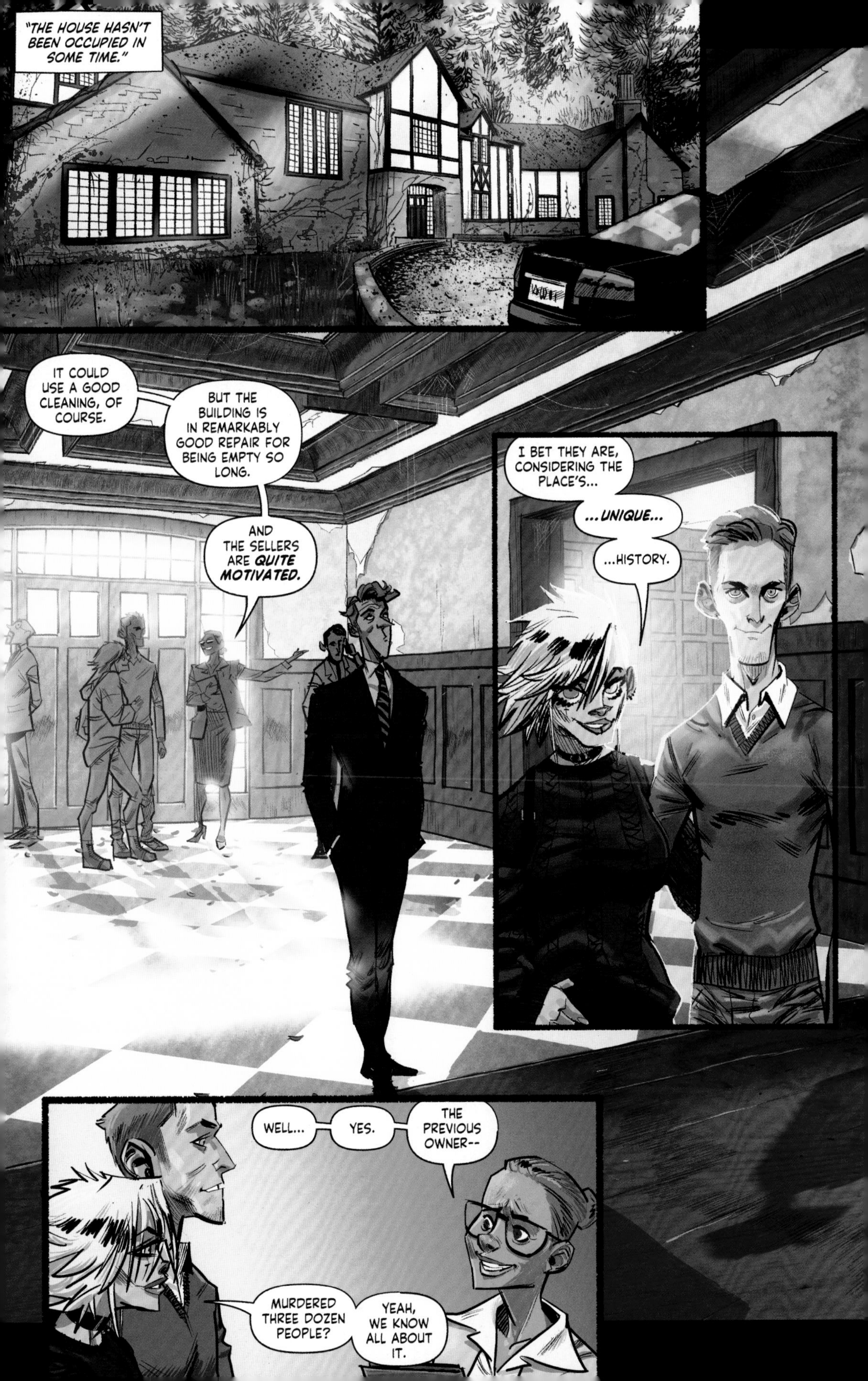
"THE HOUSE HASN'T BEEN OCCUPIED IN SOME TIME."
IT COULD USE A GOOD CLEANING, OF COURSE.
BUT THE BUILDING IS IN REMARKABLY GOOD REPAIR FOR BEING EMPTY SO LONG.
AND THE SELLERS ARE QUITE MOTIVATED.
I BET THEY ARE, CONSIDERING THE PLACE'S...
...UNIQUE...
...HISTORY.
WELL...
YES.
THE PREVIOUS OWNER--
MURDERED THREE DOZEN PEOPLE?
YEAH, WE KNOW ALL ABOUT IT.

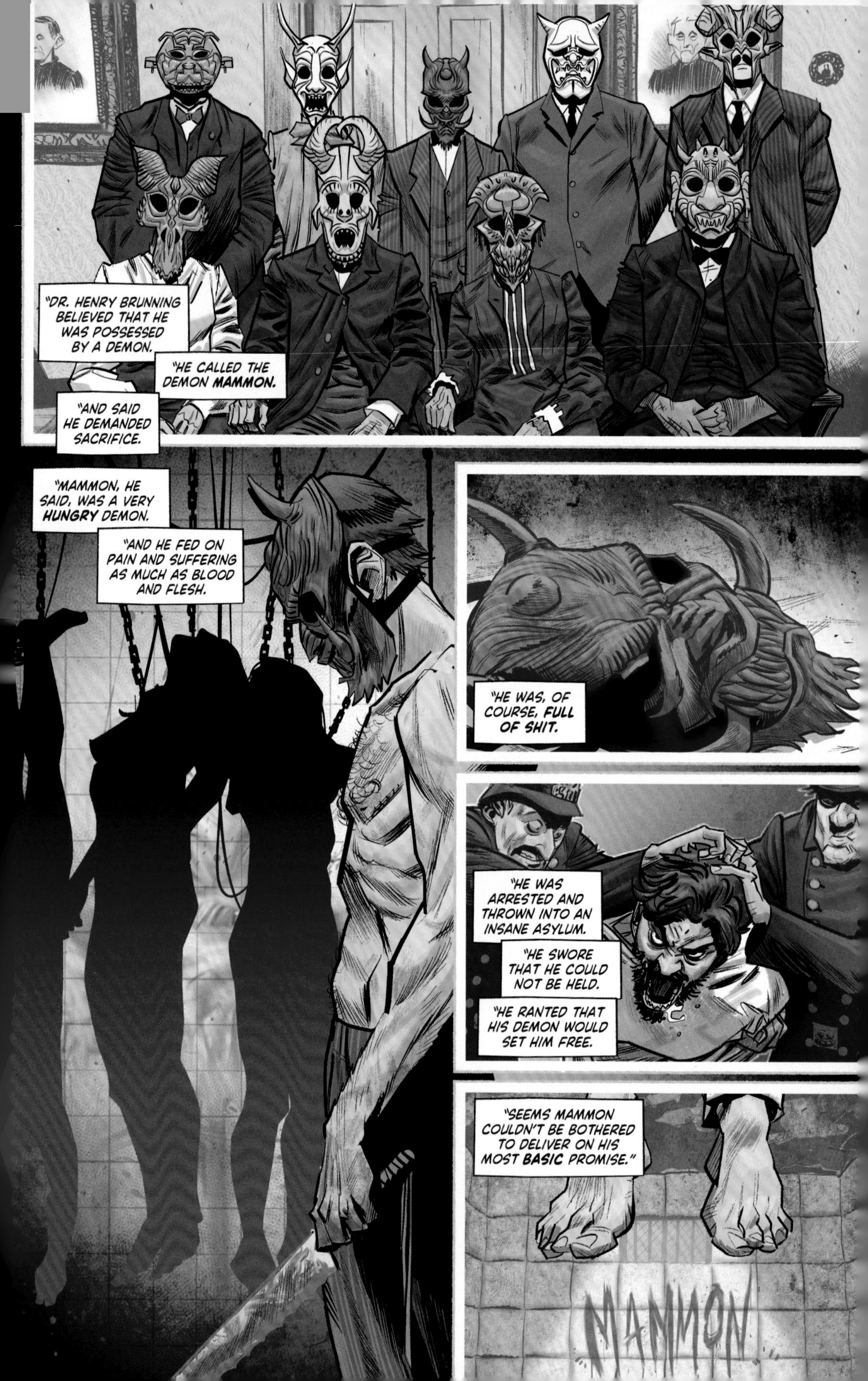
"DR. HENRY BRUNNING BELIEVED THAT HE WAS POSSESSED BY A DEMON.
"HE CALLED THE DEMON MAMMON.
"AND SAID HE DEMANDED SACRIFICE.
"MAMMON, HE SAID, WAS A VERY HUNGRY DEMON.
"AND HE FED ON PAIN AND SUFFERING AS MUCH AS BLOOD AND FLESH.
"HE WAS, OF COURSE, FULL OF SHIT.
"HE WAS ARRESTED AND THROWN INTO AN INSANE ASYLUM.
"HE SWORE THAT HE COULD NOT BE HELD.
"HE RANTED THAT HIS DEMON WOULD SET HIM FREE.
"SEEMS MAMMON COULDN'T BE BOTHERED TO DELIVER ON HIS MOST BASIC PROMISE."
MAMMON

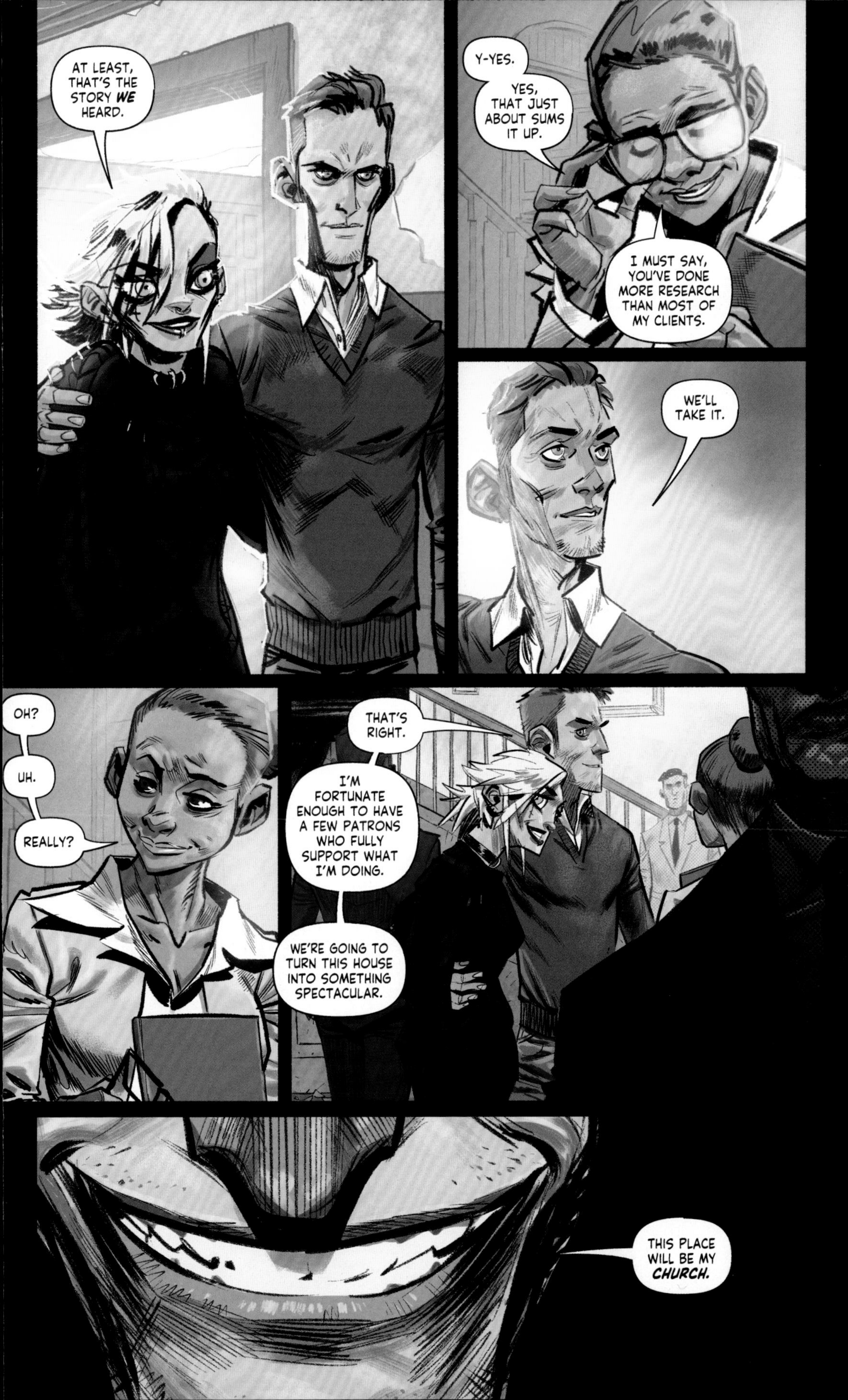
AT LEAST, THAT'S THE STORY *WE* HEARD.
Y-YES.
YES, THAT JUST ABOUT SUMS IT UP.
I MUST SAY, YOU'VE DONE MORE RESEARCH THAN MOST OF MY CLIENTS.
WE'LL TAKE IT.
OH?
UH.
REALLY?
THAT'S RIGHT.
I'M FORTUNATE ENOUGH TO HAVE A FEW PATRONS WHO FULLY SUPPORT WHAT I'M DOING.
WE'RE GOING TO TURN THIS HOUSE INTO SOMETHING SPECTACULAR.
THIS PLACE WILL BE MY ***CHURCH.***

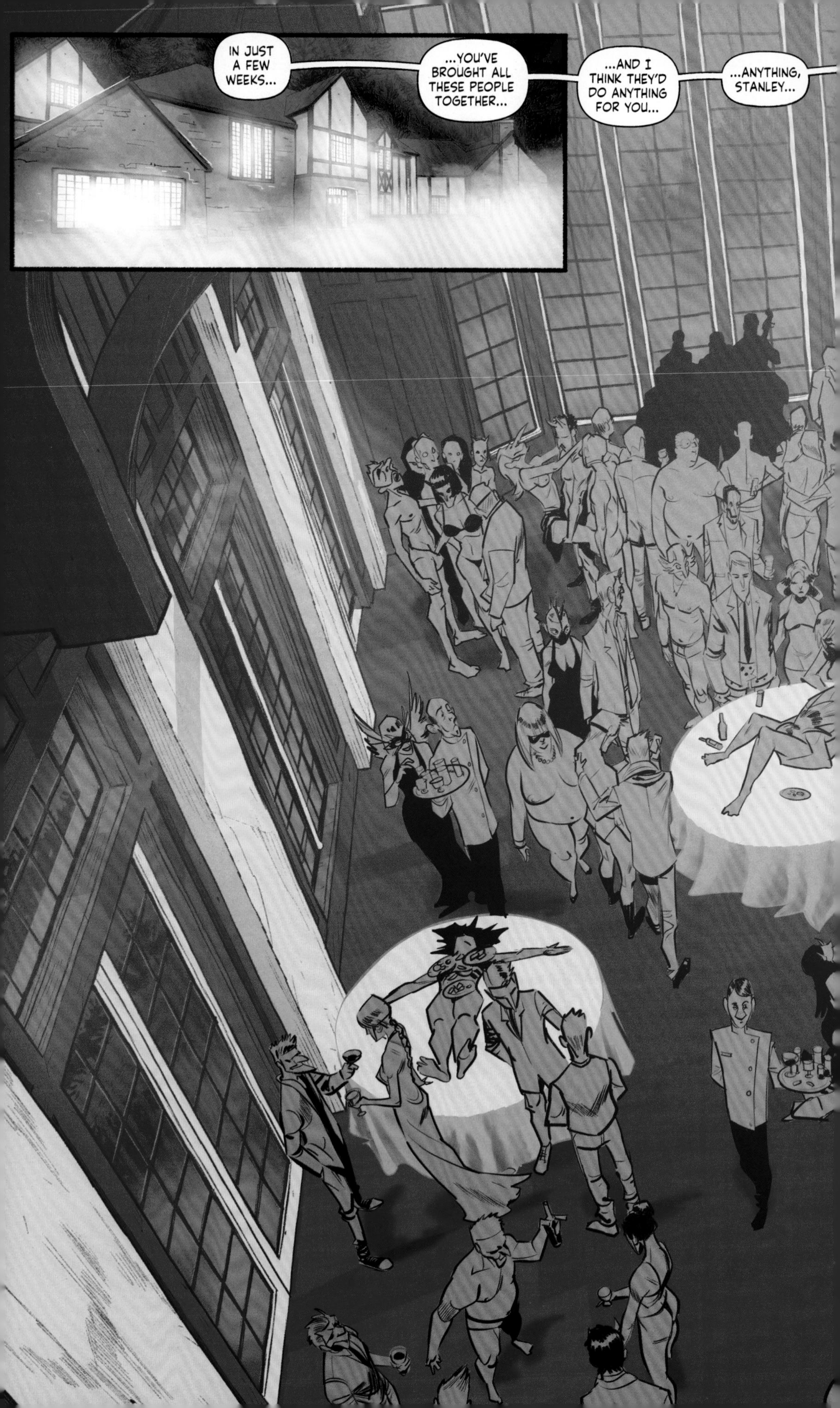

IN JUST A FEW WEEKS...
...YOU'VE BROUGHT ALL THESE PEOPLE TOGETHER...
...AND I THINK THEY'D DO ANYTHING FOR YOU...
...ANYTHING, STANLEY...

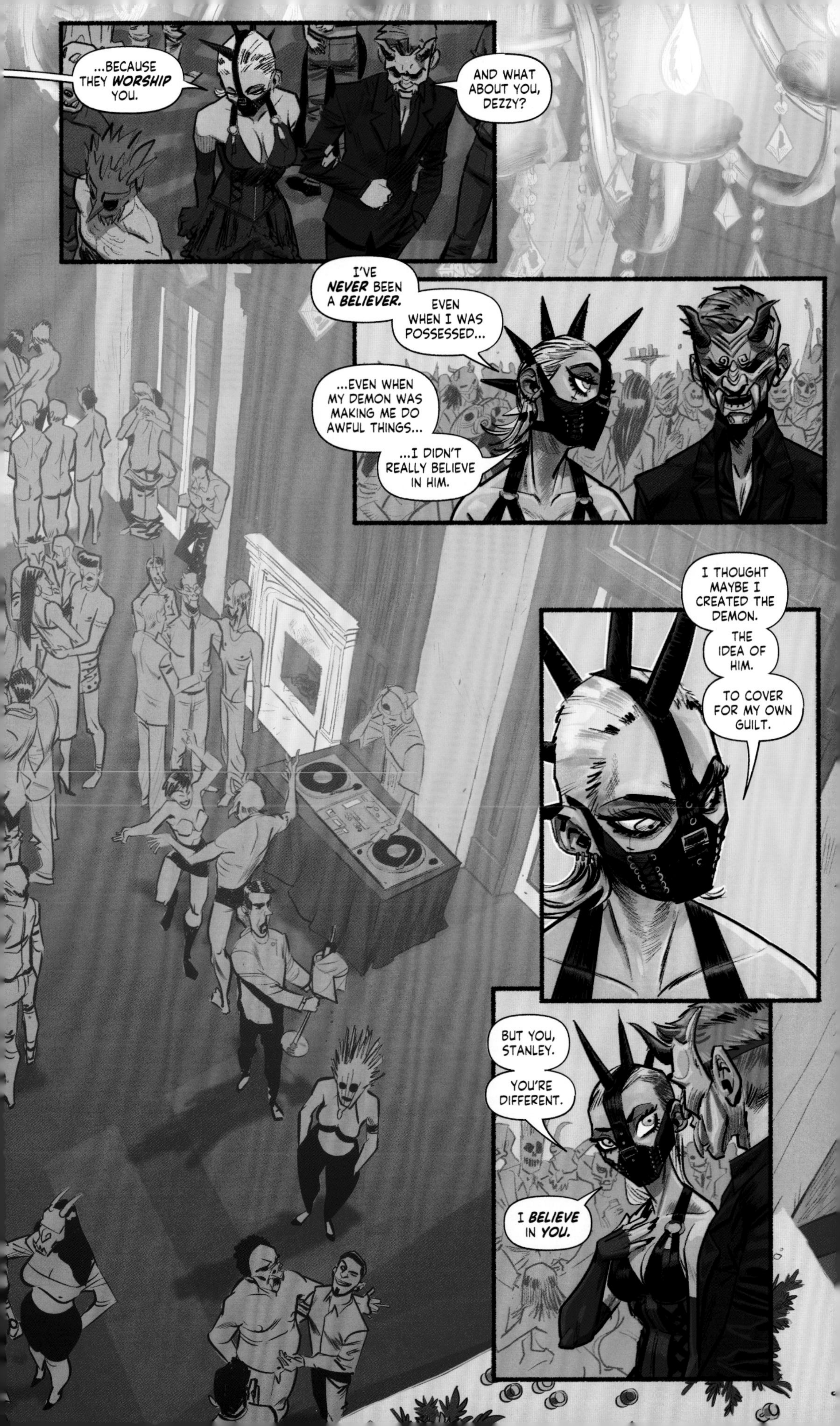
...BECAUSE THEY *WORSHIP* YOU.
AND WHAT ABOUT YOU, DEZZY?
I'VE *NEVER* BEEN A *BELIEVER.*
EVEN WHEN I WAS POSSESSED...
...EVEN WHEN MY DEMON WAS MAKING ME DO AWFUL THINGS...
...I DIDN'T REALLY BELIEVE IN HIM.
I THOUGHT MAYBE I CREATED THE DEMON.
THE IDEA OF HIM.
TO COVER FOR MY OWN GUILT.
BUT YOU, STANLEY.
YOU'RE DIFFERENT.
I *BELIEVE* IN *YOU.*

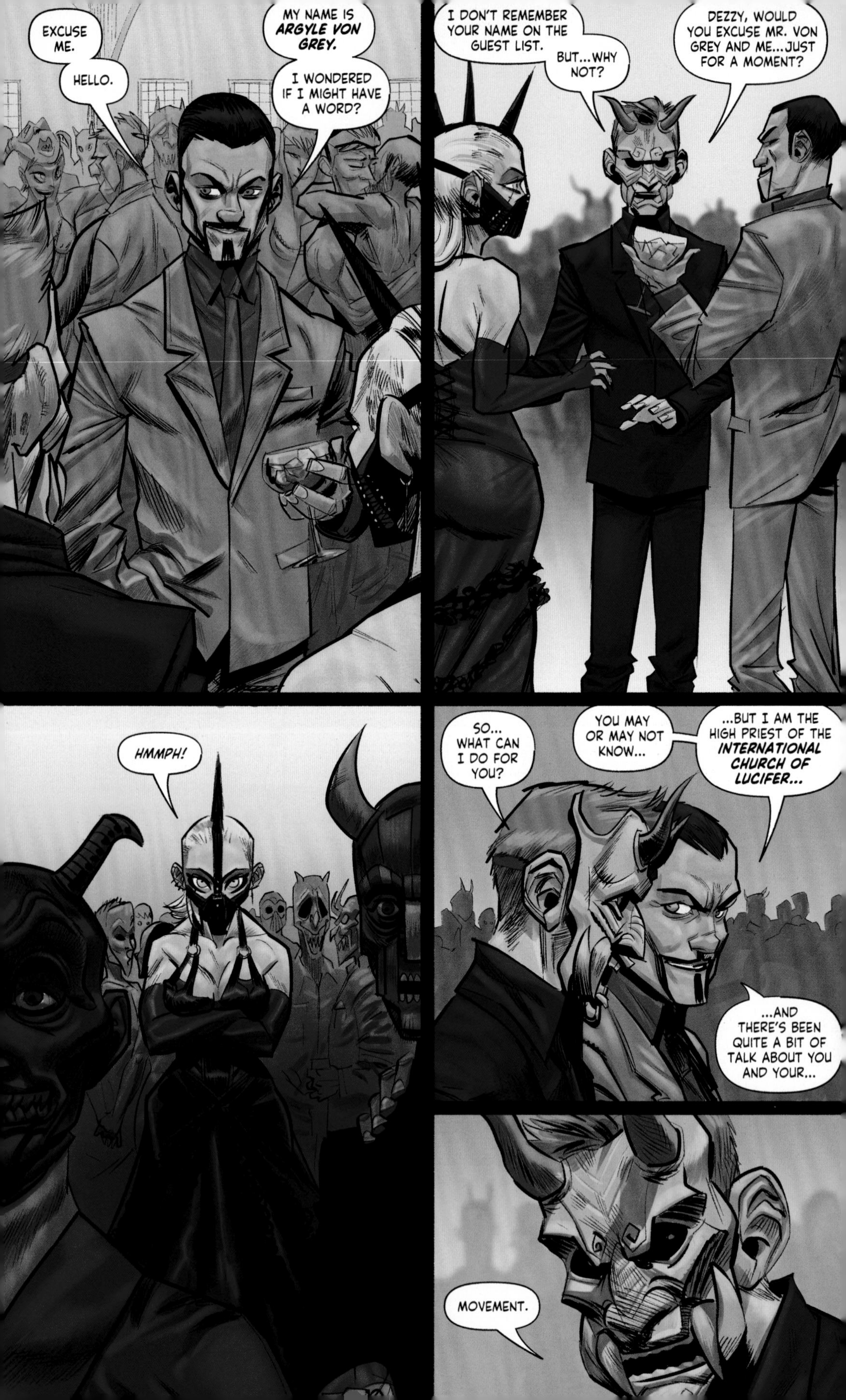
EXCUSE ME.
HELLO.
MY NAME IS ARGYLE VON GREY.
I WONDERED IF I MIGHT HAVE A WORD?
I DON'T REMEMBER YOUR NAME ON THE GUEST LIST.
BUT...WHY NOT?
DEZZY, WOULD YOU EXCUSE MR. VON GREY AND ME...JUST FOR A MOMENT?
HMMPH!
SO... WHAT CAN I DO FOR YOU?
YOU MAY OR MAY NOT KNOW...
...BUT I AM THE HIGH PRIEST OF THE INTERNATIONAL CHURCH OF LUCIFER...
...AND THERE'S BEEN QUITE A BIT OF TALK ABOUT YOU AND YOUR...
MOVEMENT.

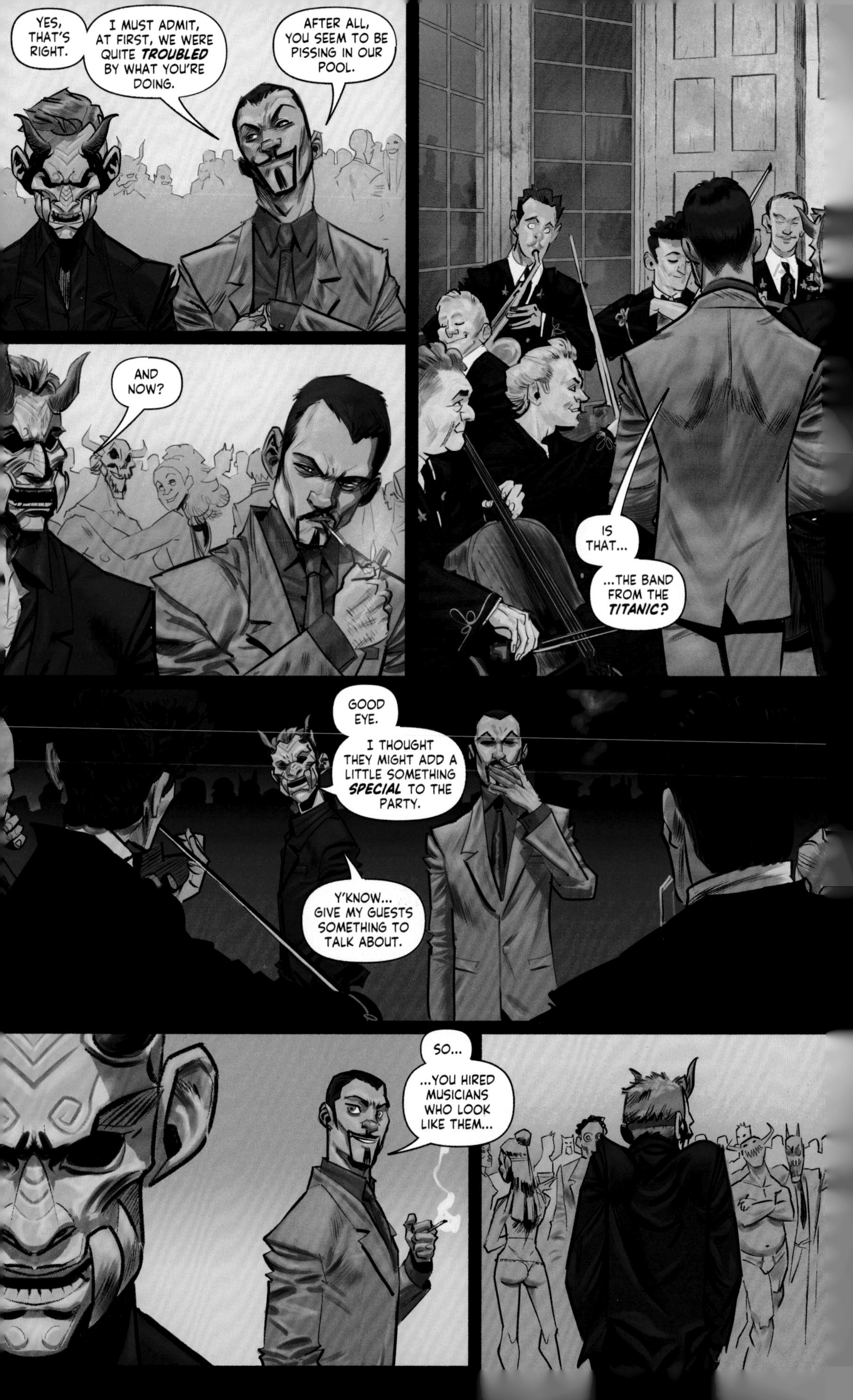
YES, THAT'S RIGHT.
I MUST ADMIT, AT FIRST, WE WERE QUITE **TROUBLED** BY WHAT YOU'RE DOING.
AFTER ALL, YOU SEEM TO BE PISSING IN OUR POOL.
AND NOW?
IS THAT...
...THE BAND FROM THE ***TITANIC?***
GOOD EYE.
I THOUGHT THEY MIGHT ADD A LITTLE SOMETHING ***SPECIAL*** TO THE PARTY.
Y'KNOW... GIVE MY GUESTS SOMETHING TO TALK ABOUT.
SO...
...YOU HIRED MUSICIANS WHO LOOK LIKE THEM...

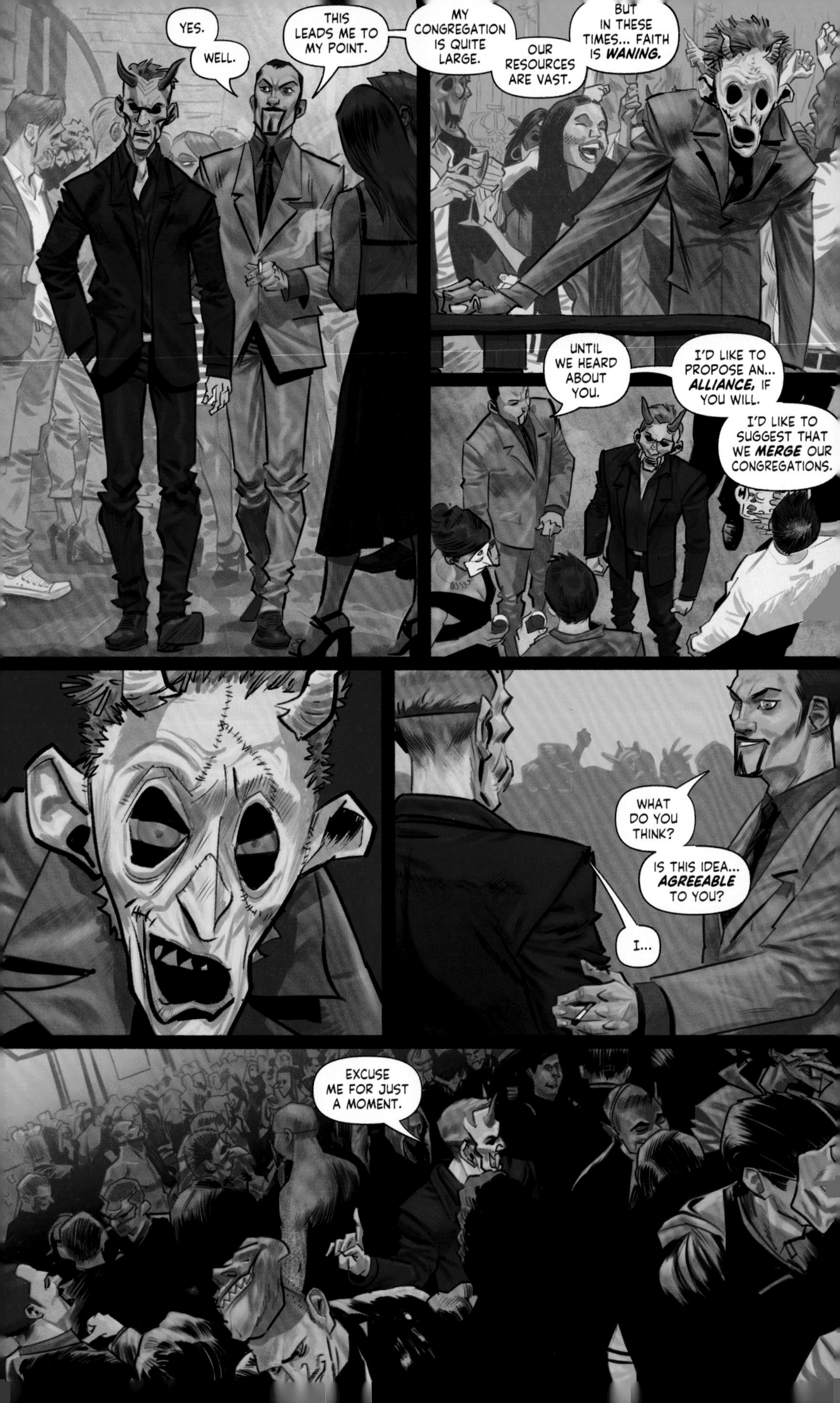
YES.
WELL.
THIS LEADS ME TO MY POINT.
MY CONGREGATION IS QUITE LARGE.
OUR RESOURCES ARE VAST.
BUT IN THESE TIMES... FAITH IS ***WANING.***
UNTIL WE HEARD ABOUT YOU.
I'D LIKE TO PROPOSE AN... ***ALLIANCE,*** IF YOU WILL.
I'D LIKE TO SUGGEST THAT WE ***MERGE*** OUR CONGREGATIONS.
WHAT DO YOU THINK?
IS THIS IDEA... ***AGREEABLE*** TO YOU?
I...
EXCUSE ME FOR JUST A MOMENT.

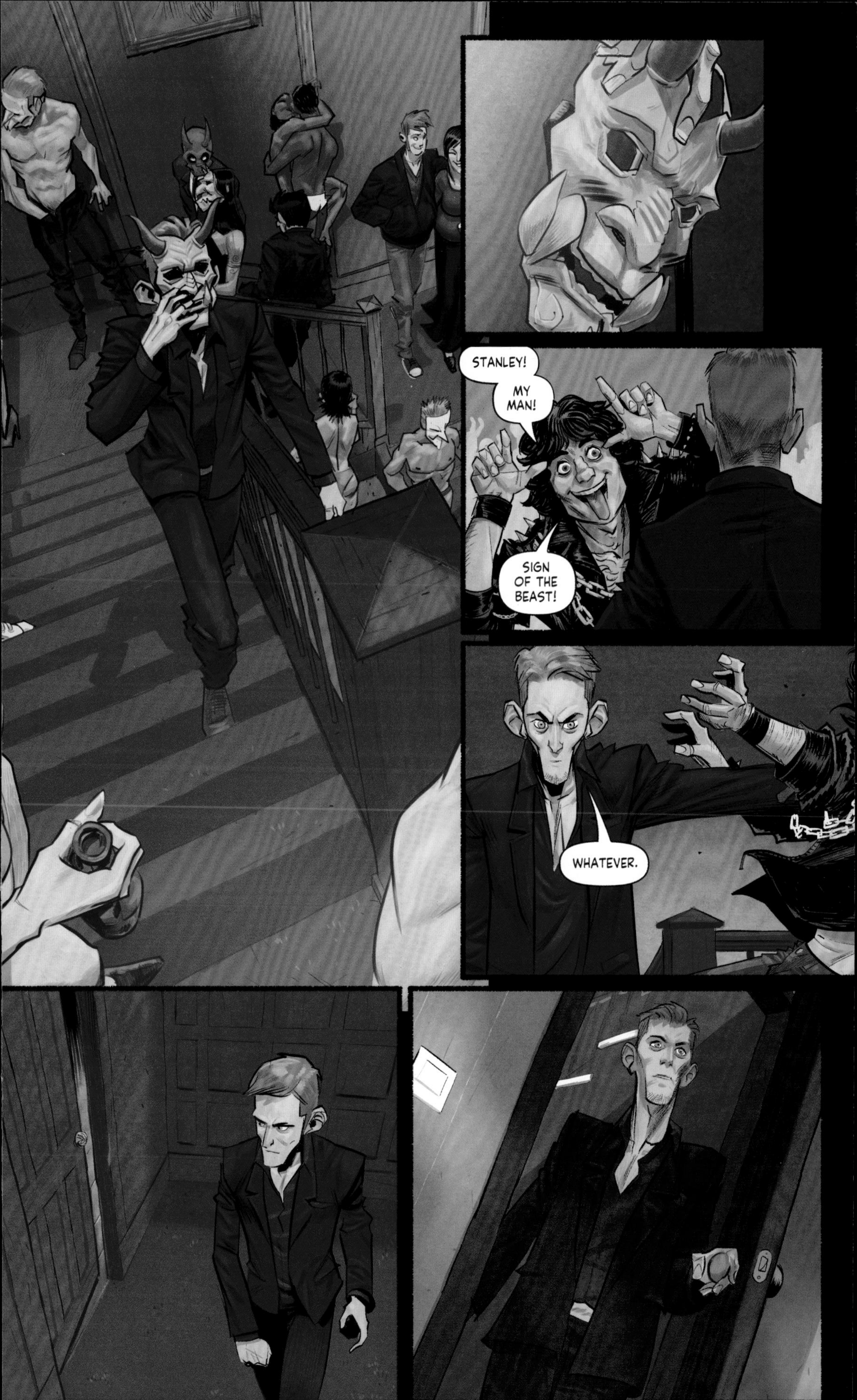
STANLEY!
MY MAN!
SIGN OF THE BEAST!
WHATEVER.

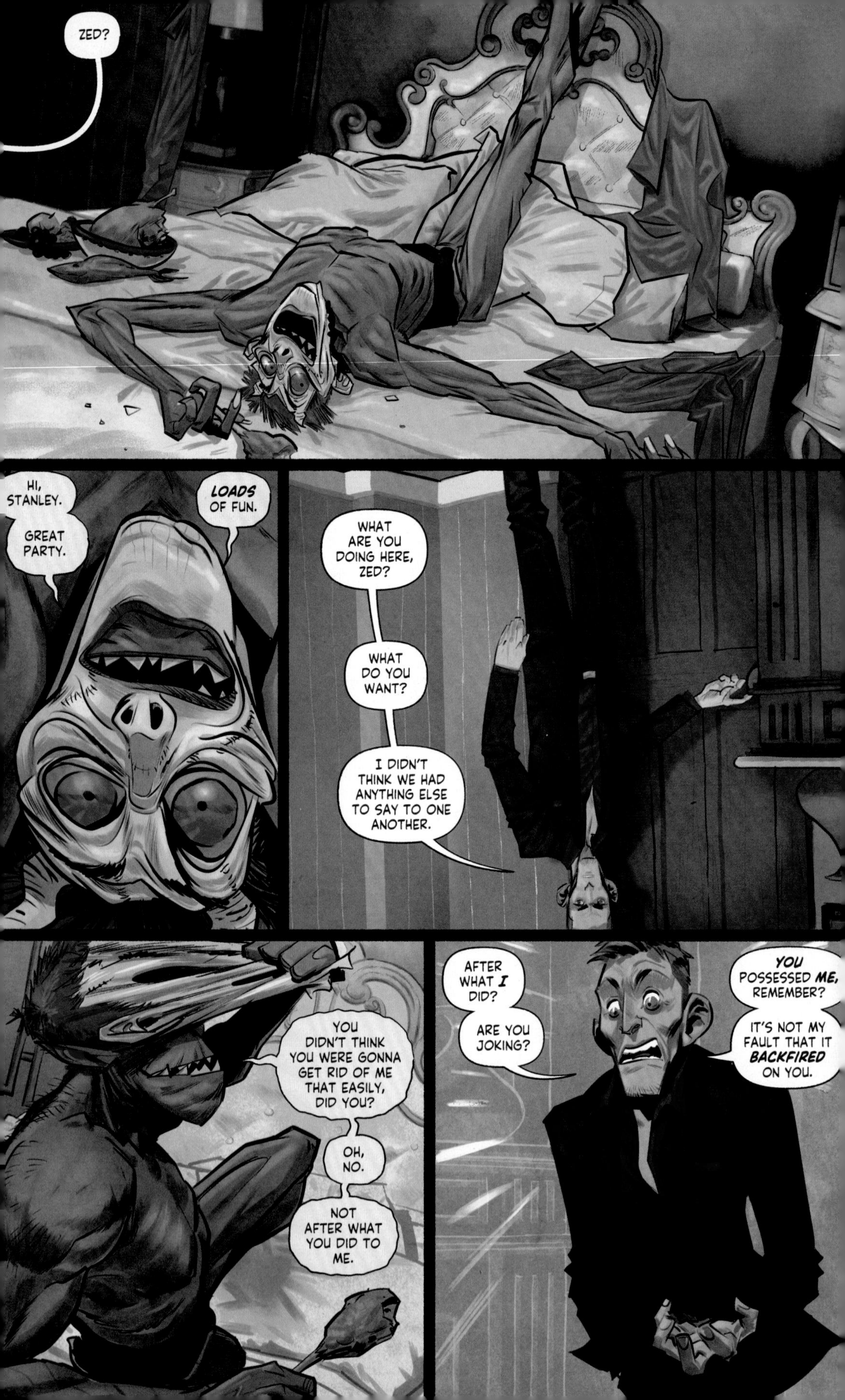
ZED?
HI, STANLEY.
GREAT PARTY.
LOADS OF FUN.
WHAT ARE YOU DOING HERE, ZED?
WHAT DO YOU WANT?
I DIDN'T THINK WE HAD ANYTHING ELSE TO SAY TO ONE ANOTHER.
YOU DIDN'T THINK YOU WERE GONNA GET RID OF ME THAT EASILY, DID YOU?
OH, NO.
NOT AFTER WHAT YOU DID TO ME.
AFTER WHAT I DID?
ARE YOU JOKING?
YOU POSSESSED ME, REMEMBER?
IT'S NOT MY FAULT THAT IT BACKFIRED ON YOU.

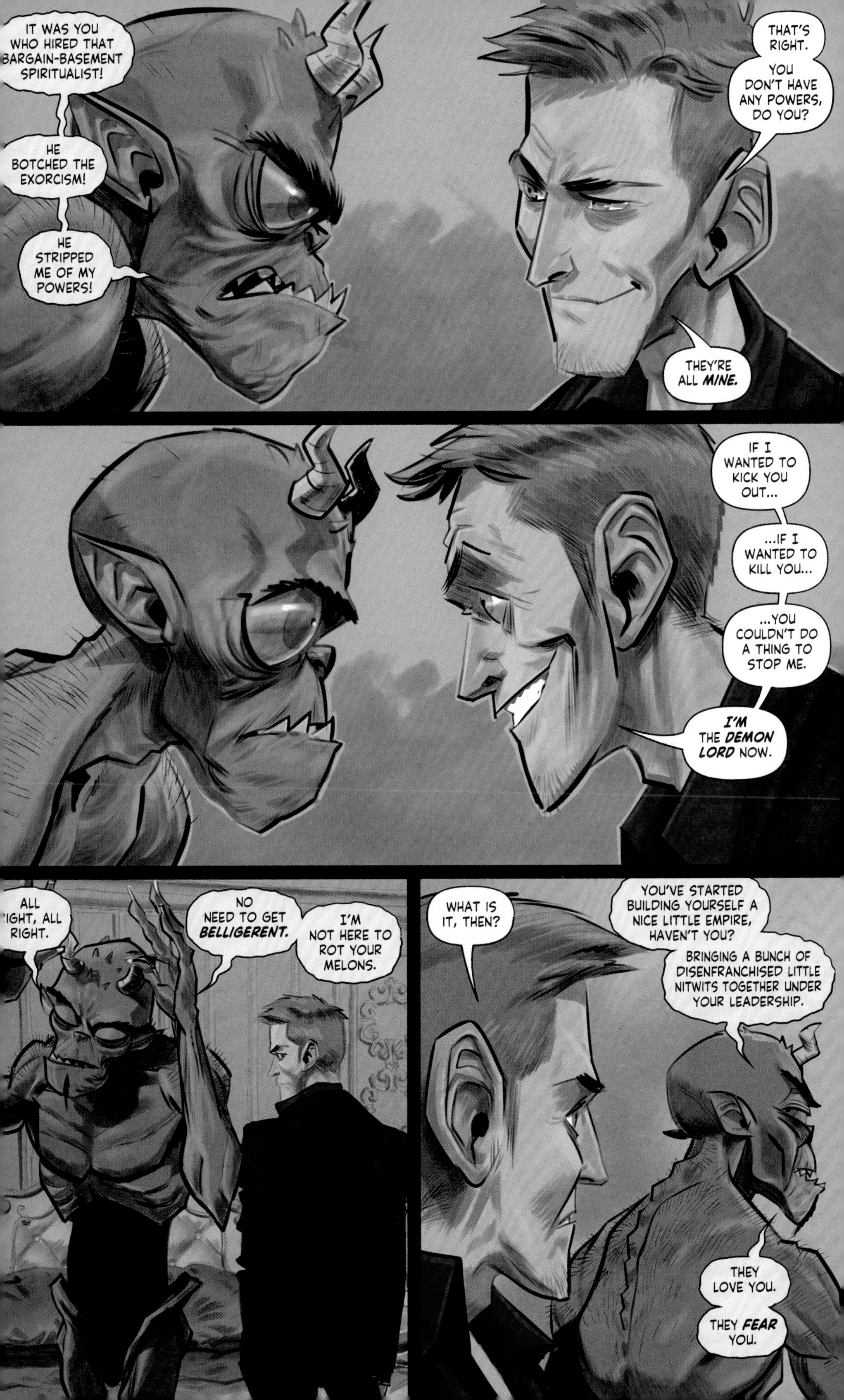
IT WAS YOU WHO HIRED THAT BARGAIN-BASEMENT SPIRITUALIST!
HE BOTCHED THE EXORCISM!
HE STRIPPED ME OF MY POWERS!
THAT'S RIGHT.
YOU DON'T HAVE ANY POWERS, DO YOU?
THEY'RE ALL *MINE.*
IF I WANTED TO KICK YOU OUT...
...IF I WANTED TO KILL YOU...
...YOU COULDN'T DO A THING TO STOP ME.
I'M THE *DEMON LORD* NOW.
ALL RIGHT, ALL RIGHT.
NO NEED TO GET *BELLIGERENT.*
I'M NOT HERE TO ROT YOUR MELONS.
WHAT IS IT, THEN?
YOU'VE STARTED BUILDING YOURSELF A NICE LITTLE EMPIRE, HAVEN'T YOU?
BRINGING A BUNCH OF DISENFRANCHISED LITTLE NITWITS TOGETHER UNDER YOUR LEADERSHIP.
THEY LOVE YOU.
THEY *FEAR* YOU.

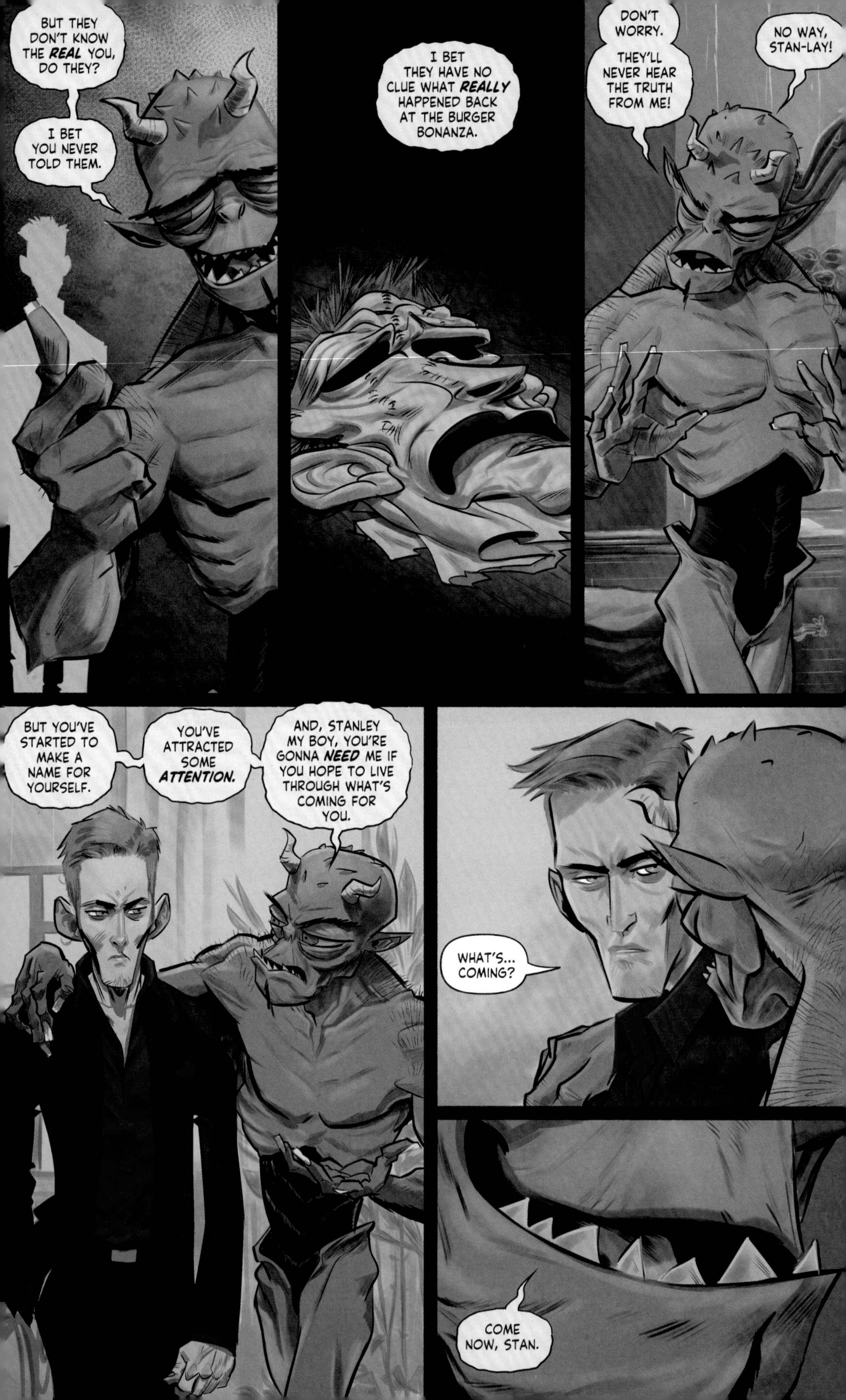
BUT THEY DON'T KNOW THE REAL YOU, DO THEY?
I BET YOU NEVER TOLD THEM.
I BET THEY HAVE NO CLUE WHAT REALLY HAPPENED BACK AT THE BURGER BONANZA.
DON'T WORRY.
THEY'LL NEVER HEAR THE TRUTH FROM ME!
NO WAY, STAN-LAY!
BUT YOU'VE STARTED TO MAKE A NAME FOR YOURSELF.
YOU'VE ATTRACTED SOME ATTENTION.
AND, STANLEY MY BOY, YOU'RE GONNA NEED ME IF YOU HOPE TO LIVE THROUGH WHAT'S COMING FOR YOU.
WHAT'S... COMING?
COME NOW, STAN.

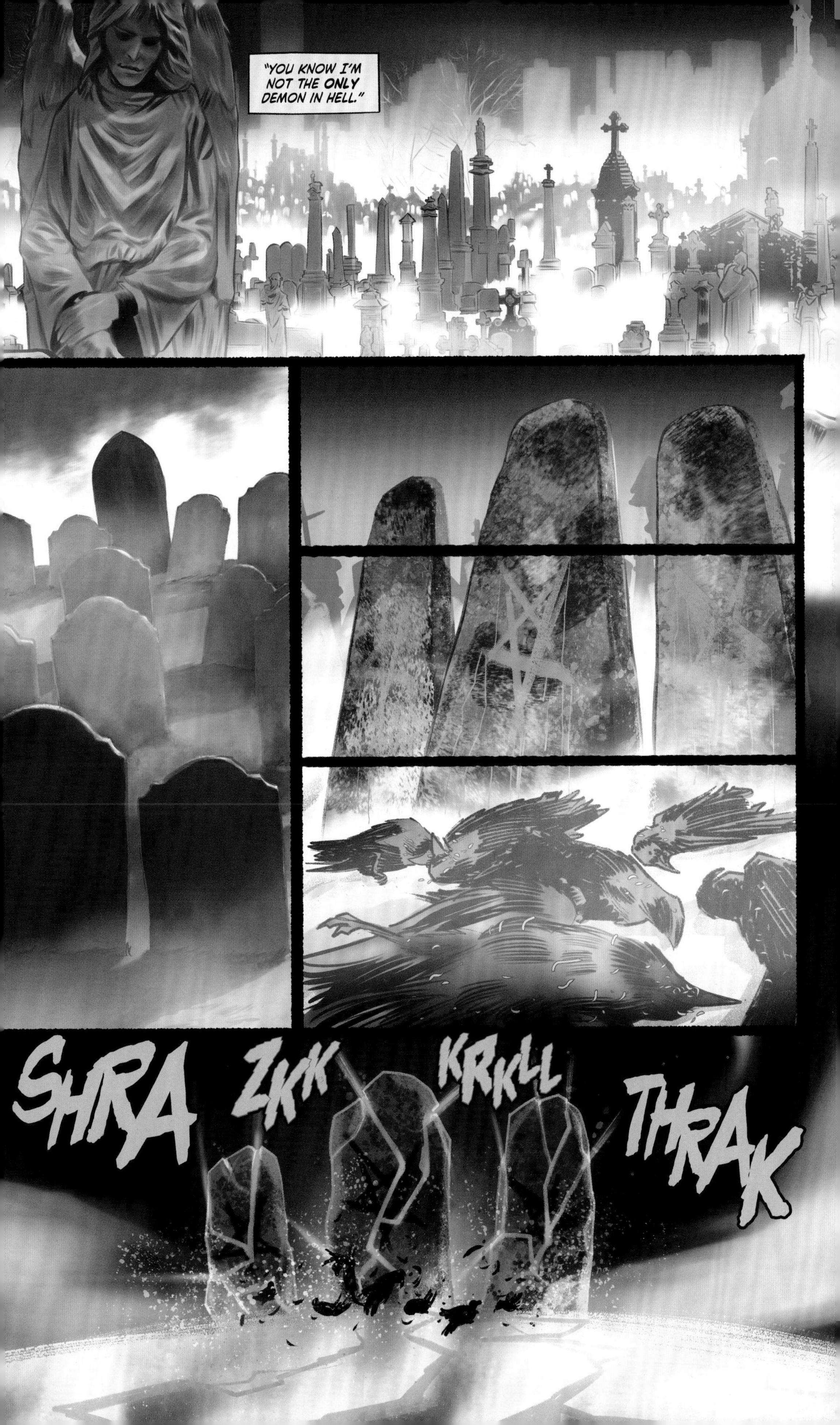
"YOU KNOW I'M NOT THE ONLY DEMON IN HELL."
SHRA
ZKK
KRKLL
THRAK

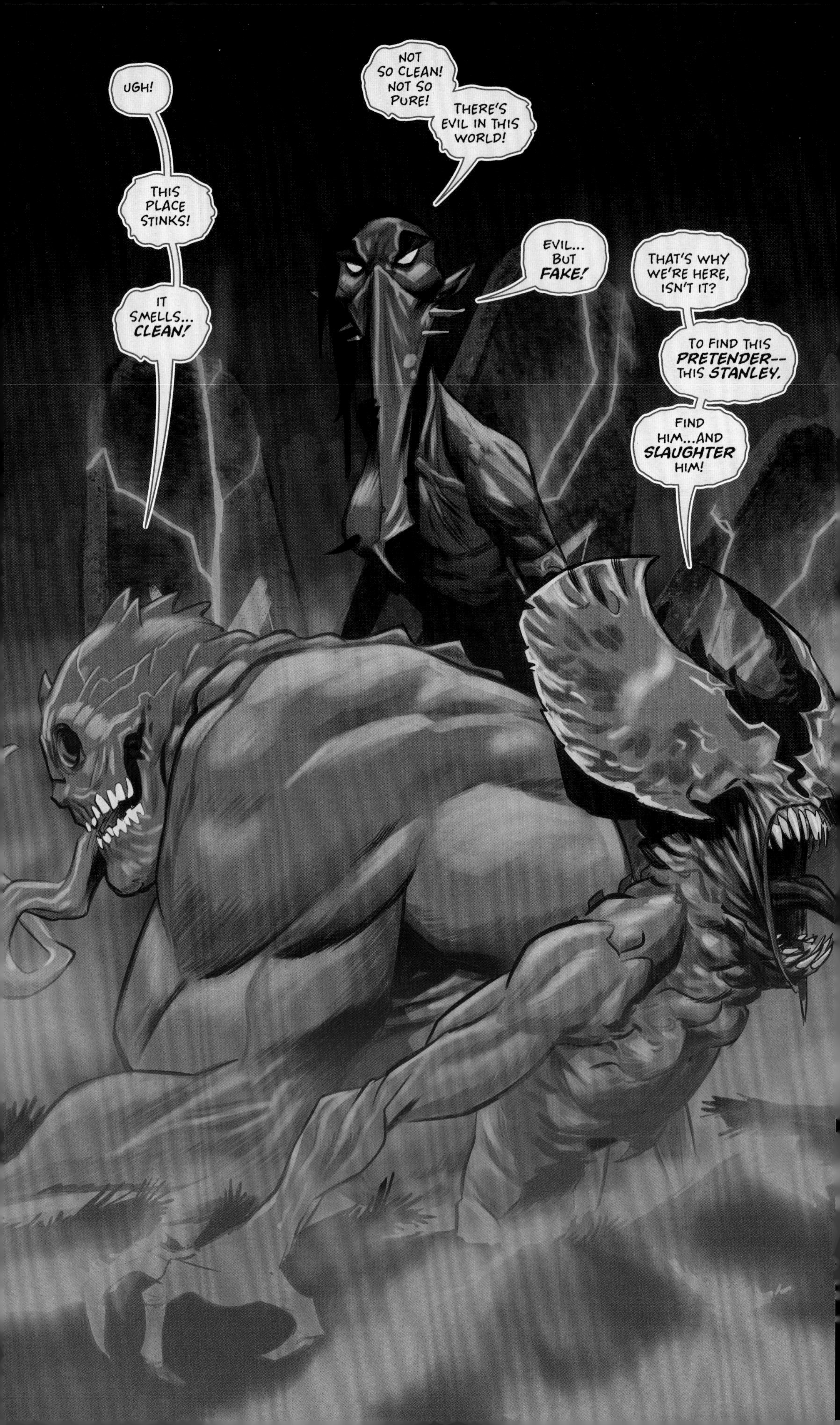
UGH!
THIS PLACE STINKS!
IT SMELLS... CLEAN!
NOT SO CLEAN! NOT SO PURE!
THERE'S EVIL IN THIS WORLD!
EVIL... BUT FAKE!
THAT'S WHY WE'RE HERE, ISN'T IT?
TO FIND THIS PRETENDER-- THIS STANLEY.
FIND HIM...AND SLAUGHTER HIM!

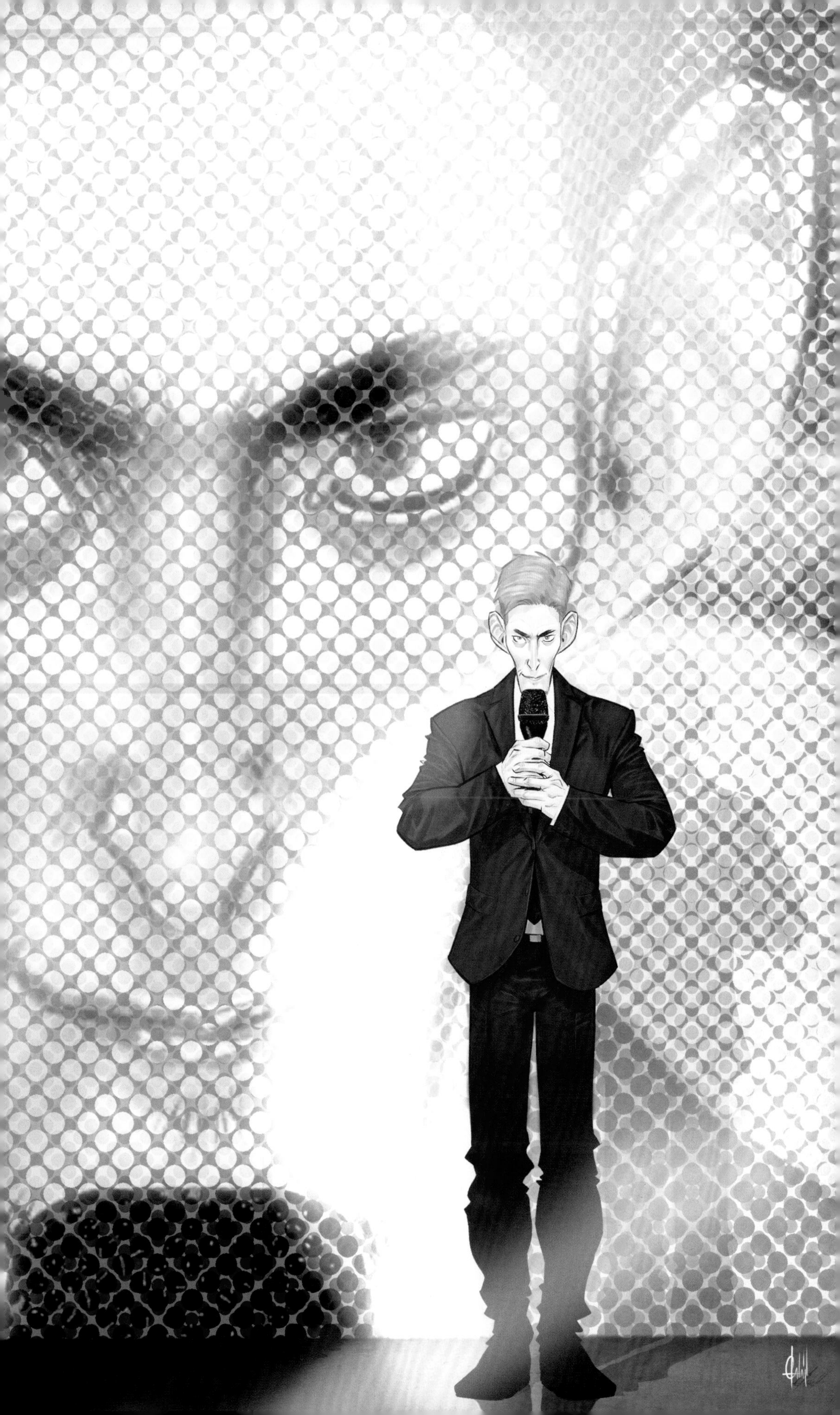

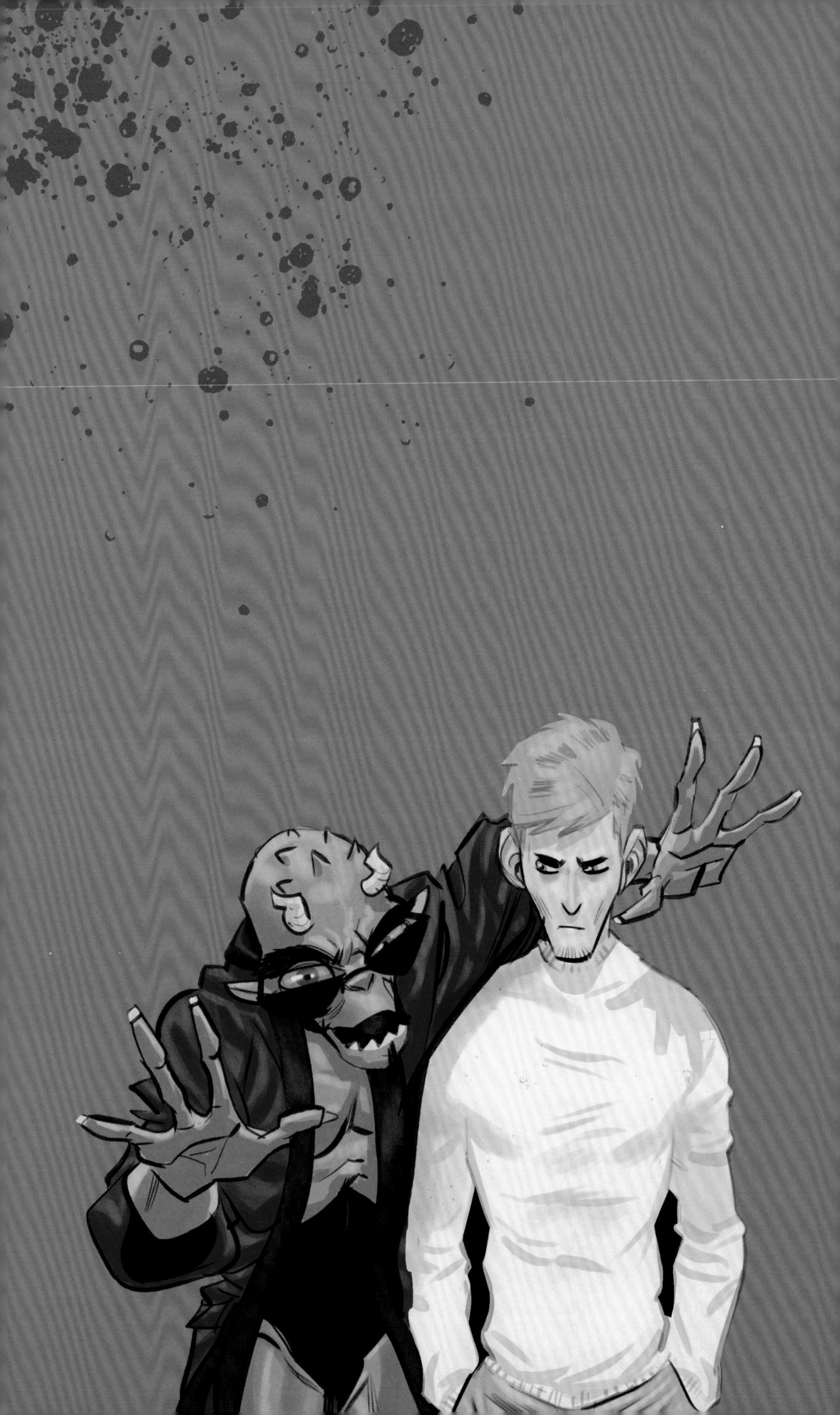

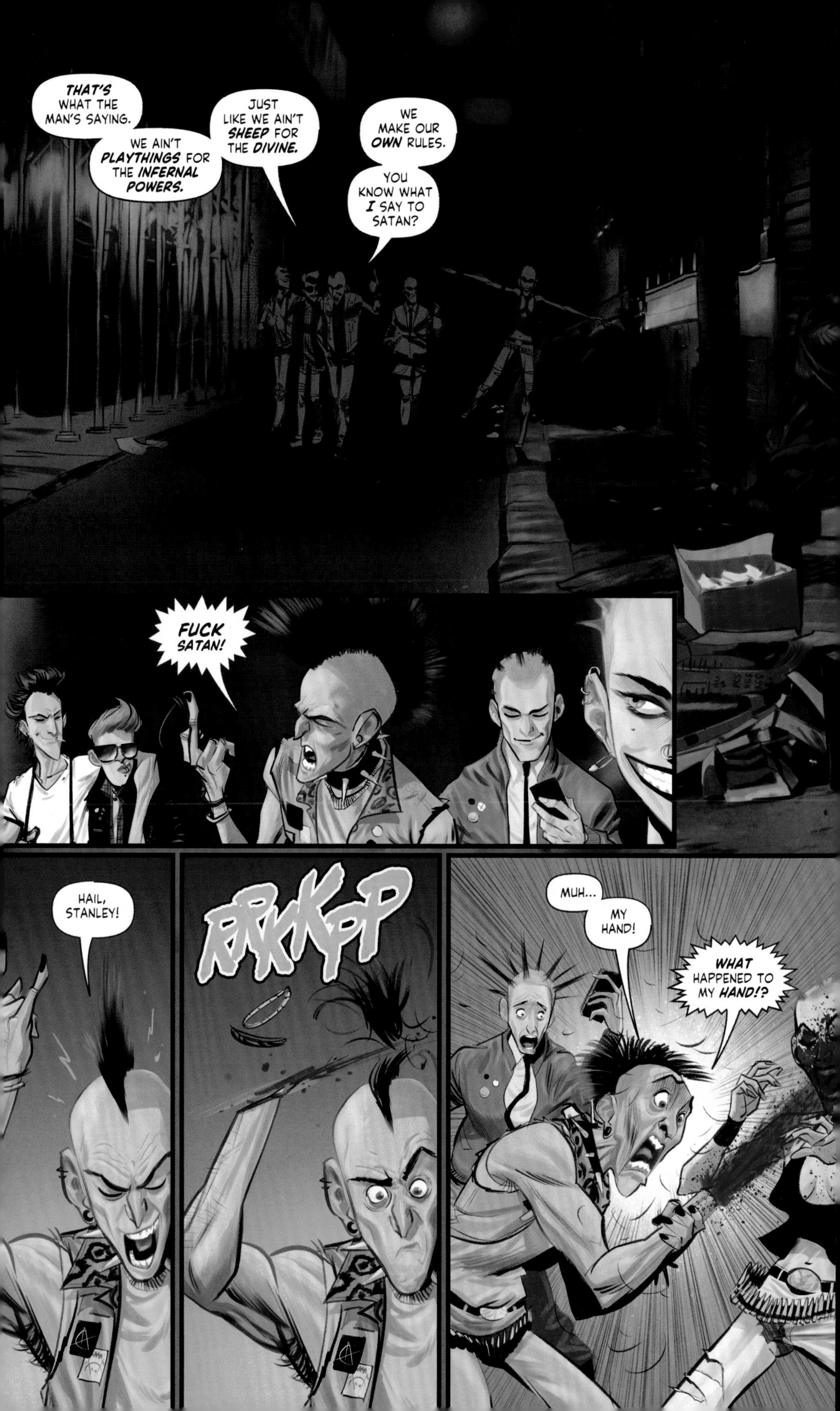
THAT'S WHAT THE MAN'S SAYING.
WE AIN'T PLAYTHINGS FOR THE INFERNAL POWERS.
JUST LIKE WE AIN'T SHEEP FOR THE DIVINE.
WE MAKE OUR OWN RULES.
YOU KNOW WHAT I SAY TO SATAN?
FUCK SATAN!
HAIL, STANLEY!
RRKKPP
MUH...
MY HAND!
WHAT HAPPENED TO MY HAND!?

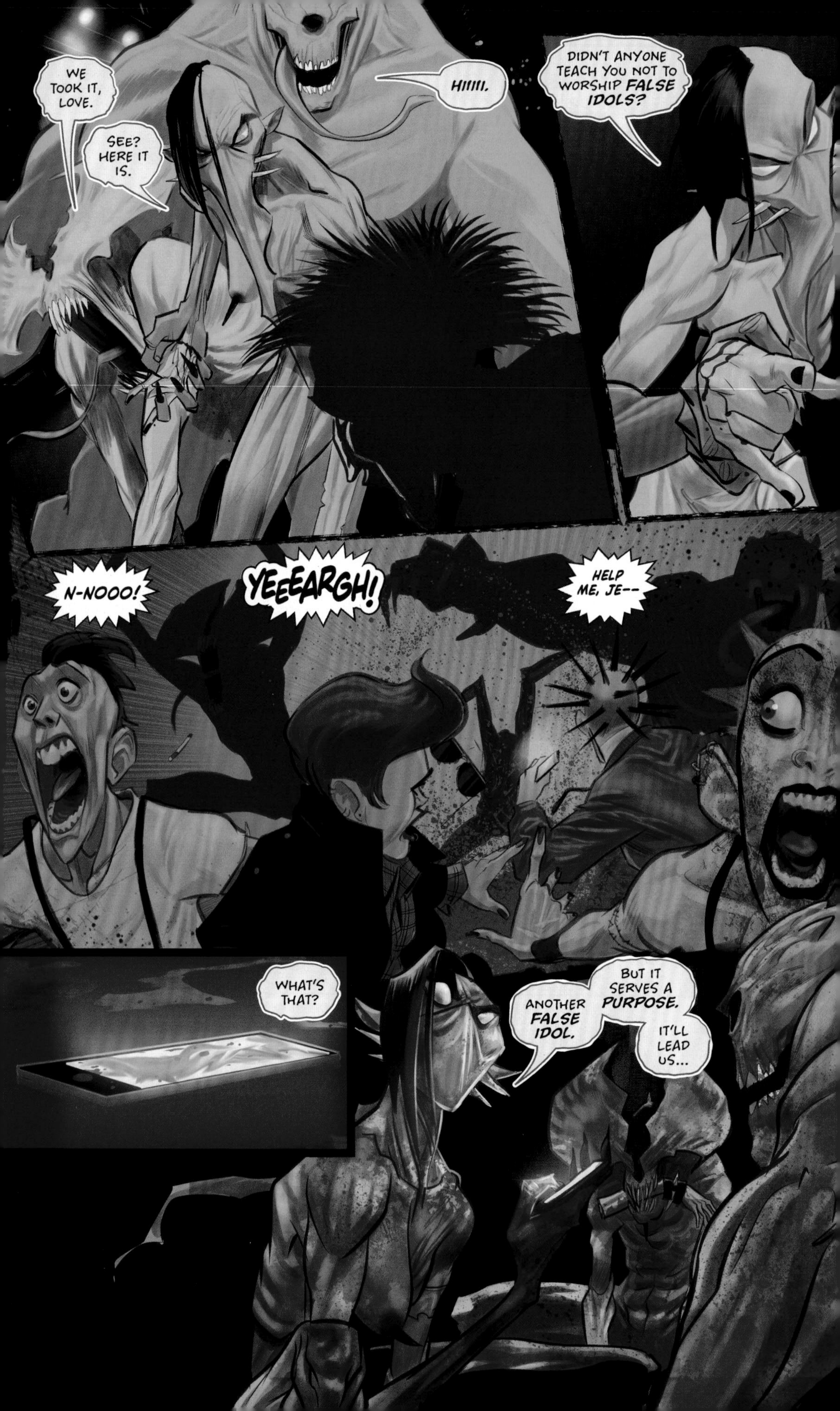

WE TOOK IT, LOVE.
SEE? HERE IT IS.
HIIIII.
DIDN'T ANYONE TEACH YOU NOT TO WORSHIP FALSE IDOLS?
N-NOOO!
YEEEARGH!
HELP ME, JE--
WHAT'S THAT?
ANOTHER FALSE IDOL.
BUT IT SERVES A PURPOSE.
IT'LL LEAD US...

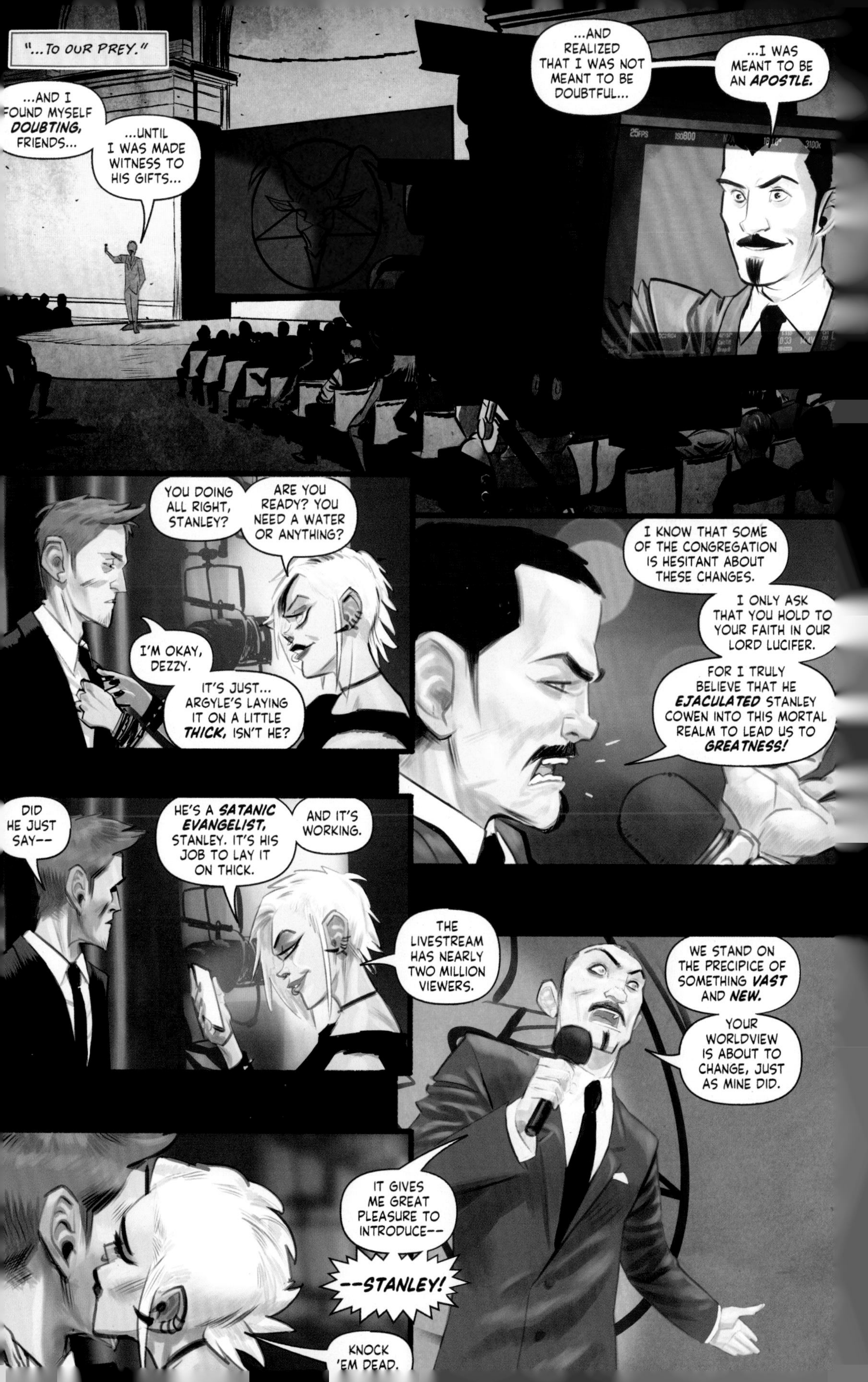
"...TO OUR PREY."
...AND I FOUND MYSELF DOUBTING, FRIENDS...
...UNTIL I WAS MADE WITNESS TO HIS GIFTS...
...AND REALIZED THAT I WAS NOT MEANT TO BE DOUBTFUL...
...I WAS MEANT TO BE AN APOSTLE.
YOU DOING ALL RIGHT, STANLEY?
ARE YOU READY? YOU NEED A WATER OR ANYTHING?
I'M OKAY, DEZZY.
IT'S JUST... ARGYLE'S LAYING IT ON A LITTLE THICK, ISN'T HE?
I KNOW THAT SOME OF THE CONGREGATION IS HESITANT ABOUT THESE CHANGES.
I ONLY ASK THAT YOU HOLD TO YOUR FAITH IN OUR LORD LUCIFER.
FOR I TRULY BELIEVE THAT HE EJACULATED STANLEY COWEN INTO THIS MORTAL REALM TO LEAD US TO GREATNESS!
DID HE JUST SAY--
HE'S A SATANIC EVANGELIST, STANLEY. IT'S HIS JOB TO LAY IT ON THICK.
AND IT'S WORKING.
THE LIVESTREAM HAS NEARLY TWO MILLION VIEWERS.
WE STAND ON THE PRECIPICE OF SOMETHING VAST AND NEW.
YOUR WORLDVIEW IS ABOUT TO CHANGE, JUST AS MINE DID.
IT GIVES ME GREAT PLEASURE TO INTRODUCE--
--STANLEY!
KNOCK 'EM DEAD.

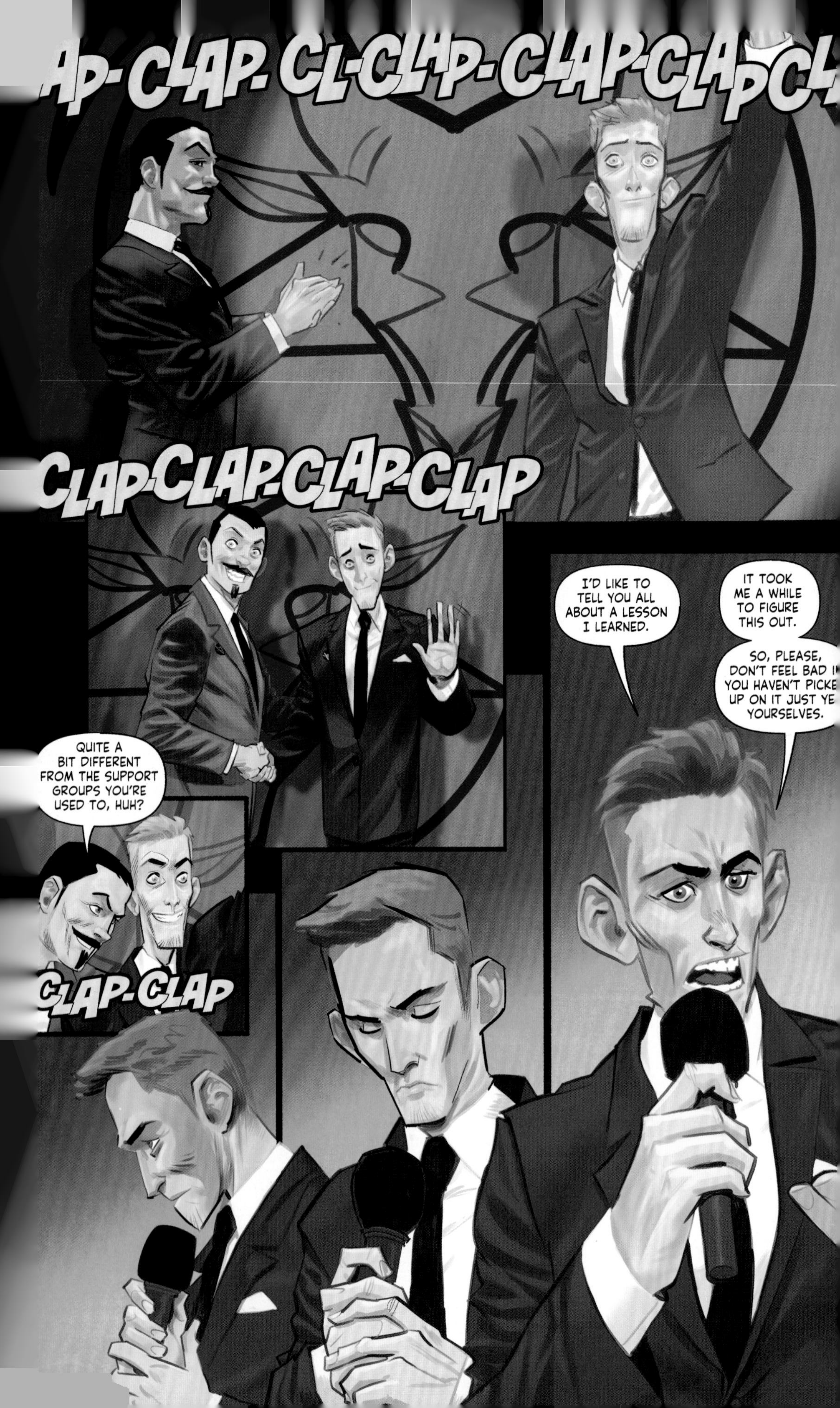

AP-CLAP. CL-CLAP-CLAP-CLAP-CLAPCL
CLAP-CLAP-CLAP-CLAP
QUITE A BIT DIFFERENT FROM THE SUPPORT GROUPS YOU'RE USED TO, HUH?
CLAP-CLAP
I'D LIKE TO TELL YOU ALL ABOUT A LESSON I LEARNED.
IT TOOK ME A WHILE TO FIGURE THIS OUT.
SO, PLEASE, DON'T FEEL BAD I YOU HAVEN'T PICKE UP ON IT JUST YE YOURSELVES.

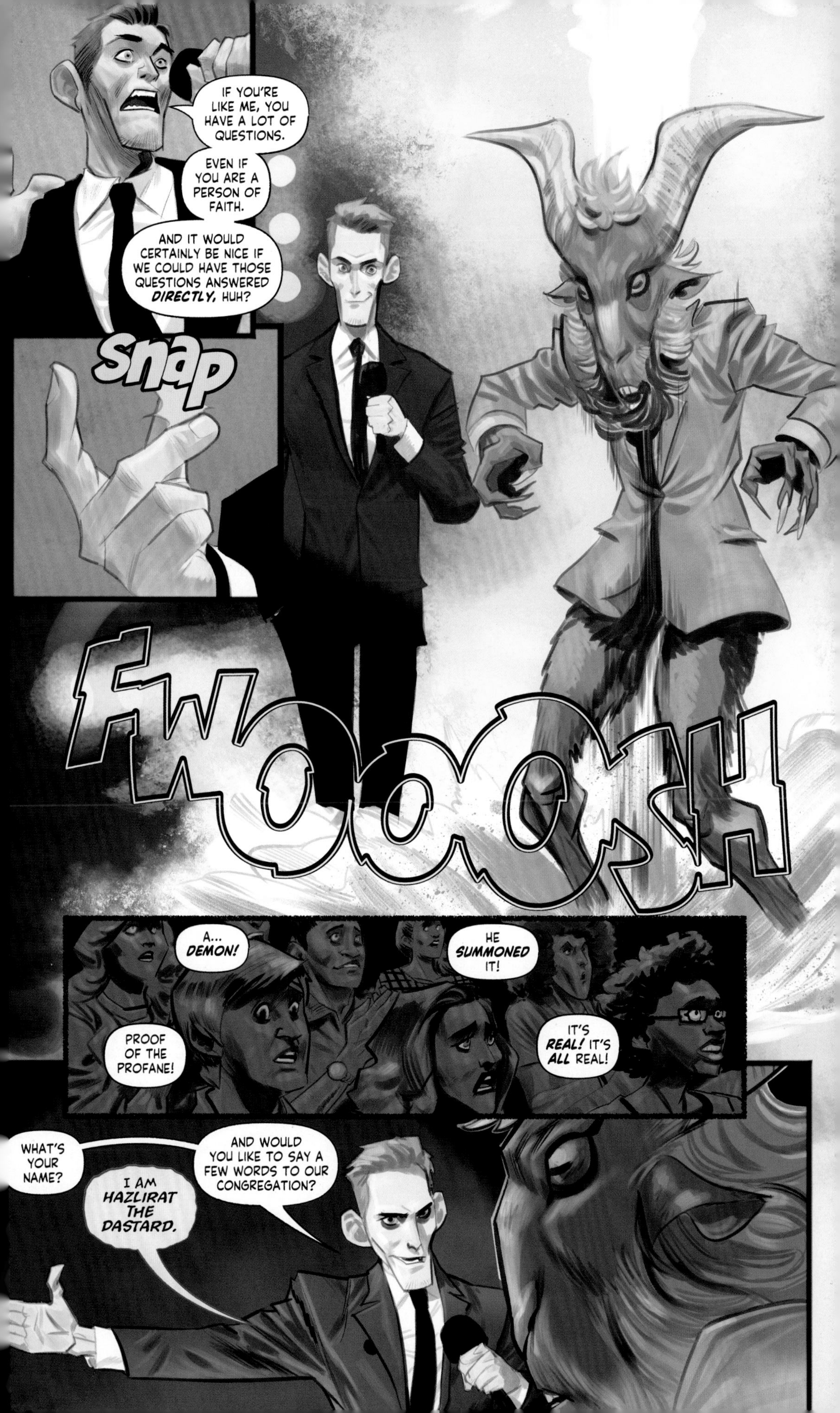
IF YOU'RE LIKE ME, YOU HAVE A LOT OF QUESTIONS.
EVEN IF YOU ARE A PERSON OF FAITH.
AND IT WOULD CERTAINLY BE NICE IF WE COULD HAVE THOSE QUESTIONS ANSWERED *DIRECTLY,* HUH?
SNAP
FWOOOSH
A... *DEMON!*
HE *SUMMONED* IT!
PROOF OF THE PROFANE!
IT'S *REAL!* IT'S *ALL* REAL!
WHAT'S YOUR NAME?
I AM *HAZLIRAT THE DASTARD.*
AND WOULD YOU LIKE TO SAY A FEW WORDS TO OUR CONGREGATION?

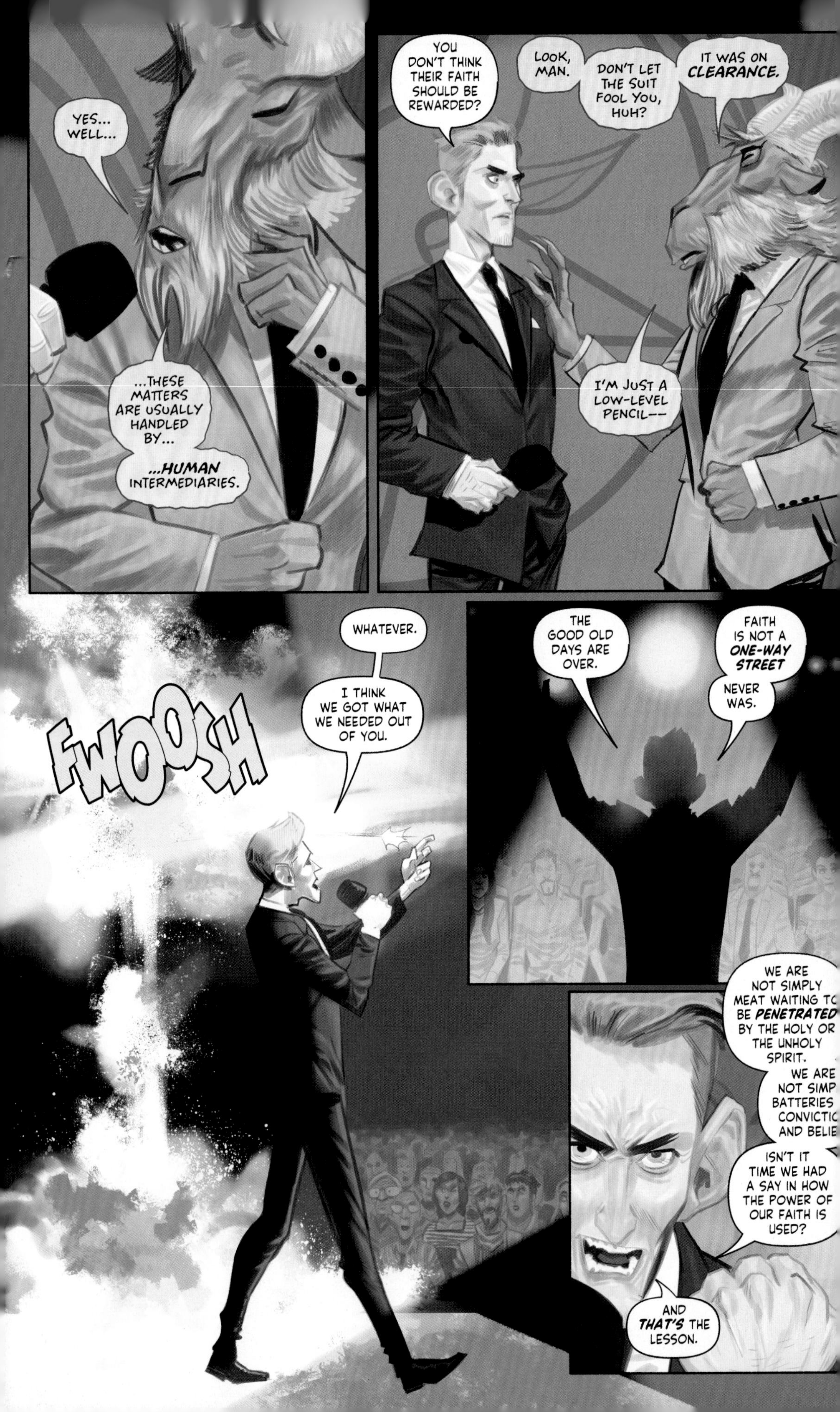
YES... WELL...
...THESE MATTERS ARE USUALLY HANDLED BY...
...HUMAN INTERMEDIARIES.
YOU DON'T THINK THEIR FAITH SHOULD BE REWARDED?
LOOK, MAN.
DON'T LET THE SUIT FOOL YOU, HUH?
IT WAS ON CLEARANCE.
I'M JUST A LOW-LEVEL PENCIL--
FWOOSH
WHATEVER.
I THINK WE GOT WHAT WE NEEDED OUT OF YOU.
THE GOOD OLD DAYS ARE OVER.
FAITH IS NOT A ONE-WAY STREET
NEVER WAS.
WE ARE NOT SIMPLY MEAT WAITING TO BE PENETRATED BY THE HOLY OR THE UNHOLY SPIRIT.
ISN'T IT TIME WE HAD A SAY IN HOW THE POWER OF OUR FAITH IS USED?
AND THAT'S THE LESSON.

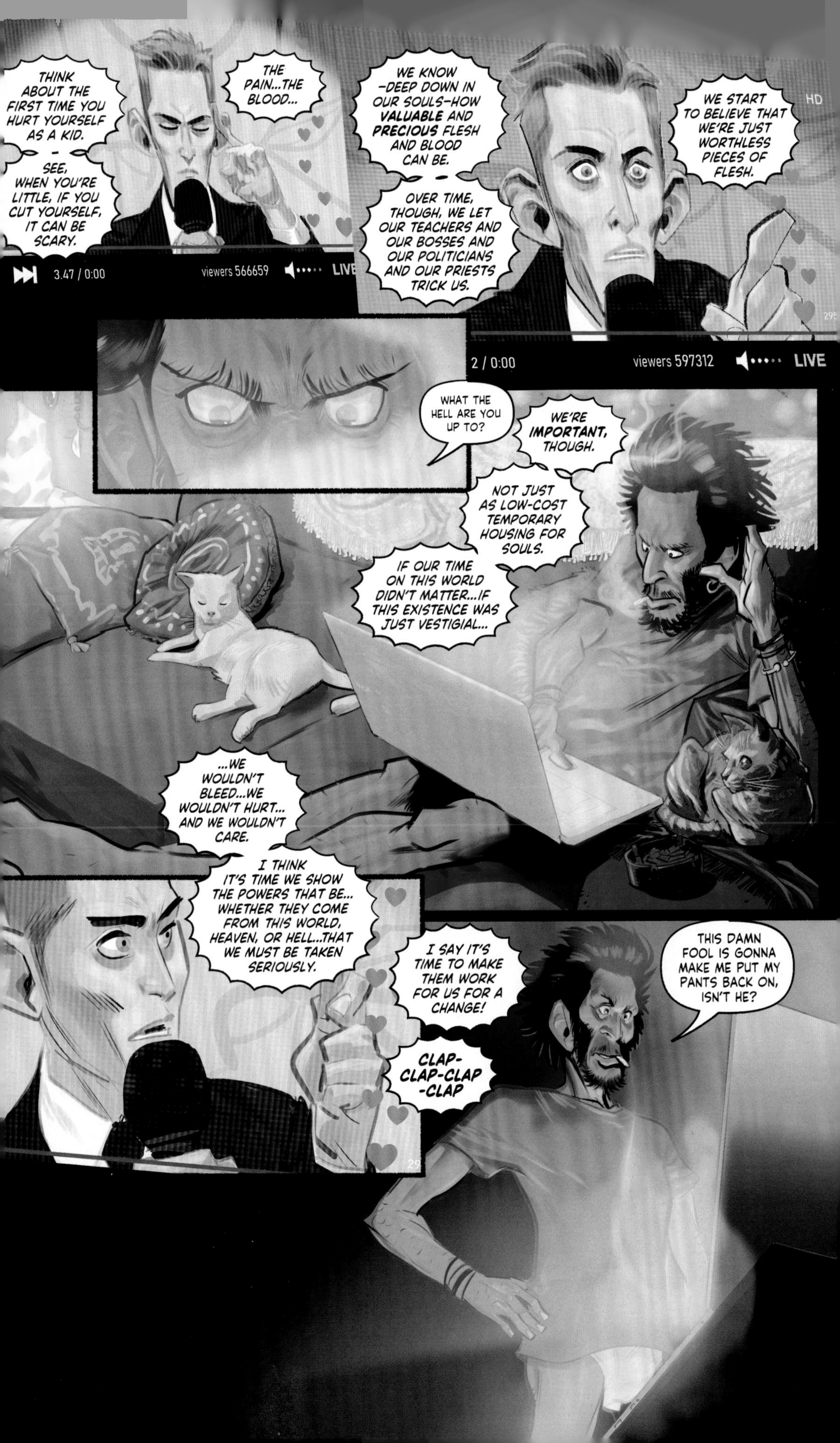
THINK ABOUT THE FIRST TIME YOU HURT YOURSELF AS A KID.
SEE, WHEN YOU'RE LITTLE, IF YOU CUT YOURSELF, IT CAN BE SCARY.
THE PAIN...THE BLOOD...
3.47 / 0:00
viewers 566659
LIVE
WE KNOW —DEEP DOWN IN OUR SOULS—HOW VALUABLE AND PRECIOUS FLESH AND BLOOD CAN BE.
OVER TIME, THOUGH, WE LET OUR TEACHERS AND OUR BOSSES AND OUR POLITICIANS AND OUR PRIESTS TRICK US.
HD
WE START TO BELIEVE THAT WE'RE JUST WORTHLESS PIECES OF FLESH.
2 / 0:00
viewers 597312
LIVE
WHAT THE HELL ARE YOU UP TO?
WE'RE IMPORTANT, THOUGH.
NOT JUST AS LOW-COST TEMPORARY HOUSING FOR SOULS.
IF OUR TIME ON THIS WORLD DIDN'T MATTER...IF THIS EXISTENCE WAS JUST VESTIGIAL...
...WE WOULDN'T BLEED...WE WOULDN'T HURT... AND WE WOULDN'T CARE.
I THINK IT'S TIME WE SHOW THE POWERS THAT BE... WHETHER THEY COME FROM THIS WORLD, HEAVEN, OR HELL...THAT WE MUST BE TAKEN SERIOUSLY.
I SAY IT'S TIME TO MAKE THEM WORK FOR US FOR A CHANGE!
CLAP-CLAP-CLAP-CLAP
THIS DAMN FOOL IS GONNA MAKE ME PUT MY PANTS BACK ON, ISN'T HE?

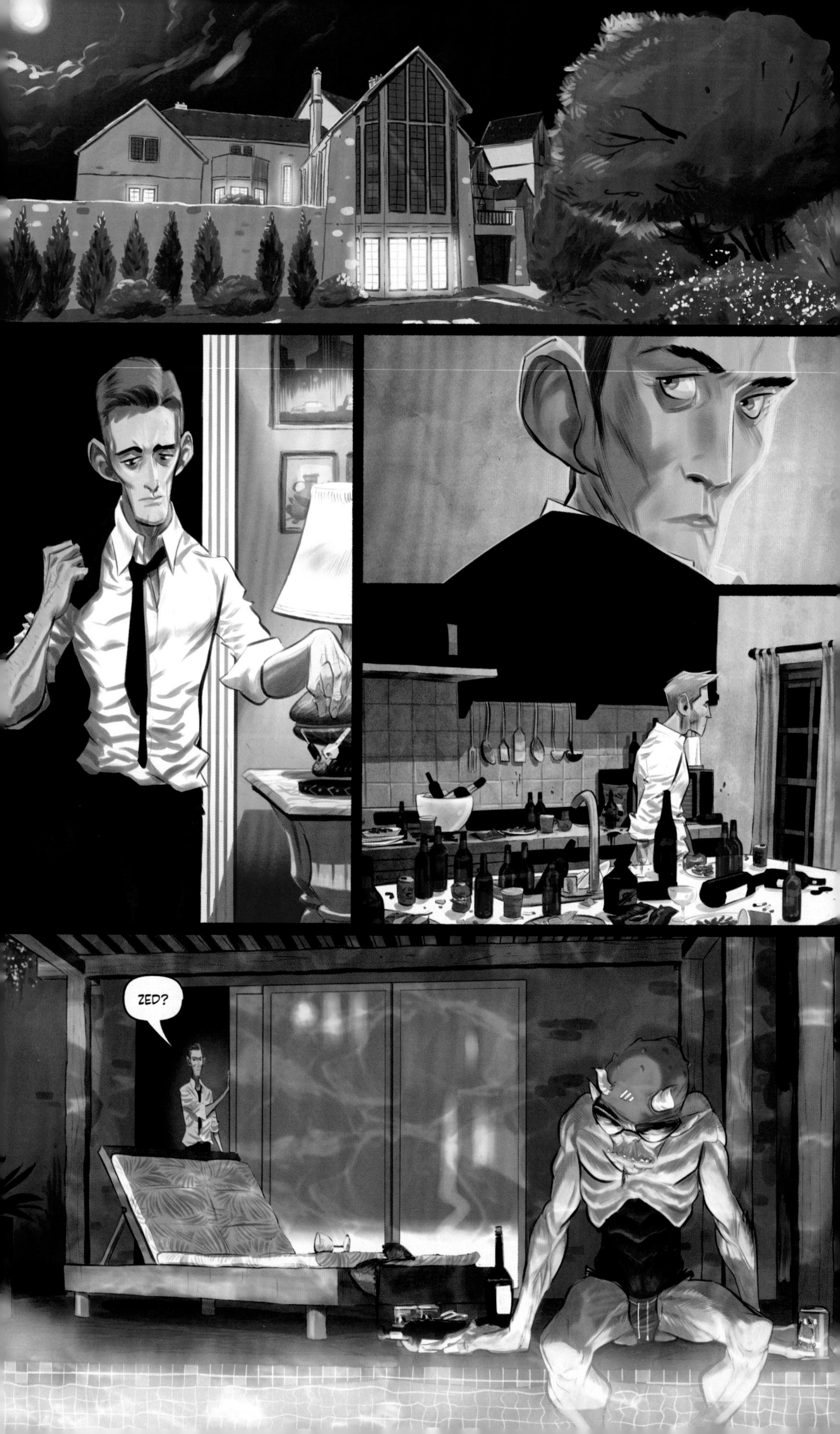
ZED?

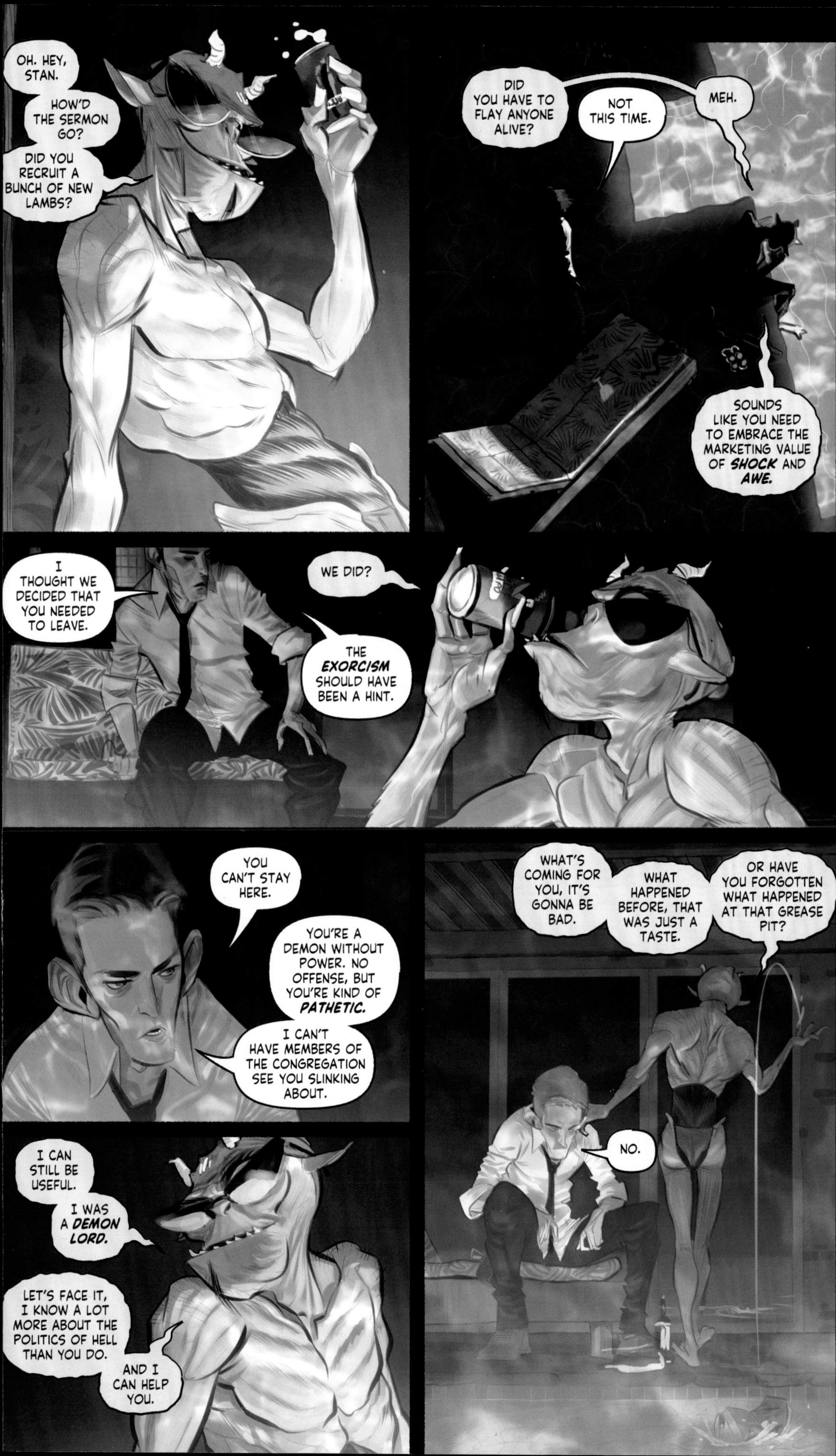
OH. HEY, STAN.
HOW'D THE SERMON GO?
DID YOU RECRUIT A BUNCH OF NEW LAMBS?
DID YOU HAVE TO FLAY ANYONE ALIVE?
NOT THIS TIME.
MEH.
SOUNDS LIKE YOU NEED TO EMBRACE THE MARKETING VALUE OF SHOCK AND AWE.
I THOUGHT WE DECIDED THAT YOU NEEDED TO LEAVE.
WE DID?
THE EXORCISM SHOULD HAVE BEEN A HINT.
YOU CAN'T STAY HERE.
YOU'RE A DEMON WITHOUT POWER. NO OFFENSE, BUT YOU'RE KIND OF PATHETIC.
I CAN'T HAVE MEMBERS OF THE CONGREGATION SEE YOU SLINKING ABOUT.
I CAN STILL BE USEFUL.
I WAS A DEMON LORD.
LET'S FACE IT, I KNOW A LOT MORE ABOUT THE POLITICS OF HELL THAN YOU DO.
AND I CAN HELP YOU.
WHAT'S COMING FOR YOU, IT'S GONNA BE BAD.
WHAT HAPPENED BEFORE, THAT WAS JUST A TASTE.
OR HAVE YOU FORGOTTEN WHAT HAPPENED AT THAT GREASE PIT?
NO.

"I REMEMBER."

BONANZA
HOME OF THE DOLLAR BURGER!

JUST THE BURGER WITHOUT THE CHEESE, THEN.

BUT I GAVE YOU—

STILL NOT ENOUGH.

YOU DON'T HAVE ENOUGH TO COVER *TAX.*

HOME OF THE DOLLAR BURGER!

HEY, BUDDY.

CLEAR OUT OF THE LINE.

US *PAYING CUSTOMERS* ARE HUNGRY.

JESUS!

WHAT THE HELL IS THAT?

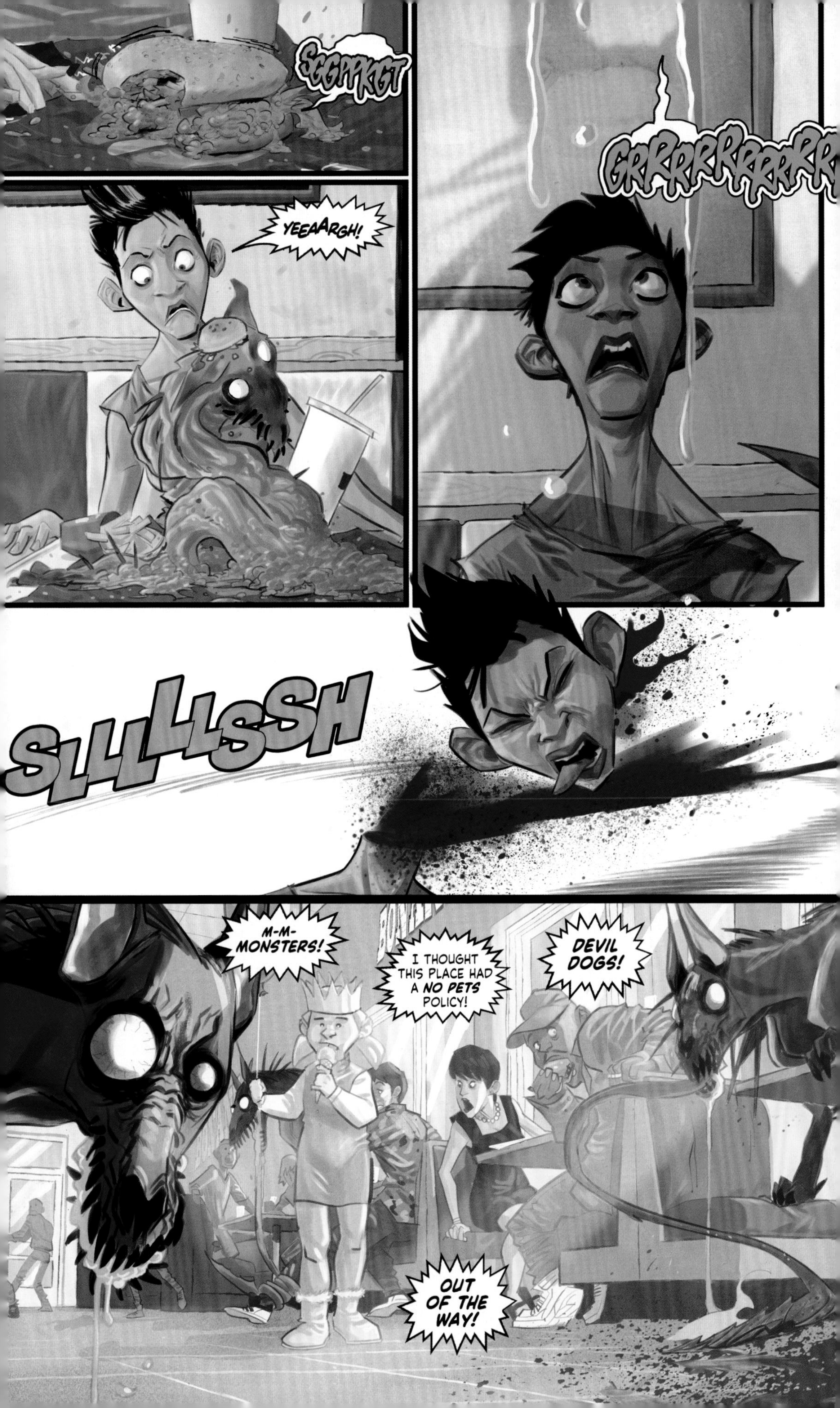
SCGPPKGT
GRRRRRRRRR
YEEAARGH!
SLLLLSSH
M-M-MONSTERS!
I THOUGHT THIS PLACE HAD A NO PETS POLICY!
DEVIL DOGS!
OUT OF THE WAY!

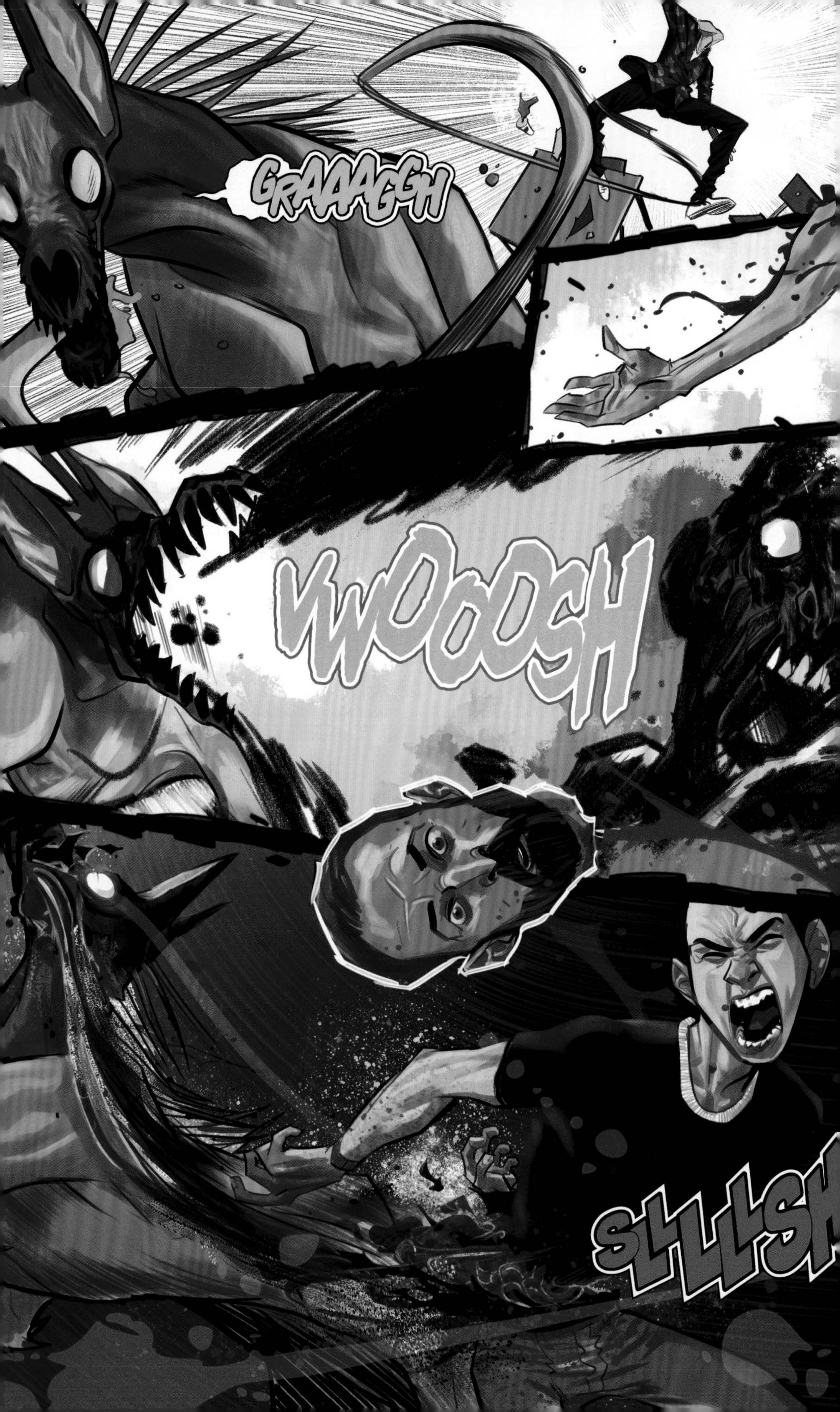
GRAAAGGH
VWOOOSH
SLLLSH

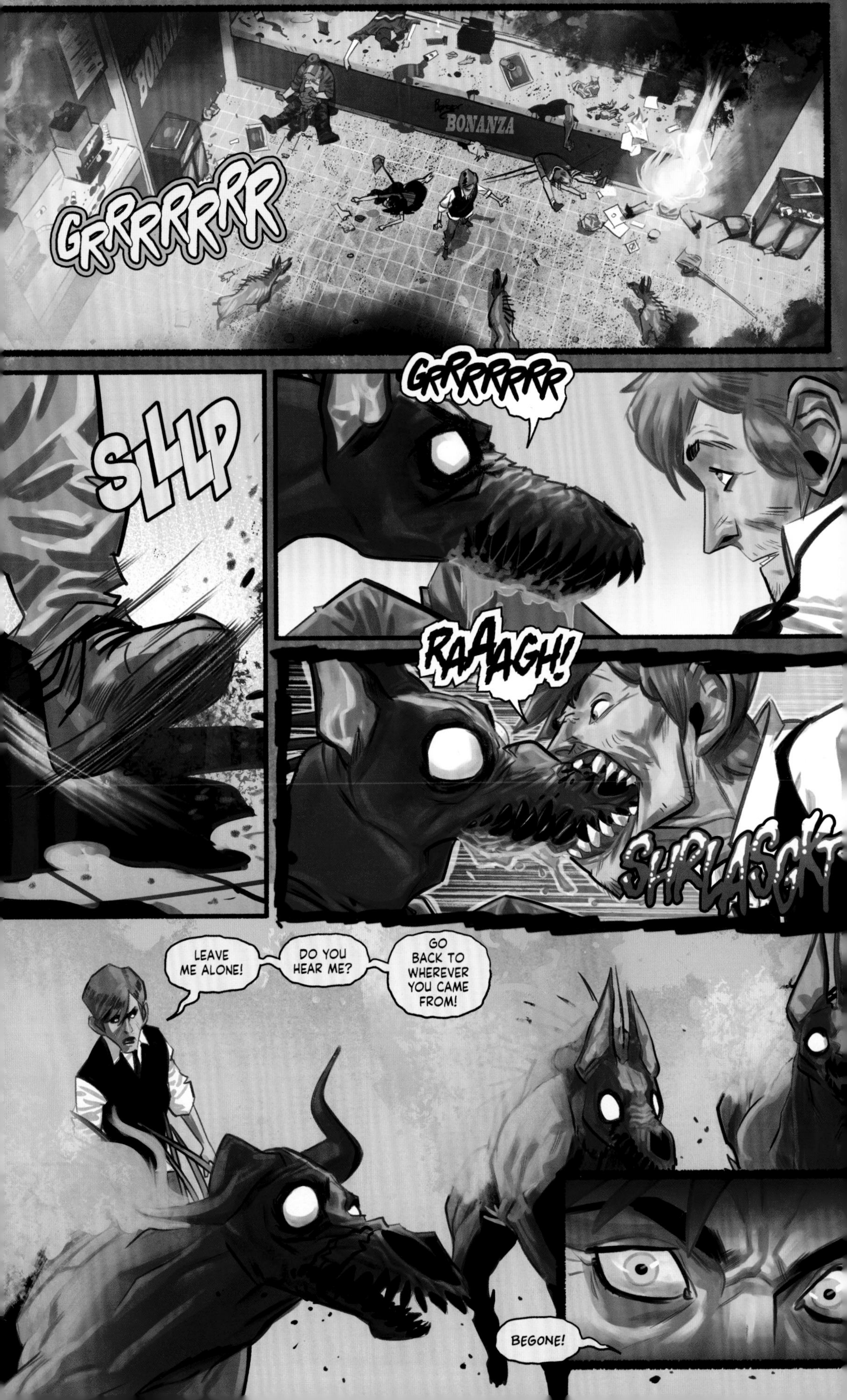
BONANZA
GRRRRRRR
SLLLP
GRRRRRRR
RAAAGH!
SHRLASCKT
LEAVE ME ALONE!
DO YOU HEAR ME?
GO BACK TO WHEREVER YOU CAME FROM!
BEGONE!

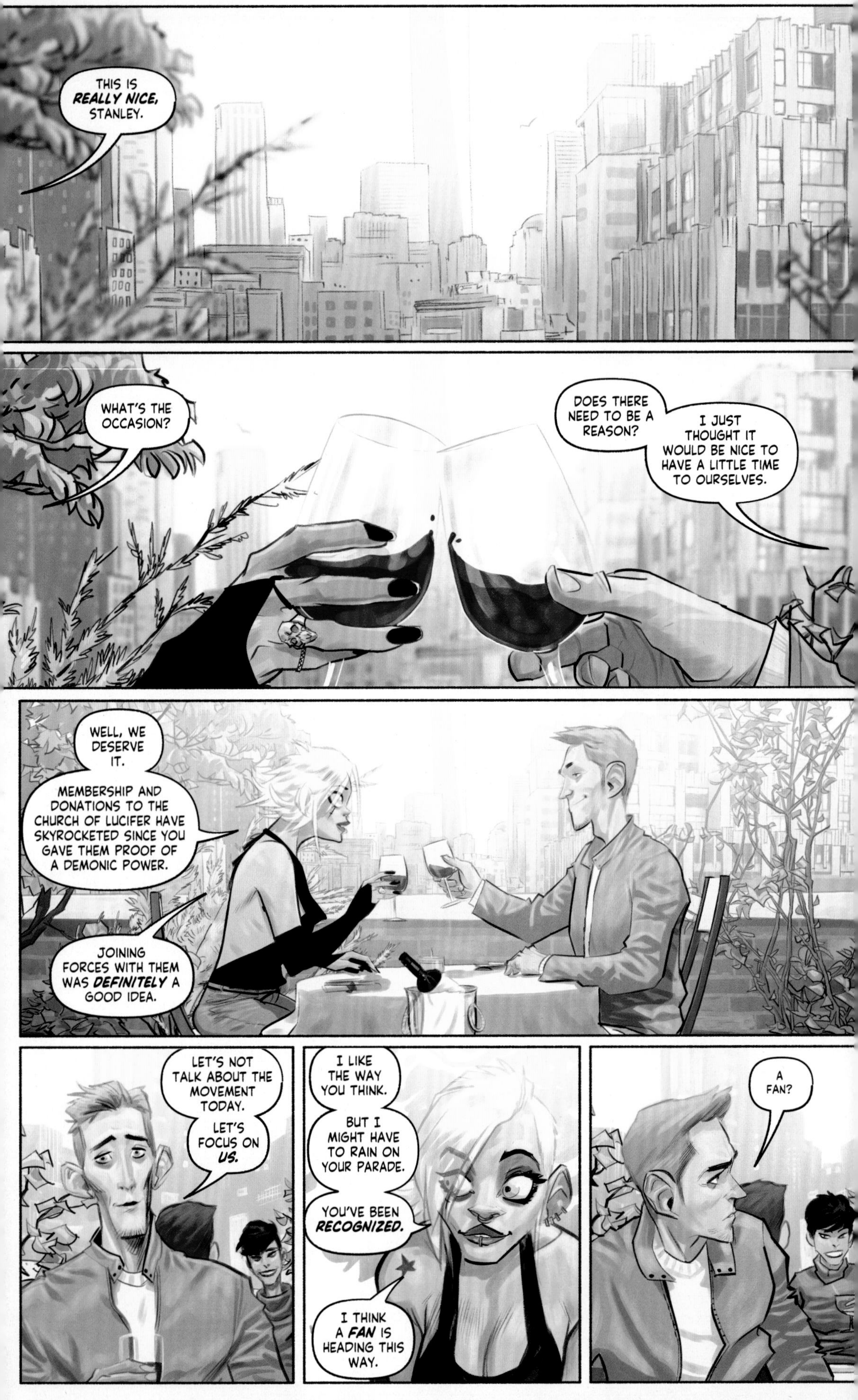
THIS IS **REALLY NICE,** STANLEY.
WHAT'S THE OCCASION?
DOES THERE NEED TO BE A REASON?
I JUST THOUGHT IT WOULD BE NICE TO HAVE A LITTLE TIME TO OURSELVES.
WELL, WE DESERVE IT.
MEMBERSHIP AND DONATIONS TO THE CHURCH OF LUCIFER HAVE SKYROCKETED SINCE YOU GAVE THEM PROOF OF A DEMONIC POWER.
JOINING FORCES WITH THEM WAS **DEFINITELY** A GOOD IDEA.
LET'S NOT TALK ABOUT THE MOVEMENT TODAY.
LET'S FOCUS ON **US.**
I LIKE THE WAY YOU THINK.
BUT I MIGHT HAVE TO RAIN ON YOUR PARADE.
YOU'VE BEEN **RECOGNIZED.**
I THINK A **FAN** IS HEADING THIS WAY.
A FAN?

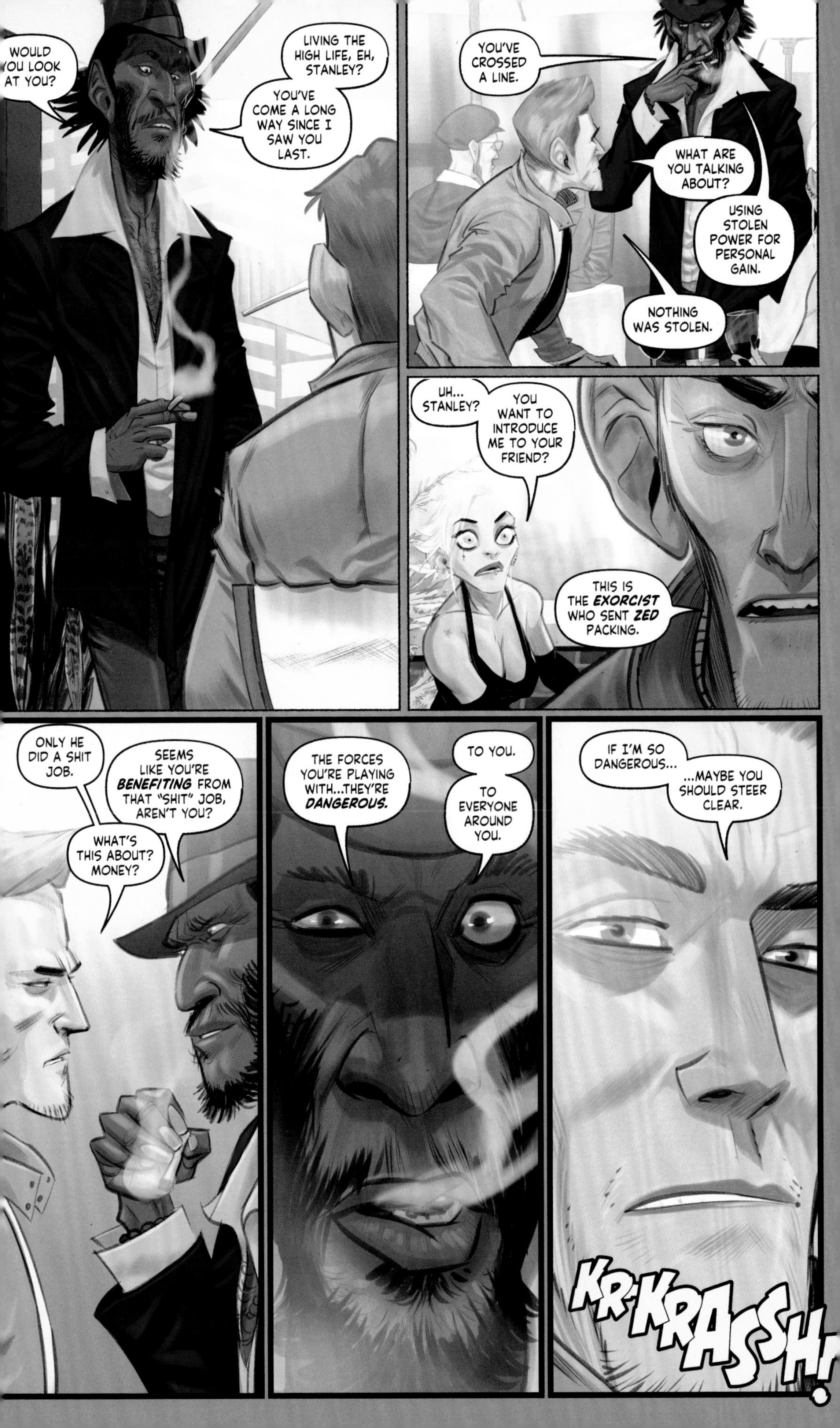
WOULD YOU LOOK AT YOU?
LIVING THE HIGH LIFE, EH, STANLEY?
YOU'VE COME A LONG WAY SINCE I SAW YOU LAST.
YOU'VE CROSSED A LINE.
WHAT ARE YOU TALKING ABOUT?
USING STOLEN POWER FOR PERSONAL GAIN.
NOTHING WAS STOLEN.
UH... STANLEY?
YOU WANT TO INTRODUCE ME TO YOUR FRIEND?
THIS IS THE **EXORCIST** WHO SENT **ZED** PACKING.
ONLY HE DID A SHIT JOB.
SEEMS LIKE YOU'RE **BENEFITING** FROM THAT "SHIT" JOB, AREN'T YOU?
WHAT'S THIS ABOUT? MONEY?
THE FORCES YOU'RE PLAYING WITH...THEY'RE **DANGEROUS.**
TO YOU.
TO EVERYONE AROUND YOU.
IF I'M SO DANGEROUS...
...MAYBE YOU SHOULD STEER CLEAR.
KR-KRASH!

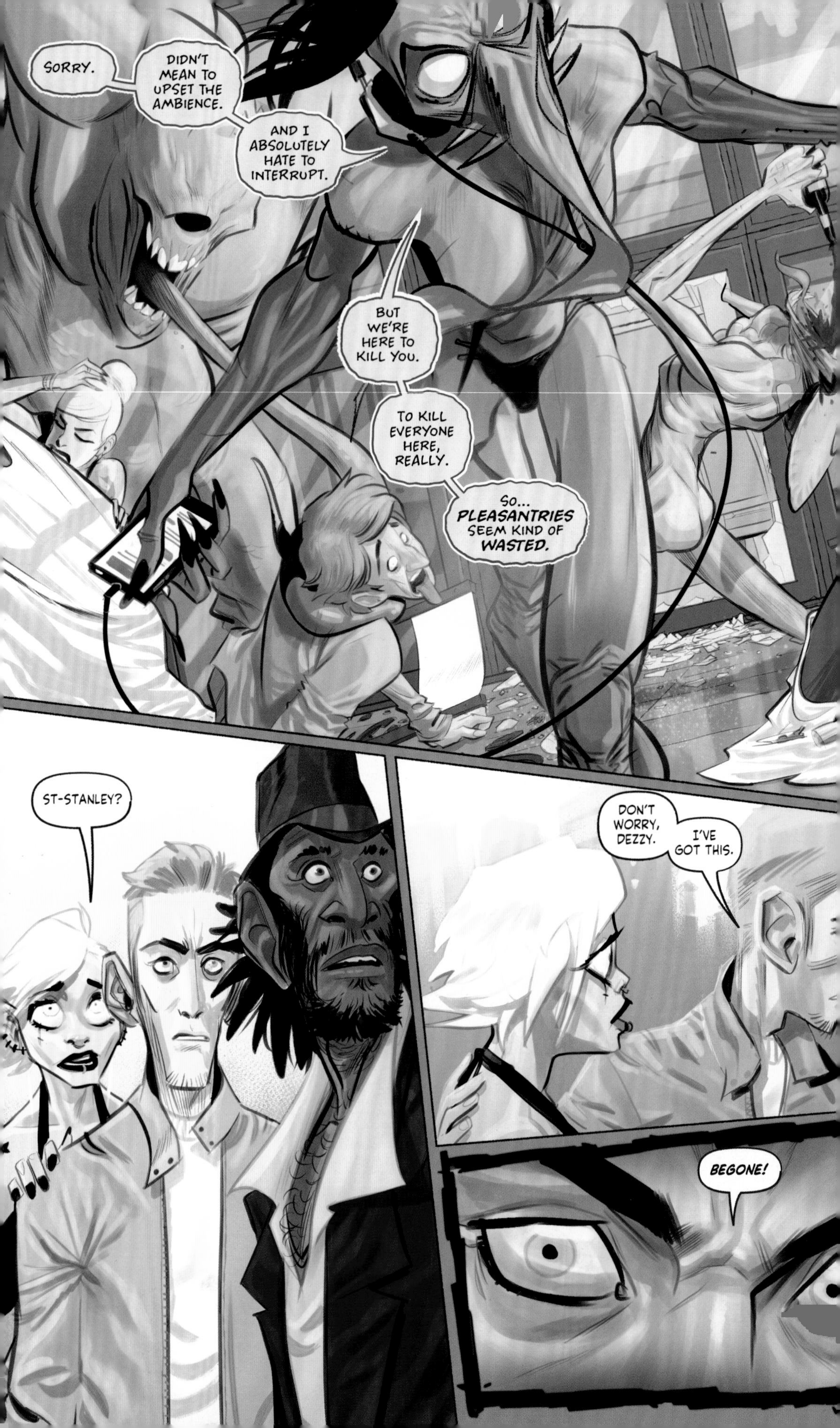

SORRY.
DIDN'T MEAN TO UPSET THE AMBIENCE.
AND I ABSOLUTELY HATE TO INTERRUPT.
BUT WE'RE HERE TO KILL YOU.
TO KILL EVERYONE HERE, REALLY.
SO... **PLEASANTRIES** SEEM KIND OF **WASTED.**
ST-STANLEY?
DON'T WORRY, DEZZY.
I'VE GOT THIS.
BEGONE!

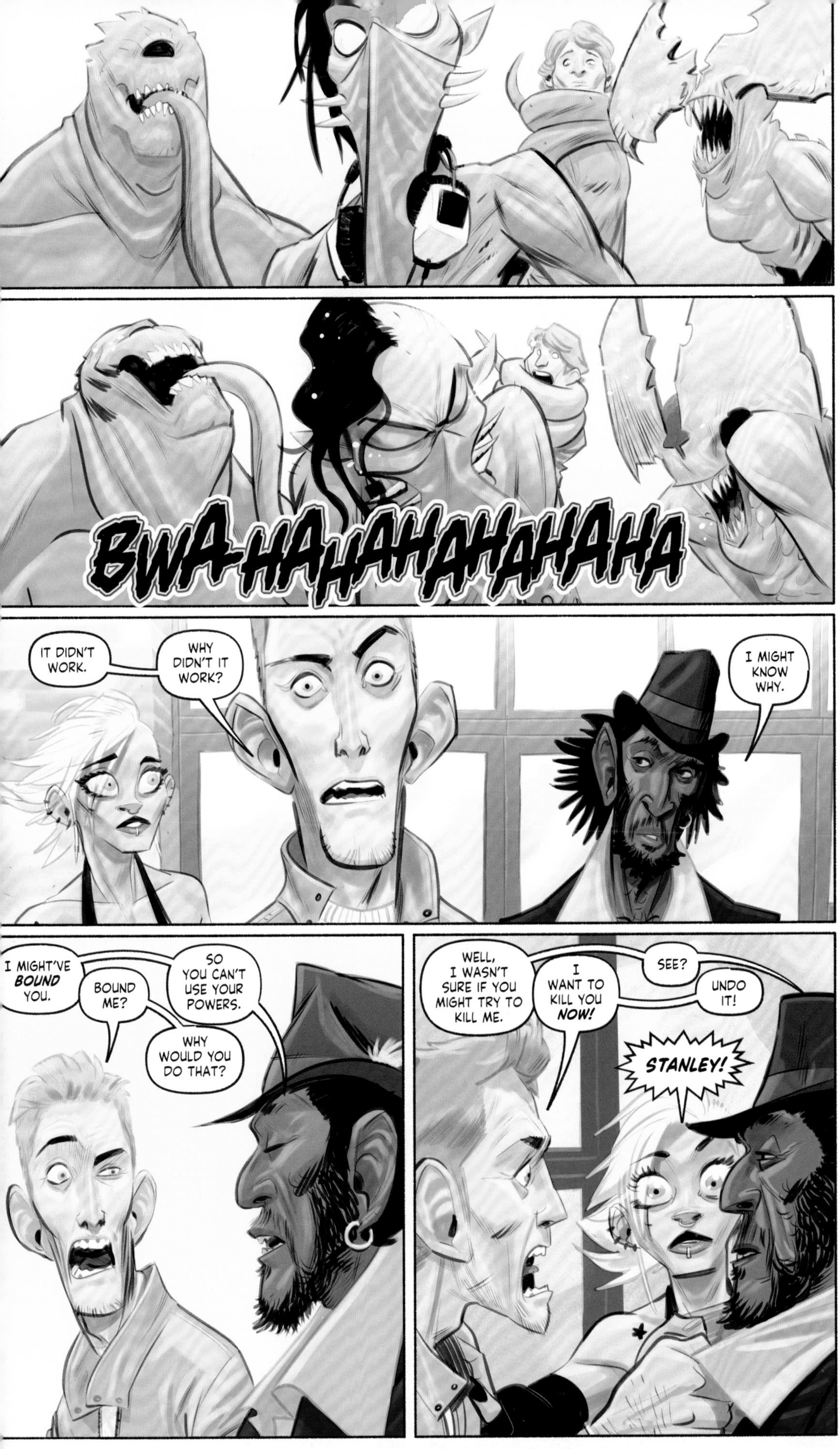
BWAHAHAHAHAHAHAHA
IT DIDN'T WORK.
WHY DIDN'T IT WORK?
I MIGHT KNOW WHY.
I MIGHT'VE *BOUND* YOU.
BOUND ME?
SO YOU CAN'T USE YOUR POWERS.
WHY WOULD YOU DO THAT?
WELL, I WASN'T SURE IF YOU MIGHT TRY TO KILL ME.
I WANT TO KILL YOU *NOW!*
SEE?
UNDO IT!
STANLEY!

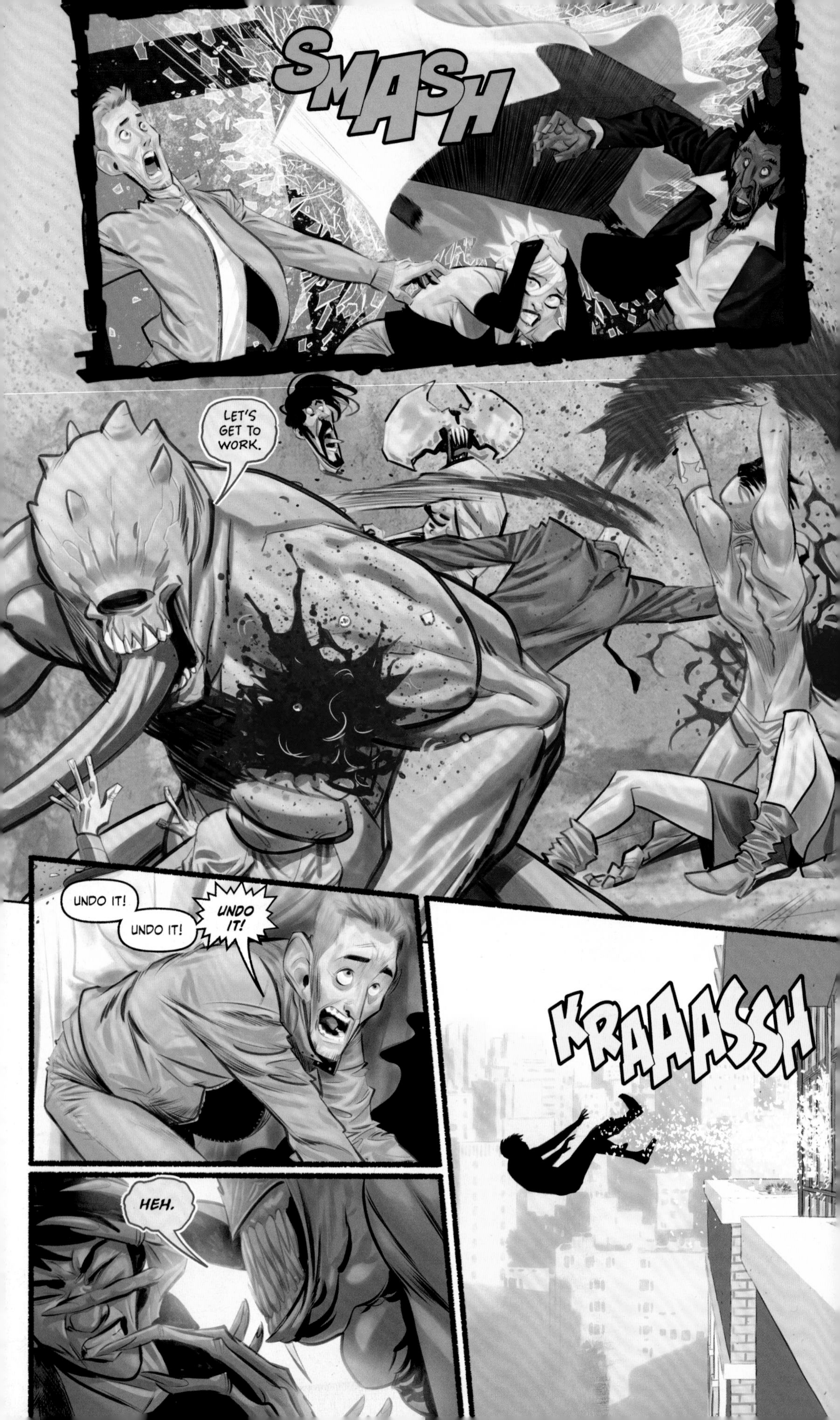
SMASH
LET'S GET TO WORK.
UNDO IT!
UNDO IT!
UNDO IT!
HEH.
KRAAASSH

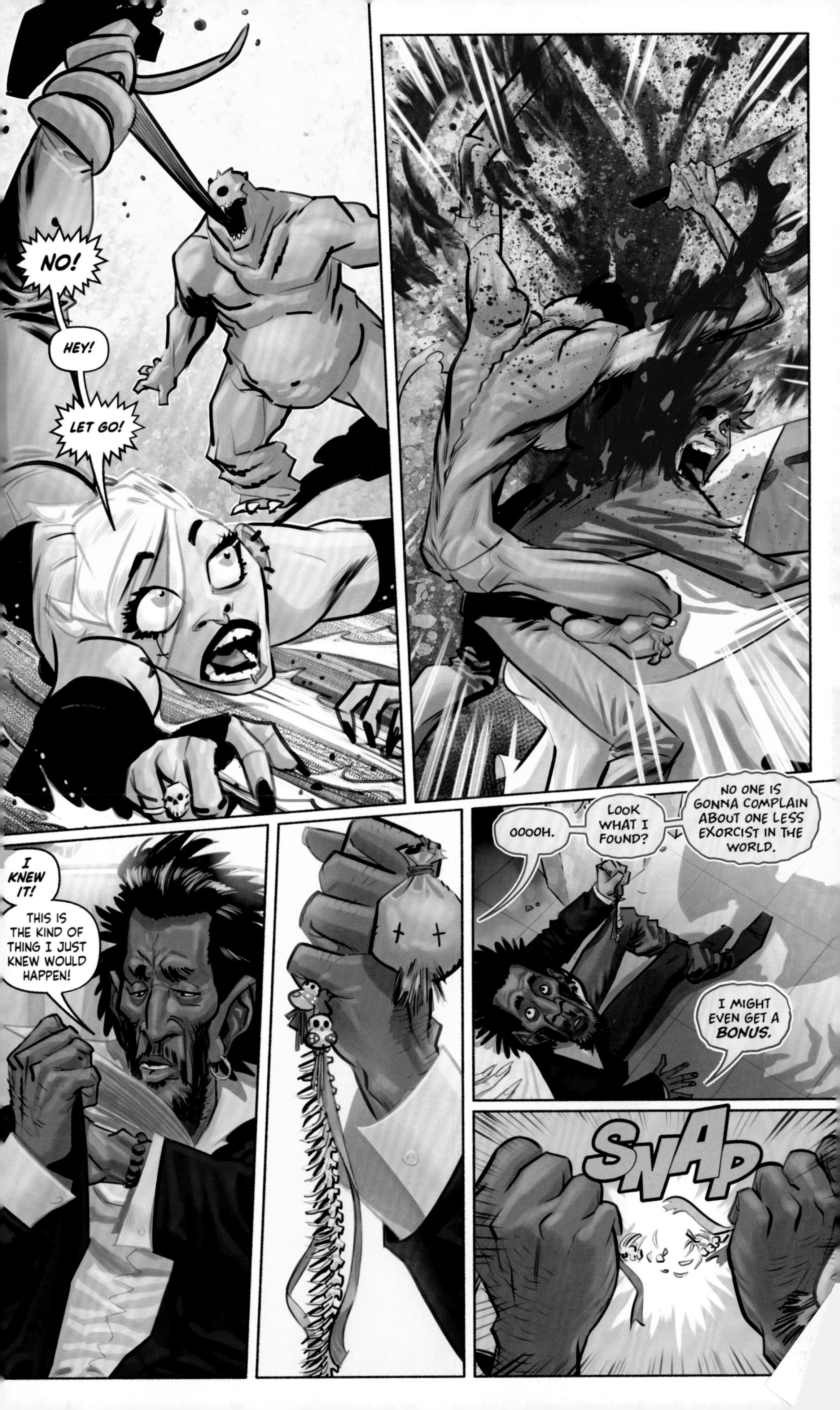

NO!
HEY!
LET GO!
I KNEW IT!
THIS IS THE KIND OF THING I JUST KNEW WOULD HAPPEN!
OOOOH.
LOOK WHAT I FOUND?
NO ONE IS GONNA COMPLAIN ABOUT ONE LESS EXORCIST IN THE WORLD.
I MIGHT EVEN GET A BONUS.
SNAP

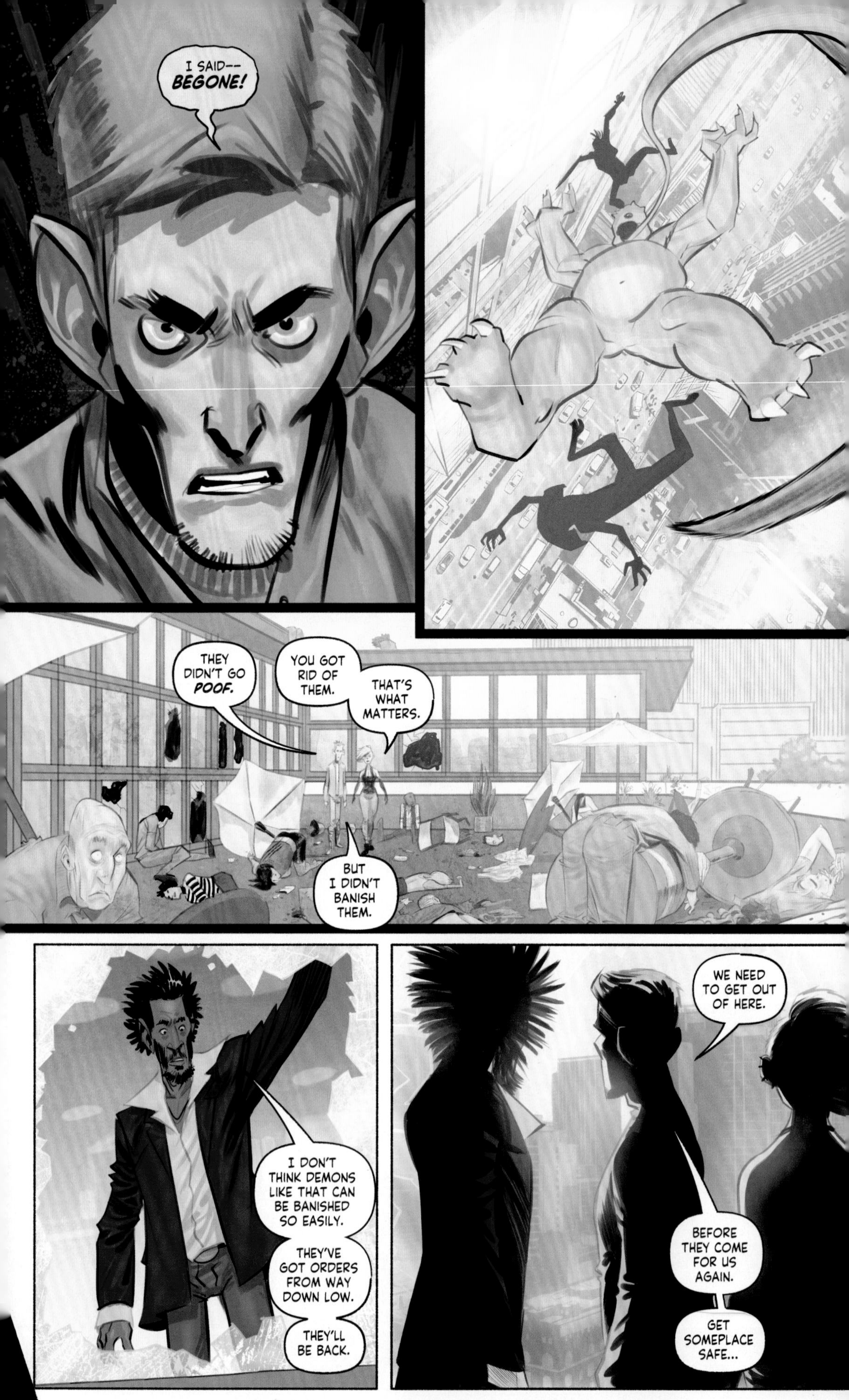
I SAID--
BEGONE!
THEY DIDN'T GO POOF.
YOU GOT RID OF THEM.
THAT'S WHAT MATTERS.
BUT I DIDN'T BANISH THEM.
I DON'T THINK DEMONS LIKE THAT CAN BE BANISHED SO EASILY.
THEY'VE GOT ORDERS FROM WAY DOWN LOW.
THEY'LL BE BACK.
WE NEED TO GET OUT OF HERE.
BEFORE THEY COME FOR US AGAIN.
GET SOMEPLACE SAFE...

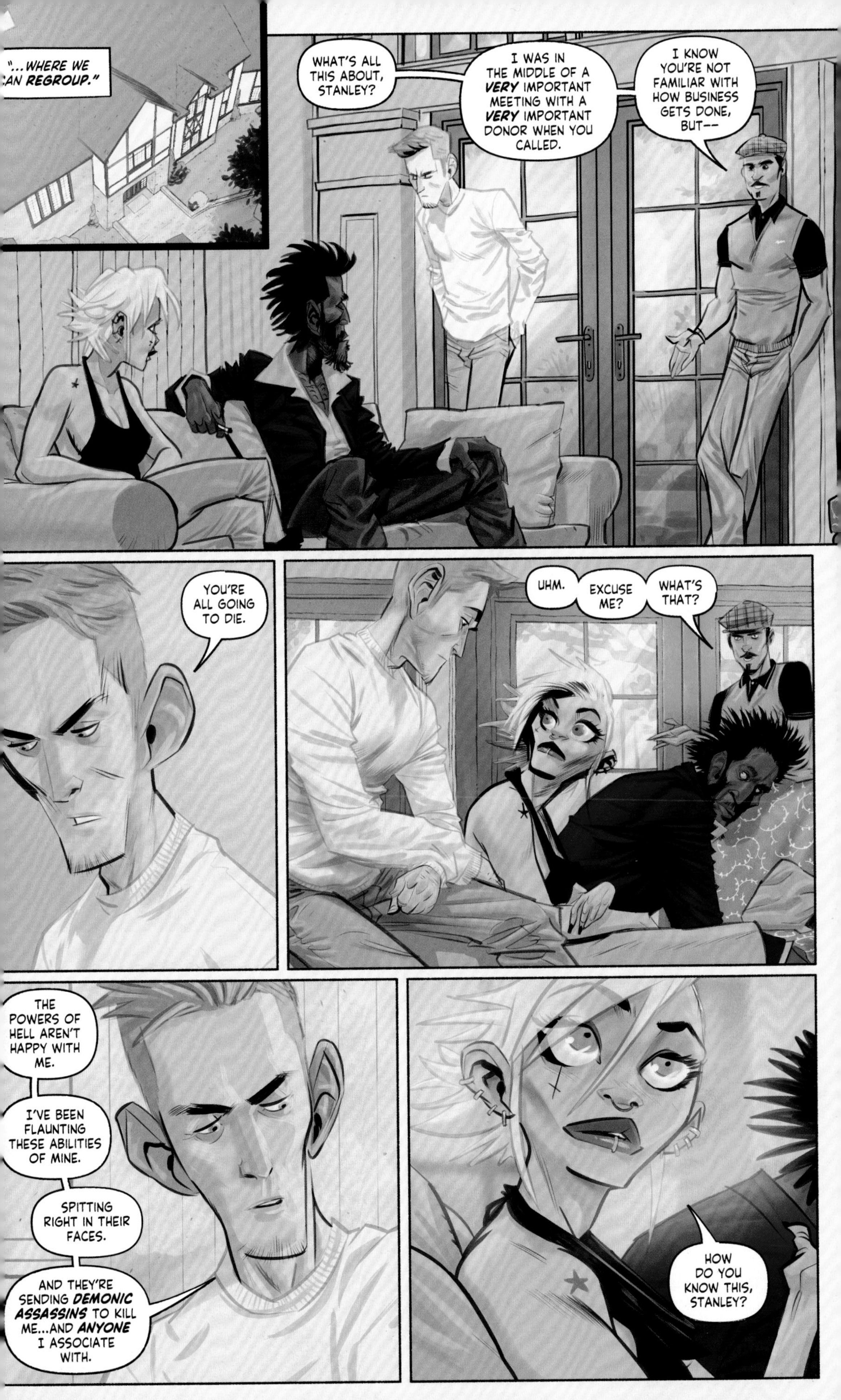
"...WHERE WE CAN REGROUP."
WHAT'S ALL THIS ABOUT, STANLEY?
I WAS IN THE MIDDLE OF A VERY IMPORTANT MEETING WITH A VERY IMPORTANT DONOR WHEN YOU CALLED.
I KNOW YOU'RE NOT FAMILIAR WITH HOW BUSINESS GETS DONE, BUT--
YOU'RE ALL GOING TO DIE.
UHM.
EXCUSE ME?
WHAT'S THAT?
THE POWERS OF HELL AREN'T HAPPY WITH ME.
I'VE BEEN FLAUNTING THESE ABILITIES OF MINE.
SPITTING RIGHT IN THEIR FACES.
AND THEY'RE SENDING DEMONIC ASSASSINS TO KILL ME...AND ANYONE I ASSOCIATE WITH.
HOW DO YOU KNOW THIS, STANLEY?

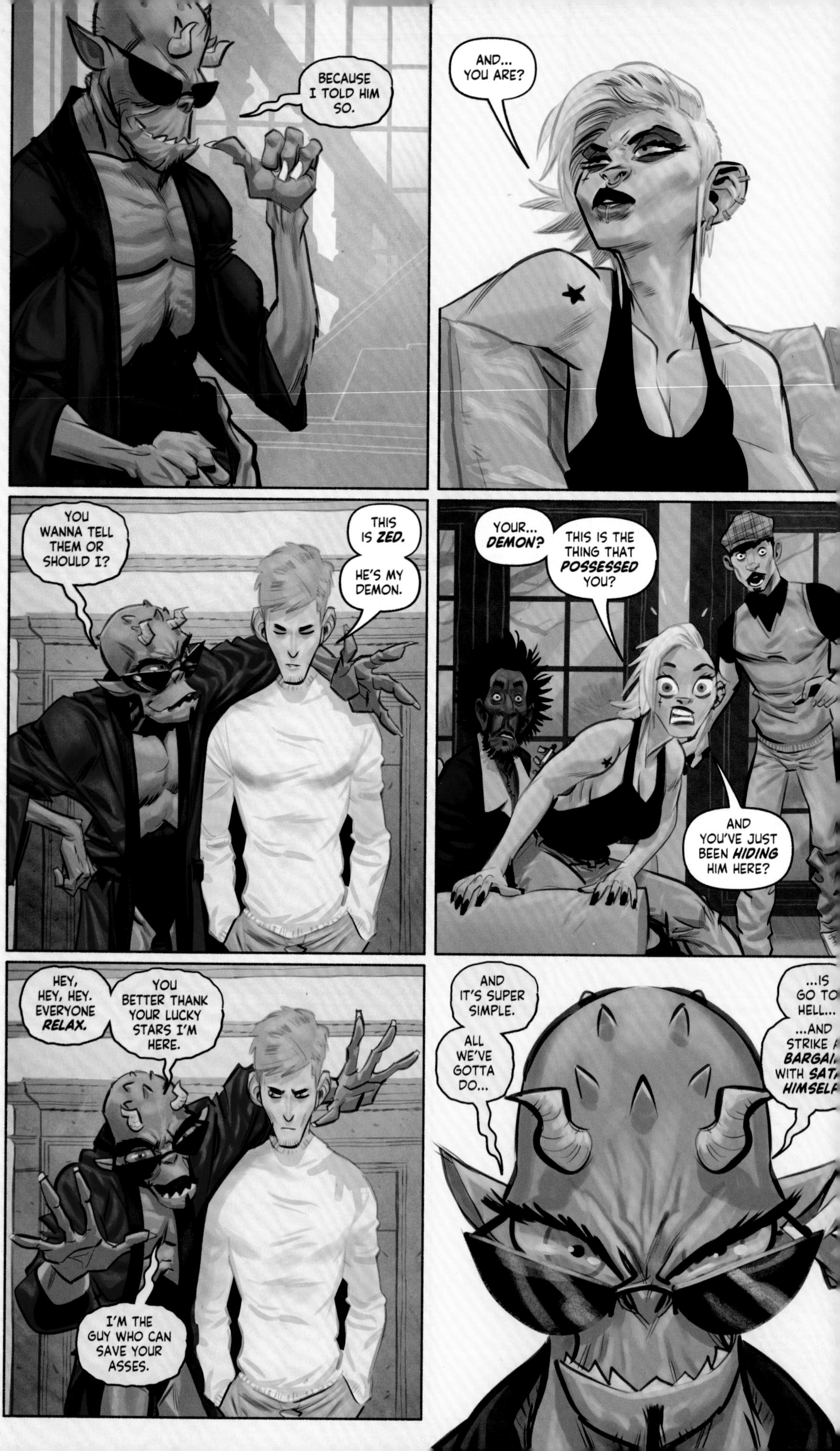
BECAUSE I TOLD HIM SO.
AND... YOU ARE?
YOU WANNA TELL THEM OR SHOULD I?
THIS IS ZED.
HE'S MY DEMON.
YOUR... DEMON?
THIS IS THE THING THAT POSSESSED YOU?
AND YOU'VE JUST BEEN HIDING HIM HERE?
HEY, HEY, HEY. EVERYONE RELAX.
YOU BETTER THANK YOUR LUCKY STARS I'M HERE.
I'M THE GUY WHO CAN SAVE YOUR ASSES.
AND IT'S SUPER SIMPLE.
ALL WE'VE GOTTA DO...
...IS GO TO HELL...
...AND STRIKE
WITH
HIMSELF

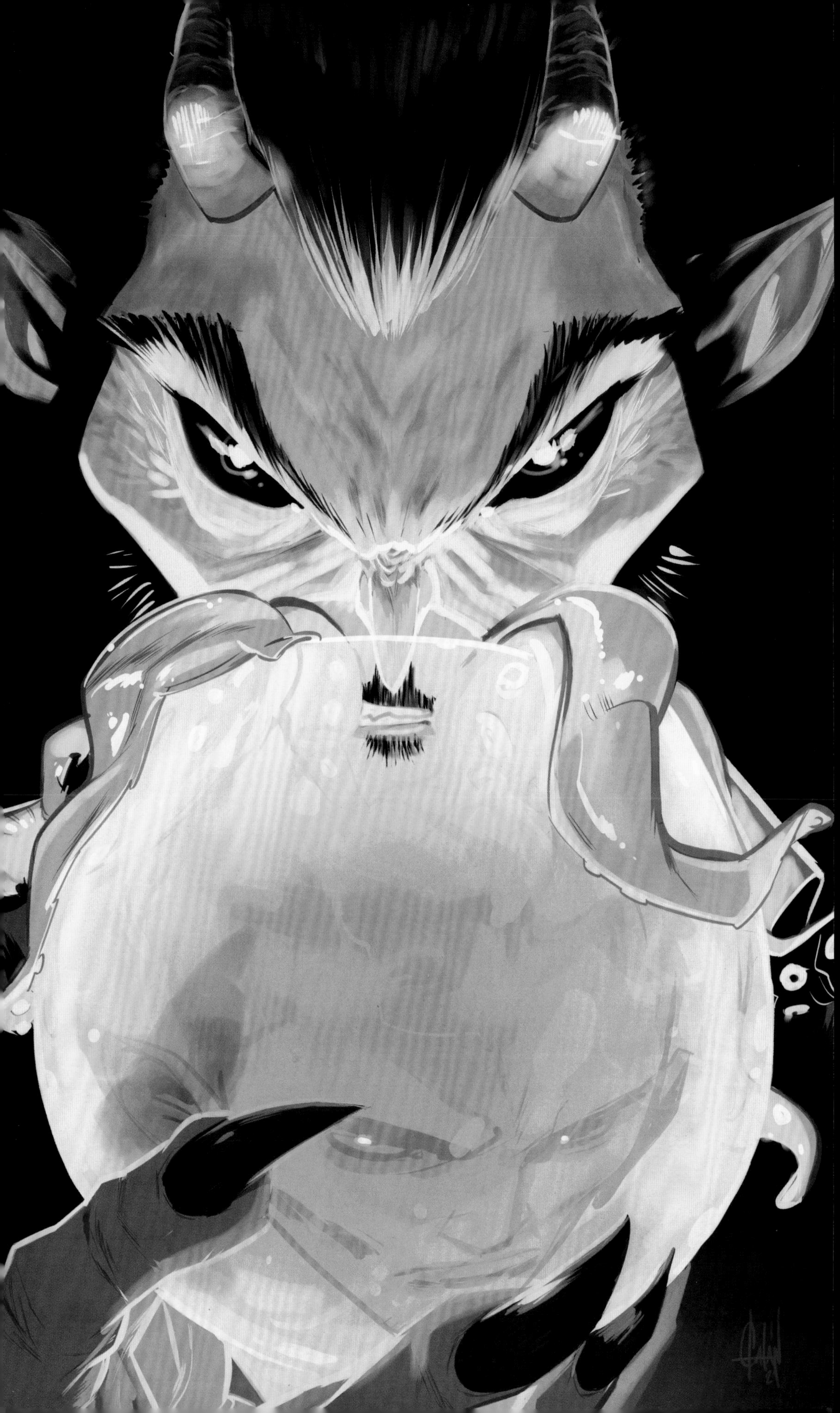

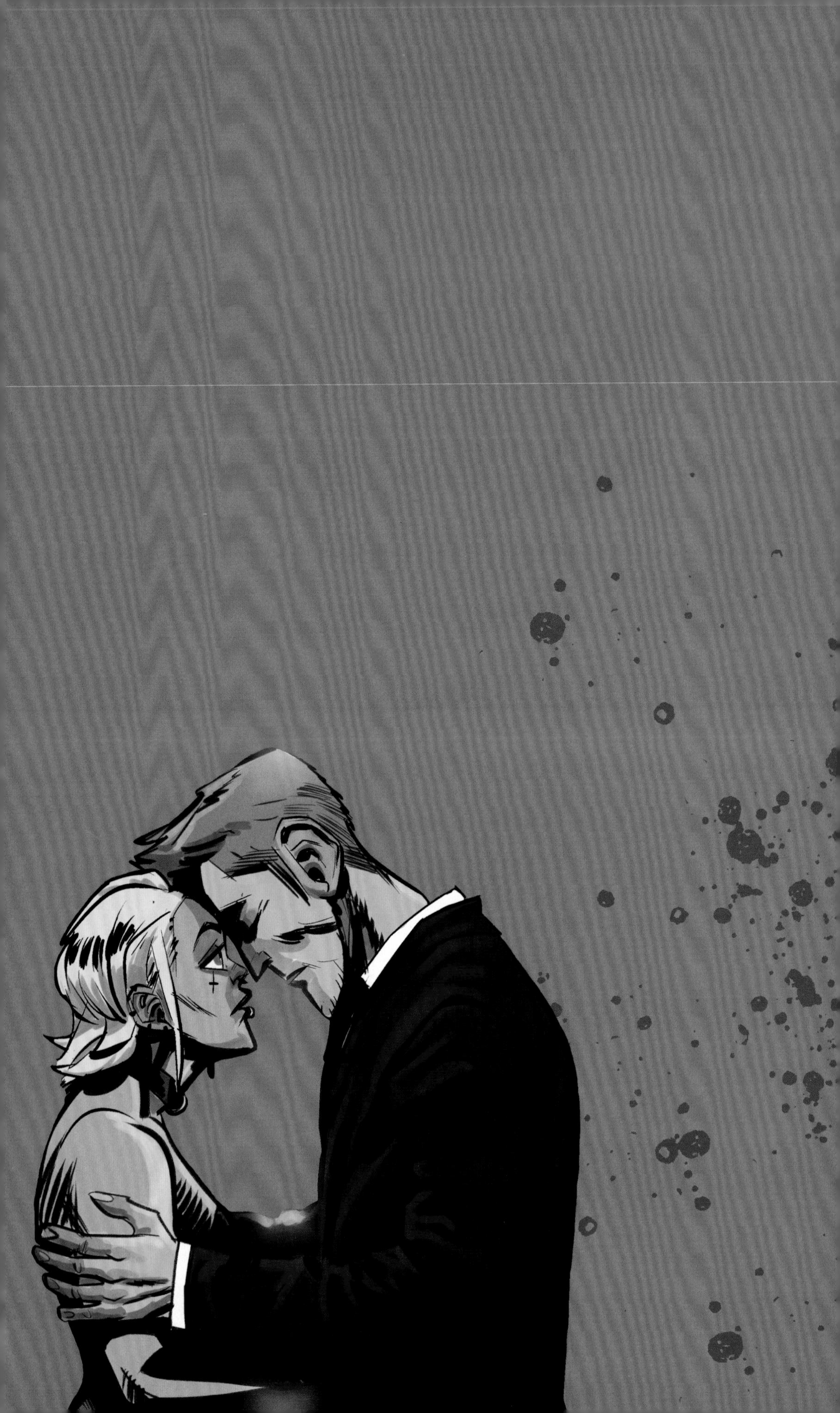

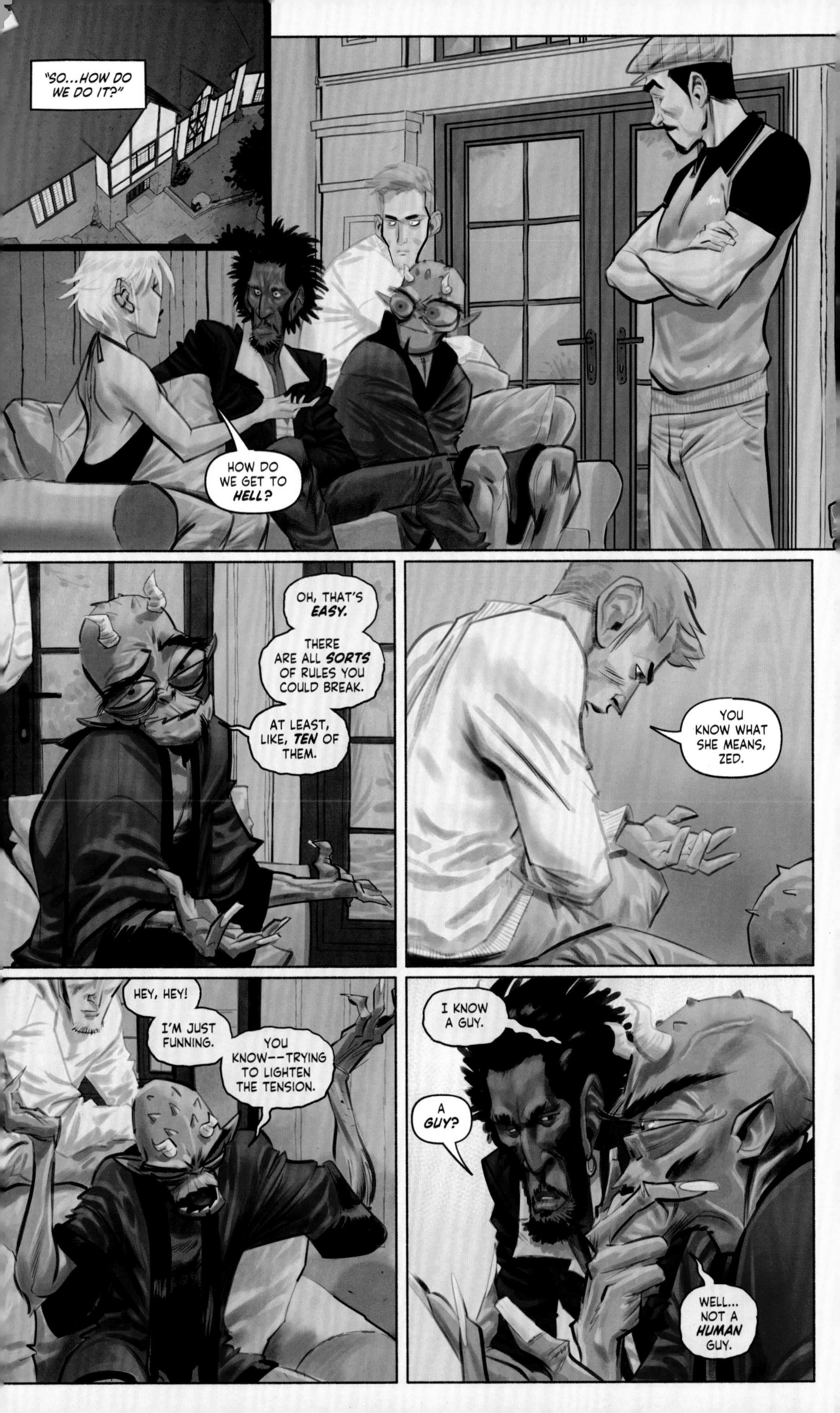
"SO...HOW DO WE DO IT?"
HOW DO WE GET TO HELL?
OH, THAT'S EASY.
THERE ARE ALL SORTS OF RULES YOU COULD BREAK.
AT LEAST, LIKE, TEN OF THEM.
YOU KNOW WHAT SHE MEANS, ZED.
HEY, HEY!
I'M JUST FUNNING.
YOU KNOW--TRYING TO LIGHTEN THE TENSION.
I KNOW A GUY.
A GUY?
WELL... NOT A HUMAN GUY.

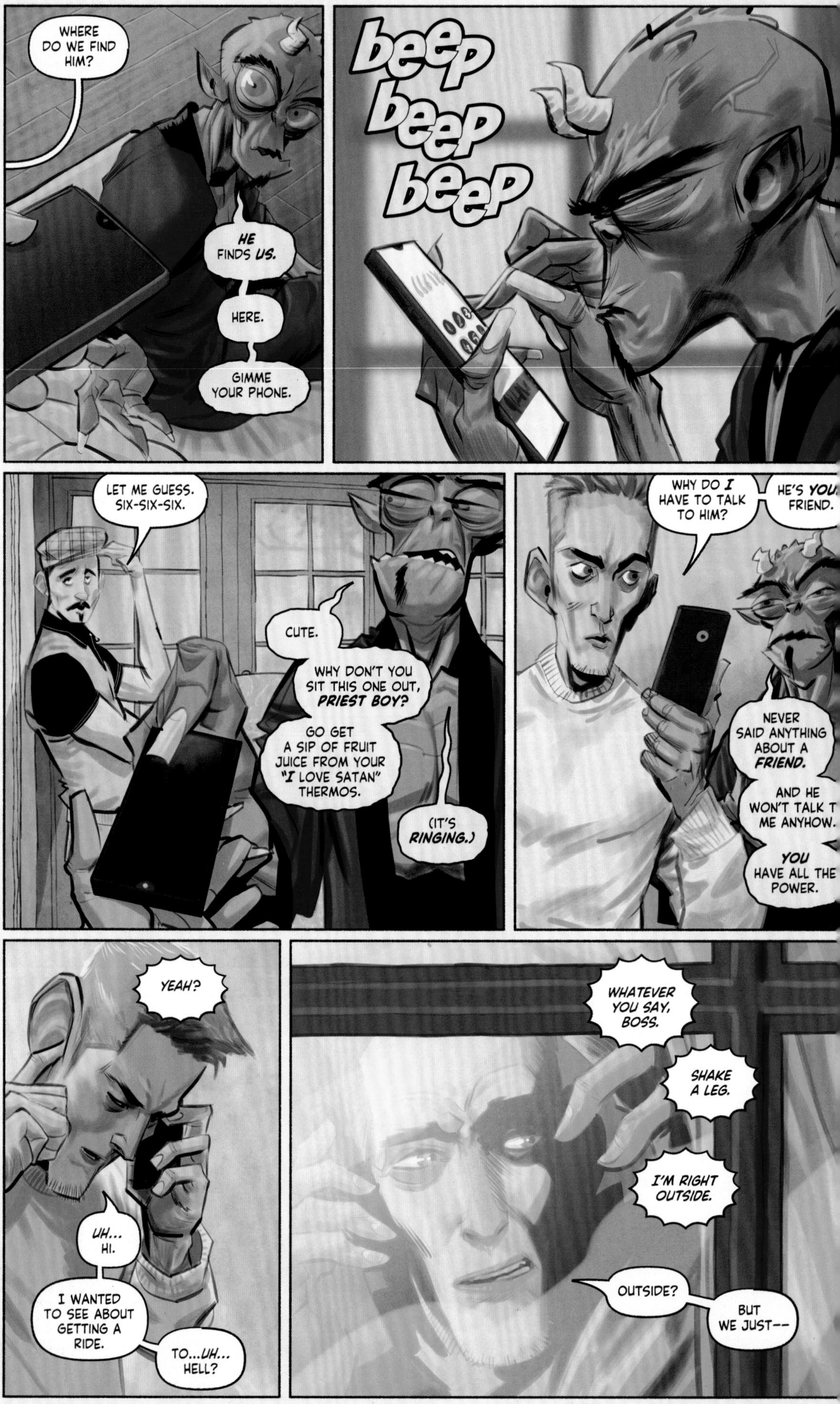
WHERE DO WE FIND HIM?
HE FINDS US.
HERE.
GIMME YOUR PHONE.
beep beep beep
LET ME GUESS. SIX-SIX-SIX.
CUTE.
WHY DON'T YOU SIT THIS ONE OUT, PRIEST BOY?
GO GET A SIP OF FRUIT JUICE FROM YOUR "I LOVE SATAN" THERMOS.
(IT'S RINGING.)
WHY DO I HAVE TO TALK TO HIM?
HE'S YOU FRIEND.
NEVER SAID ANYTHING ABOUT A FRIEND.
AND HE WON'T TALK T ME ANYHOW.
YOU HAVE ALL THE POWER.
YEAH?
UH... HI.
I WANTED TO SEE ABOUT GETTING A RIDE.
TO...UH... HELL?
WHATEVER YOU SAY, BOSS.
SHAKE A LEG.
I'M RIGHT OUTSIDE.
OUTSIDE?
BUT WE JUST--

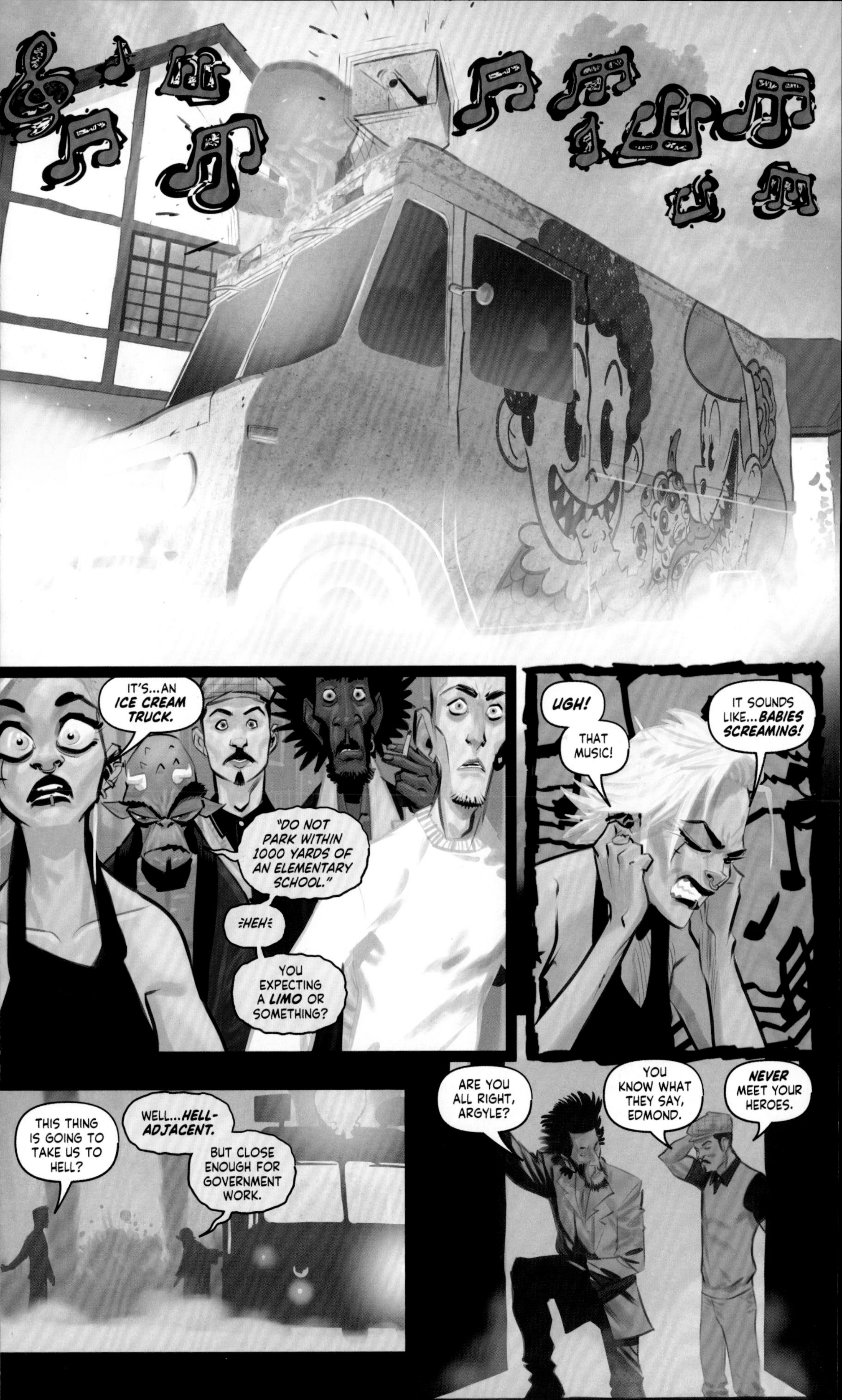
IT'S...AN ICE CREAM TRUCK.
"DO NOT PARK WITHIN 1000 YARDS OF AN ELEMENTARY SCHOOL."
HEH
YOU EXPECTING A LIMO OR SOMETHING?
UGH!
THAT MUSIC!
IT SOUNDS LIKE...BABIES SCREAMING!
THIS THING IS GOING TO TAKE US TO HELL?
WELL...HELL-ADJACENT.
BUT CLOSE ENOUGH FOR GOVERNMENT WORK.
ARE YOU ALL RIGHT, ARGYLE?
YOU KNOW WHAT THEY SAY, EDMOND.
NEVER MEET YOUR HEROES.

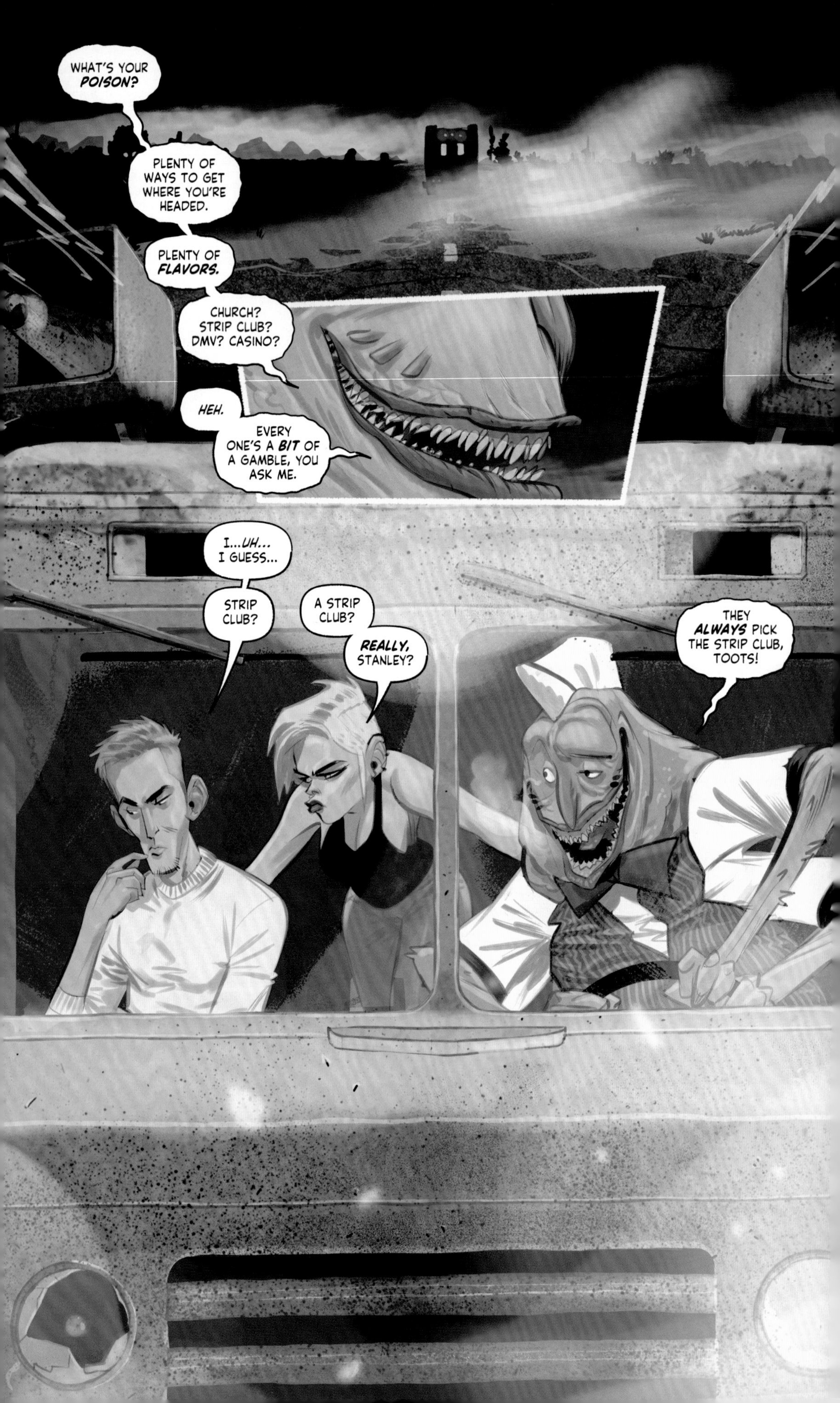
WHAT'S YOUR *POISON?*
PLENTY OF WAYS TO GET WHERE YOU'RE HEADED.
PLENTY OF *FLAVORS.*
CHURCH? STRIP CLUB? DMV? CASINO?
HEH.
EVERY ONE'S A *BIT* OF A GAMBLE, YOU ASK ME.
I...*UH*... I GUESS...
STRIP CLUB?
A STRIP CLUB?
REALLY, STANLEY?
THEY *ALWAYS* PICK THE STRIP CLUB, TOOTS!

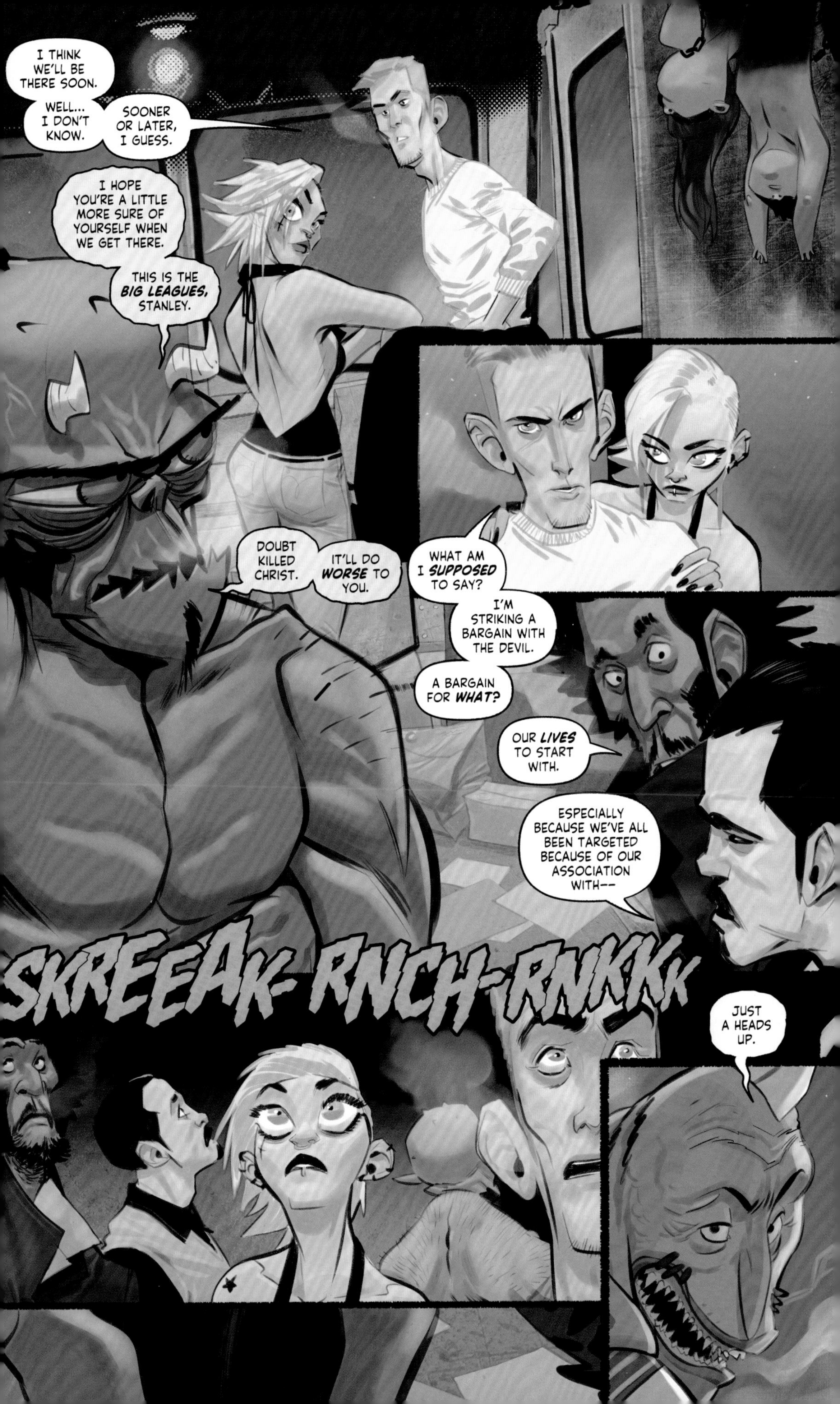

I THINK WE'LL BE THERE SOON.
WELL... I DON'T KNOW.
SOONER OR LATER, I GUESS.
I HOPE YOU'RE A LITTLE MORE SURE OF YOURSELF WHEN WE GET THERE.
THIS IS THE BIG LEAGUES, STANLEY.
DOUBT KILLED CHRIST.
IT'LL DO WORSE TO YOU.
WHAT AM I SUPPOSED TO SAY?
I'M STRIKING A BARGAIN WITH THE DEVIL.
A BARGAIN FOR WHAT?
OUR LIVES TO START WITH.
ESPECIALLY BECAUSE WE'VE ALL BEEN TARGETED BECAUSE OF OUR ASSOCIATION WITH--
SKREEAK- RNCH-RNKKK
JUST A HEADS UP.

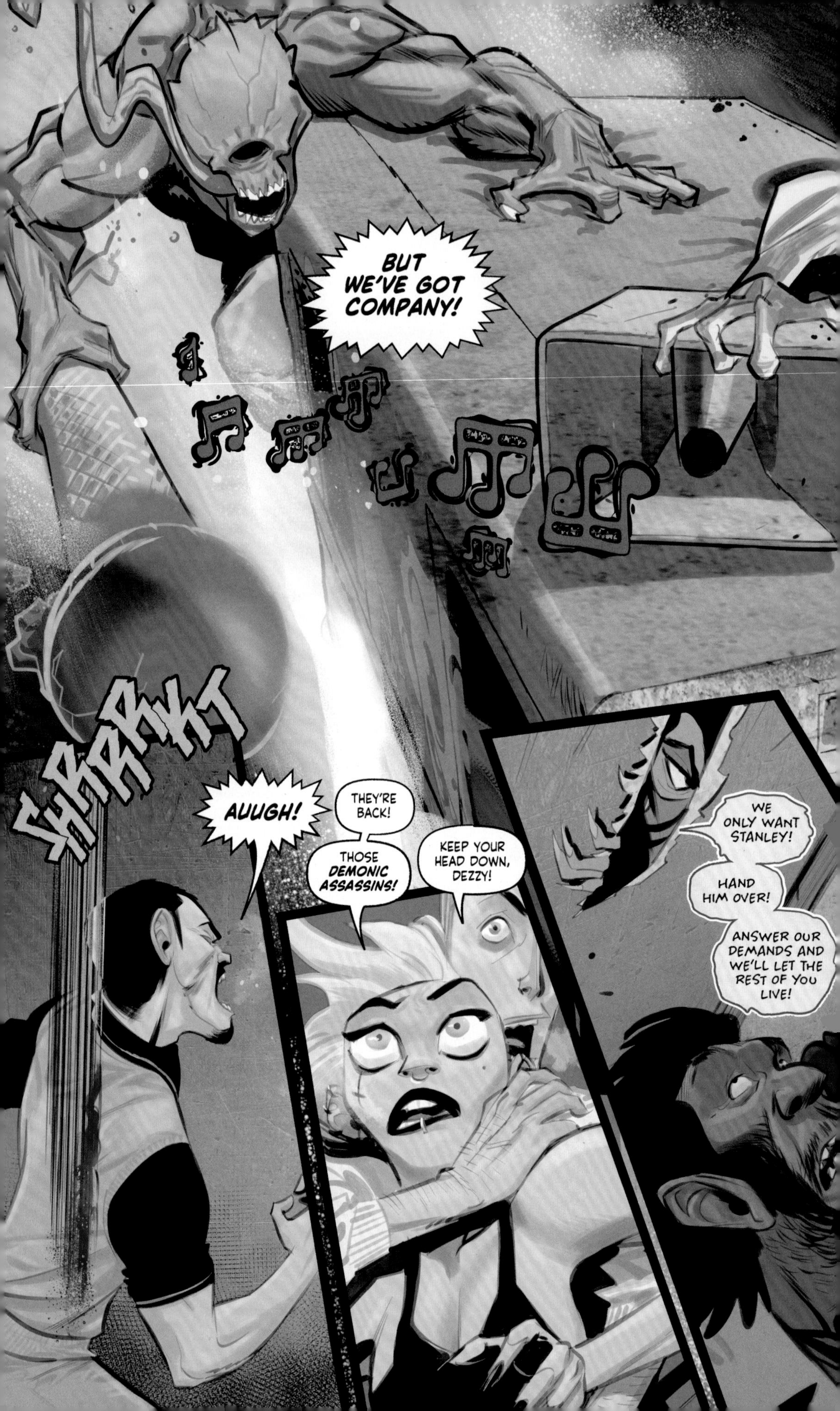
BUT WE'VE GOT COMPANY!
SHRRKT
AUUGH!
THEY'RE BACK!
THOSE DEMONIC ASSASSINS!
KEEP YOUR HEAD DOWN, DEZZY!
WE ONLY WANT STANLEY!
HAND HIM OVER!
ANSWER OUR DEMANDS AND WE'LL LET THE REST OF YOU LIVE!

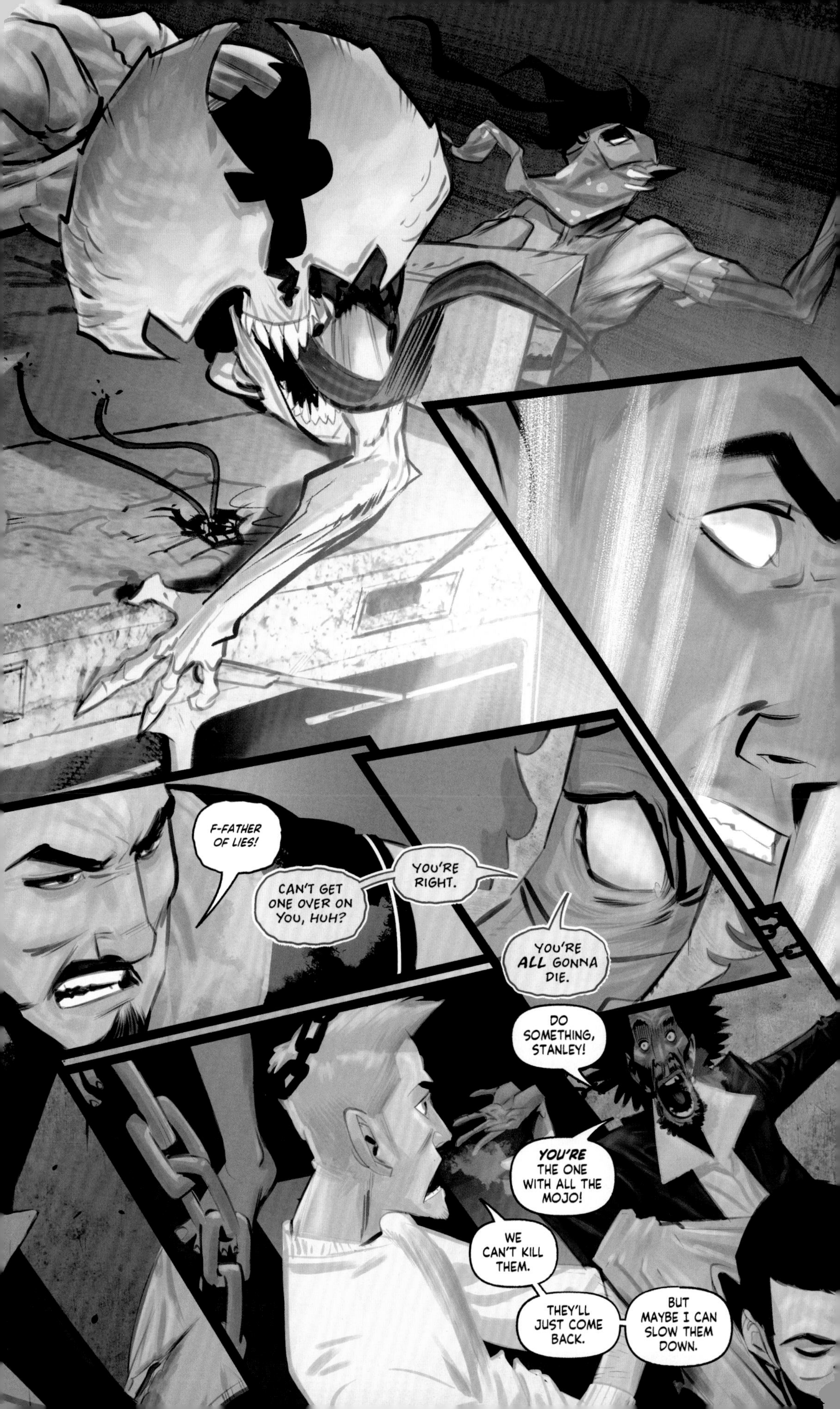
F-FATHER OF LIES!
CAN'T GET ONE OVER ON YOU, HUH?
YOU'RE RIGHT.
YOU'RE ALL GONNA DIE.
DO SOMETHING, STANLEY!
YOU'RE THE ONE WITH ALL THE MOJO!
WE CAN'T KILL THEM.
THEY'LL JUST COME BACK.
BUT MAYBE I CAN SLOW THEM DOWN.

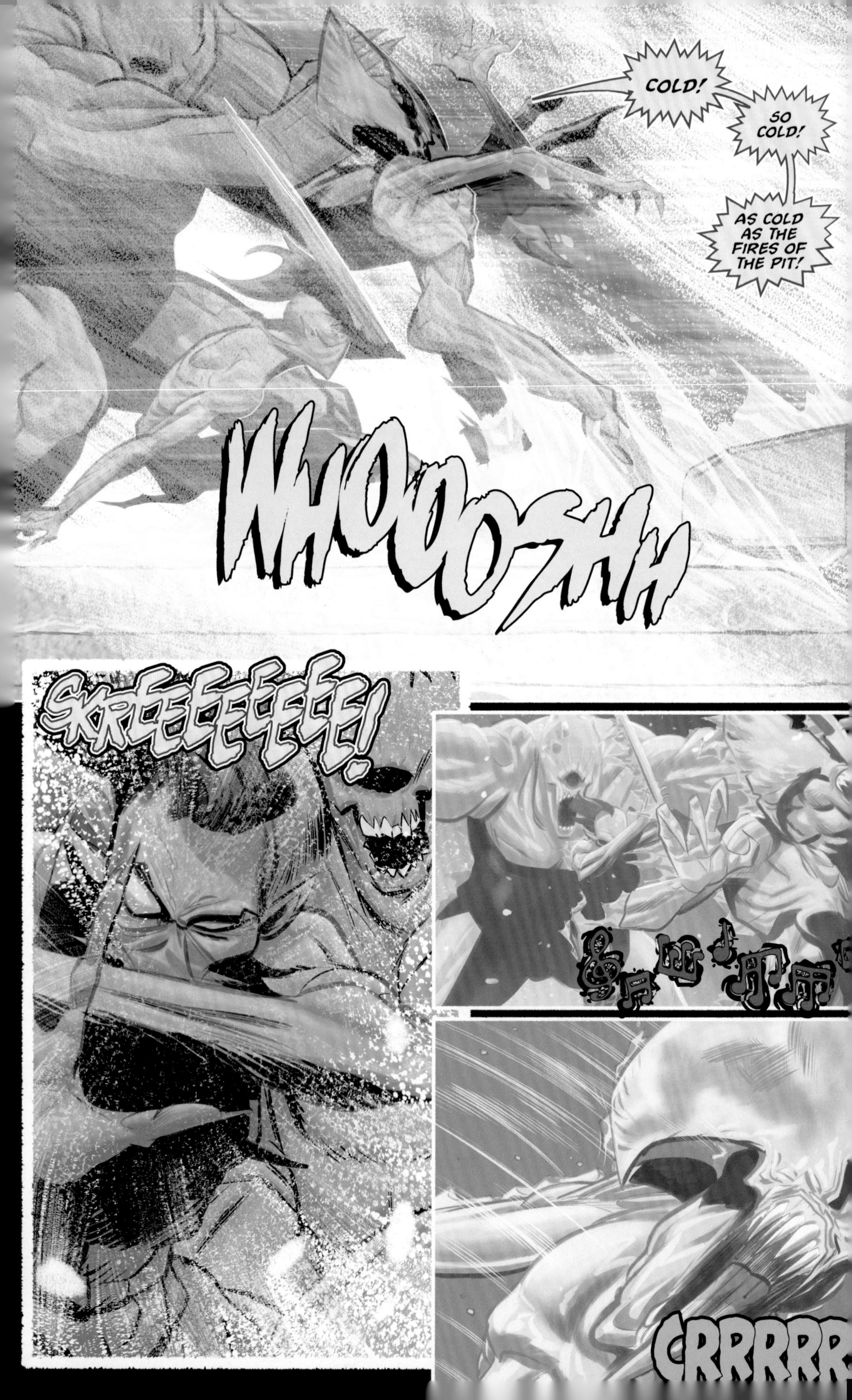
COLD!
SO COLD!
AS COLD AS THE FIRES OF THE PIT!
WHOOOSHH
SKREEEEEEEEE!
CRRRRR

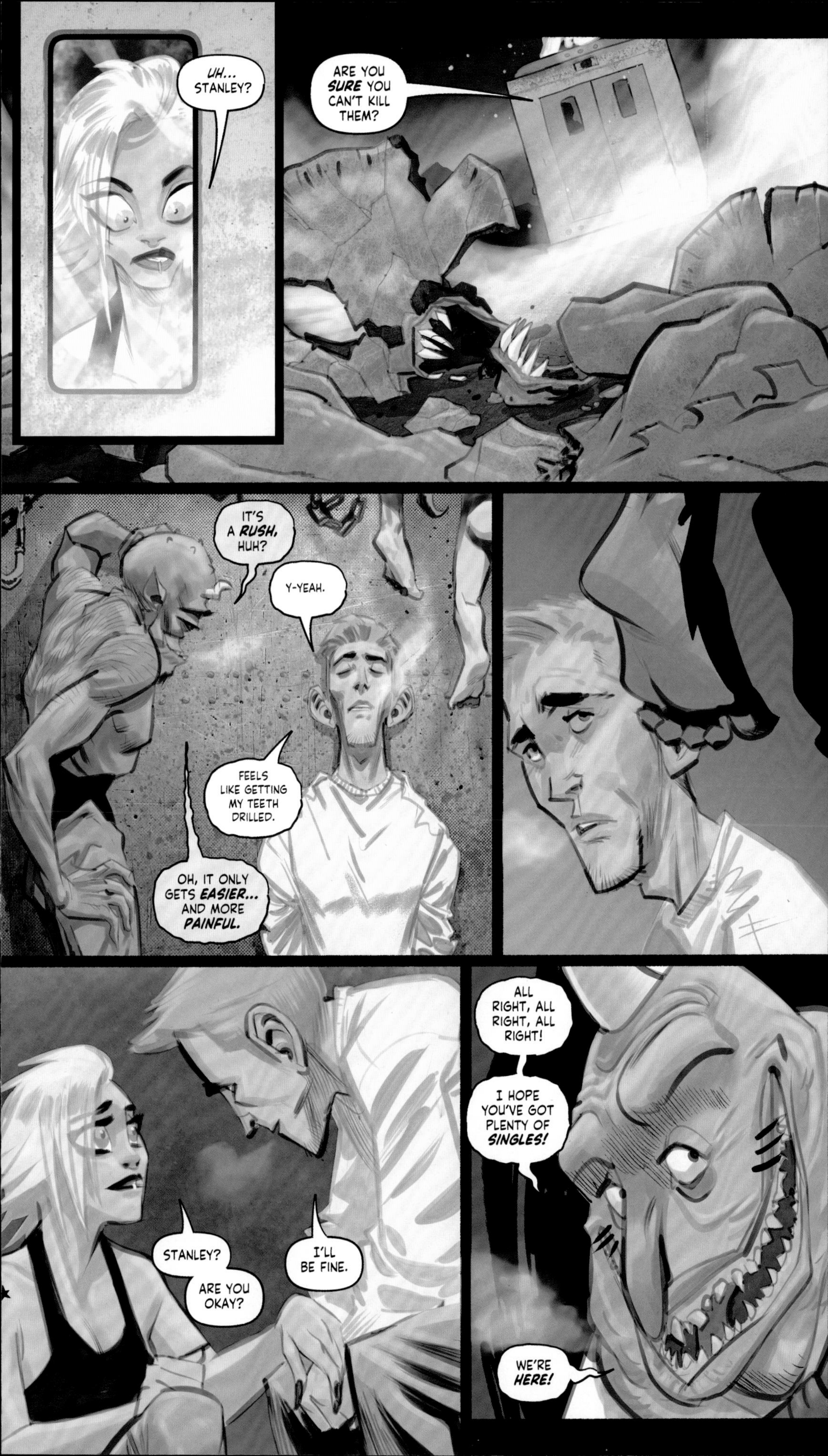
UH... STANLEY?
ARE YOU SURE YOU CAN'T KILL THEM?
IT'S A RUSH, HUH?
Y-YEAH.
FEELS LIKE GETTING MY TEETH DRILLED.
OH, IT ONLY GETS EASIER... AND MORE PAINFUL.
STANLEY?
ARE YOU OKAY?
I'LL BE FINE.
ALL RIGHT, ALL RIGHT, ALL RIGHT!
I HOPE YOU'VE GOT PLENTY OF SINGLES!
WE'RE HERE!

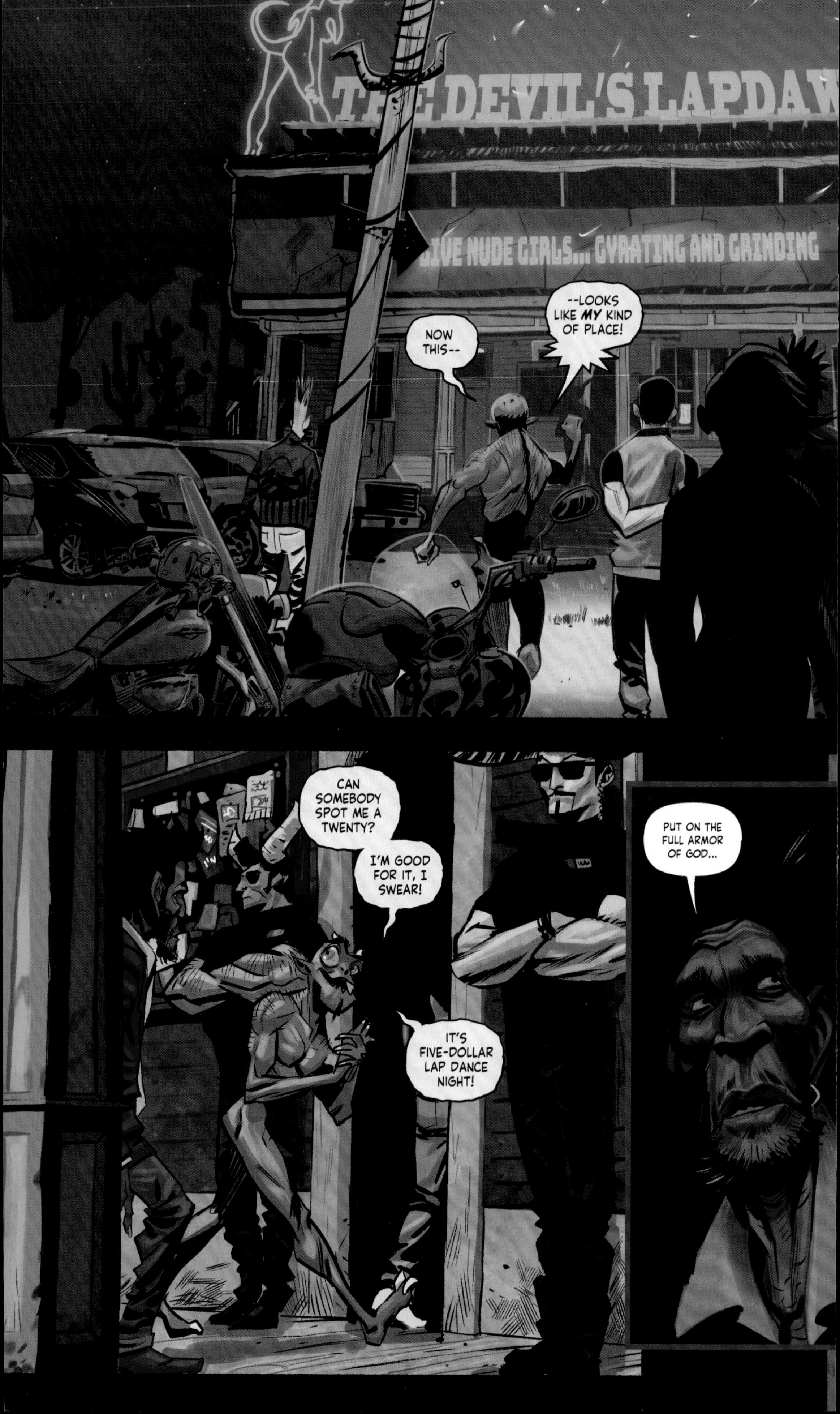
THE DEVIL'S LAPDAW
LIVE NUDE GIRLS... GYRATING AND GRINDING
NOW THIS--
--LOOKS LIKE MY KIND OF PLACE!
CAN SOMEBODY SPOT ME A TWENTY?
I'M GOOD FOR IT, I SWEAR!
IT'S FIVE-DOLLAR LAP DANCE NIGHT!
PUT ON THE FULL ARMOR OF GOD...

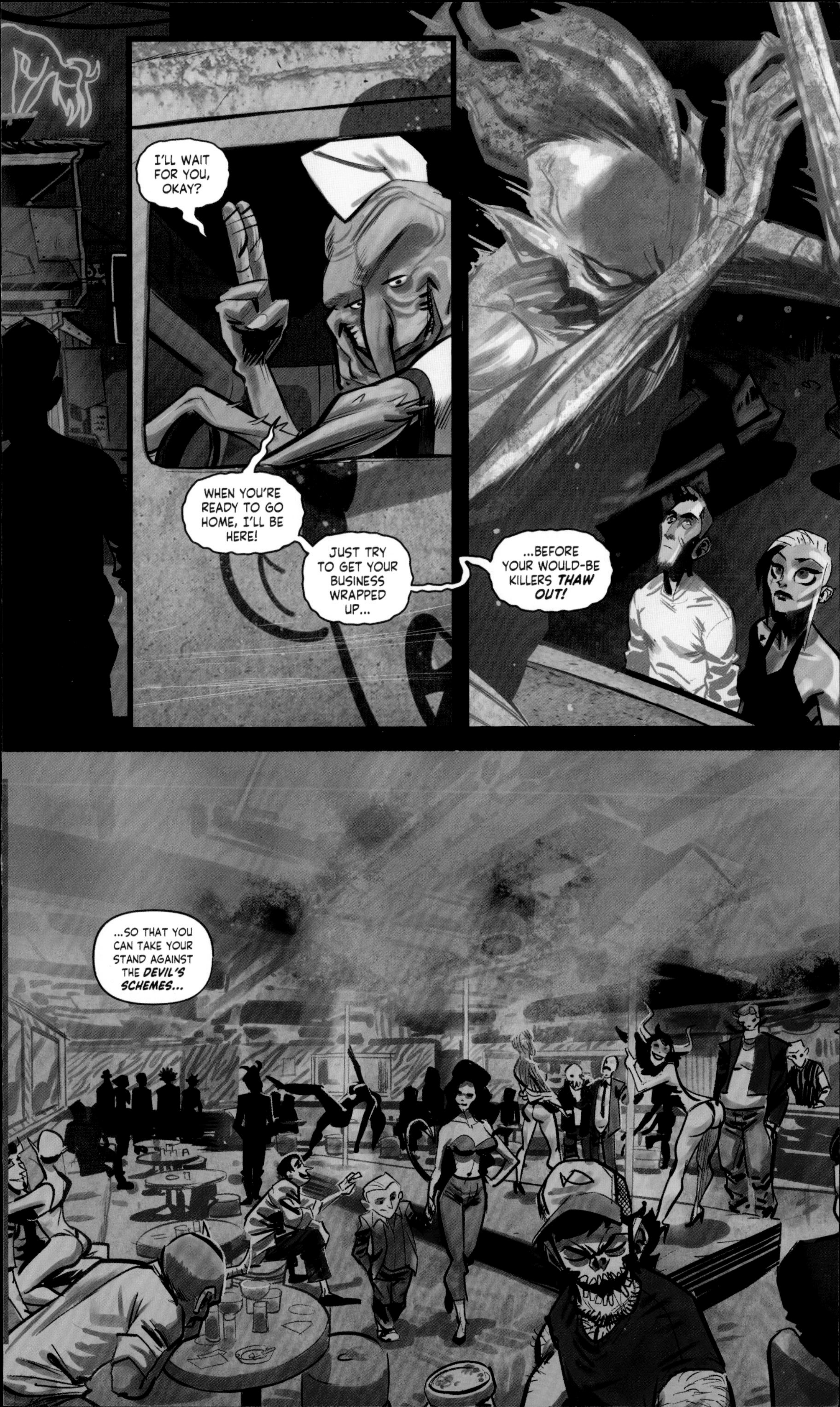
I'LL WAIT FOR YOU, OKAY?
WHEN YOU'RE READY TO GO HOME, I'LL BE HERE!
JUST TRY TO GET YOUR BUSINESS WRAPPED UP...
...BEFORE YOUR WOULD-BE KILLERS *THAW OUT!*
...SO THAT YOU CAN TAKE YOUR STAND AGAINST THE *DEVIL'S SCHEMES...*

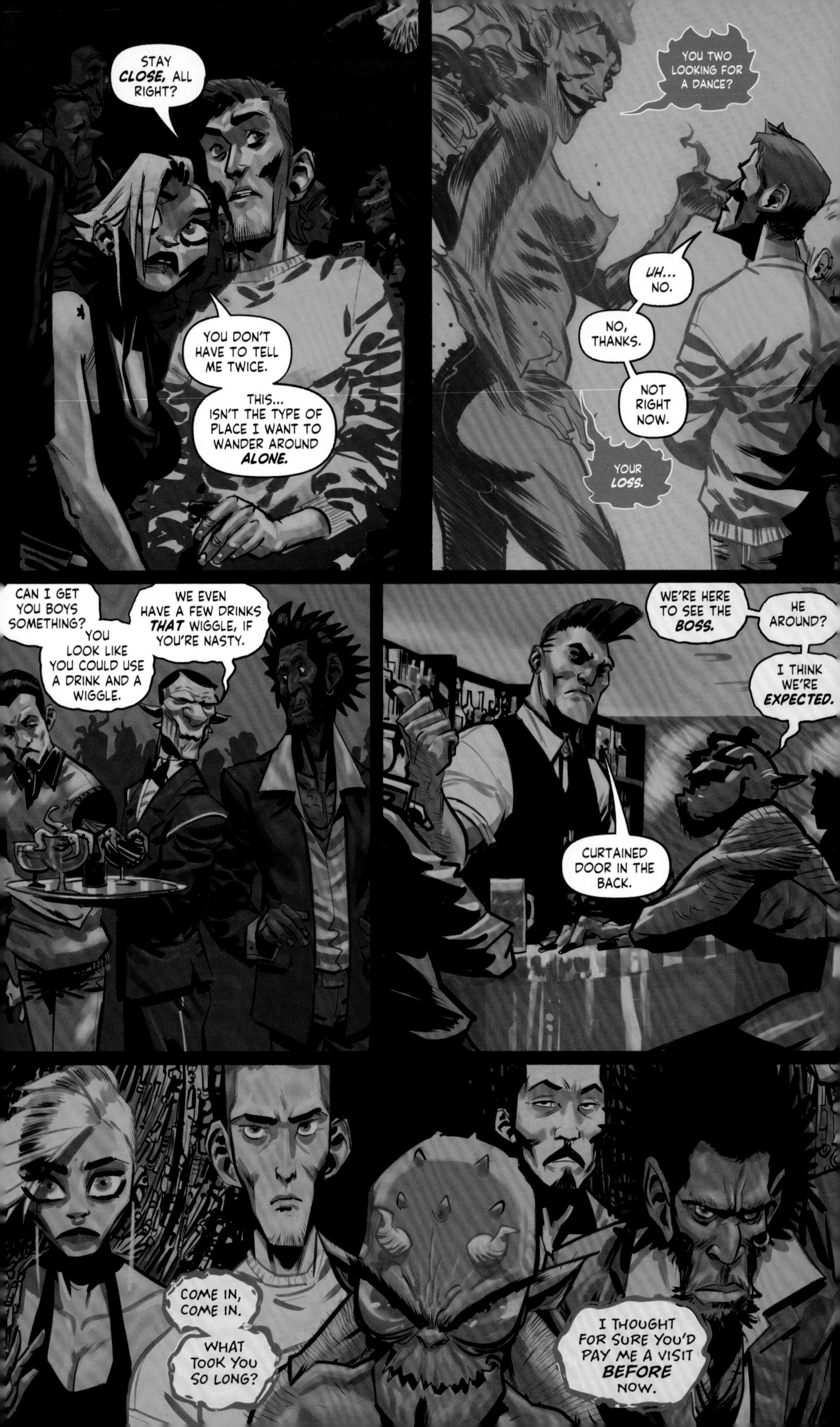

STAY CLOSE, ALL RIGHT?
YOU DON'T HAVE TO TELL ME TWICE.
THIS... ISN'T THE TYPE OF PLACE I WANT TO WANDER AROUND ALONE.
YOU TWO LOOKING FOR A DANCE?
UH... NO.
NO, THANKS.
NOT RIGHT NOW.
YOUR LOSS.
CAN I GET YOU BOYS SOMETHING? YOU LOOK LIKE YOU COULD USE A DRINK AND A WIGGLE.
WE EVEN HAVE A FEW DRINKS THAT WIGGLE, IF YOU'RE NASTY.
WE'RE HERE TO SEE THE BOSS.
HE AROUND?
I THINK WE'RE EXPECTED.
CURTAINED DOOR IN THE BACK.
COME IN, COME IN.
WHAT TOOK YOU SO LONG?
I THOUGHT FOR SURE YOU'D PAY ME A VISIT BEFORE NOW.

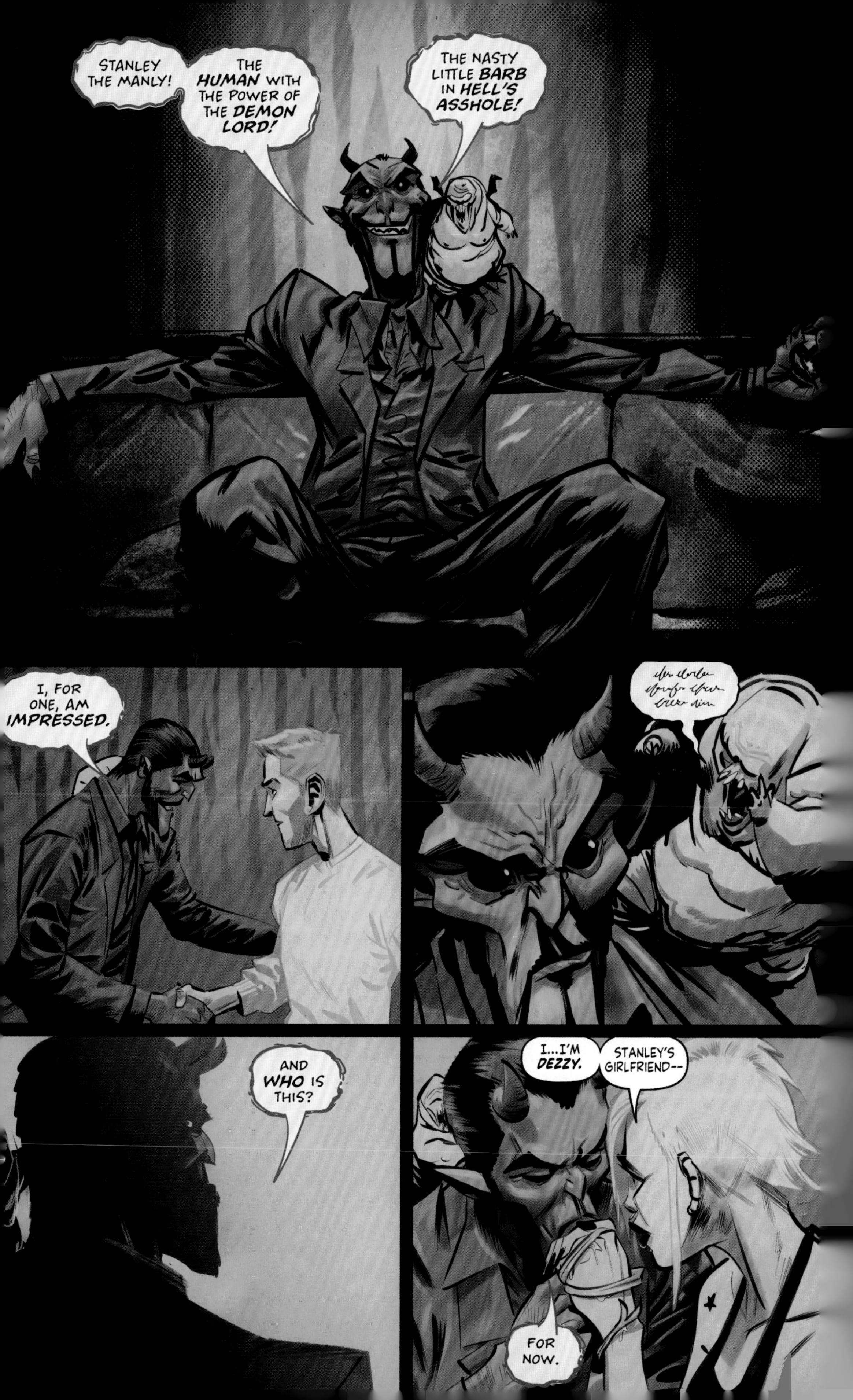
STANLEY THE MANLY!
THE HUMAN WITH THE POWER OF THE DEMON LORD!
THE NASTY LITTLE BARB IN HELL'S ASSHOLE!
I, FOR ONE, AM IMPRESSED.
AND WHO IS THIS?
I...I'M DEZZY.
STANLEY'S GIRLFRIEND--
FOR NOW.

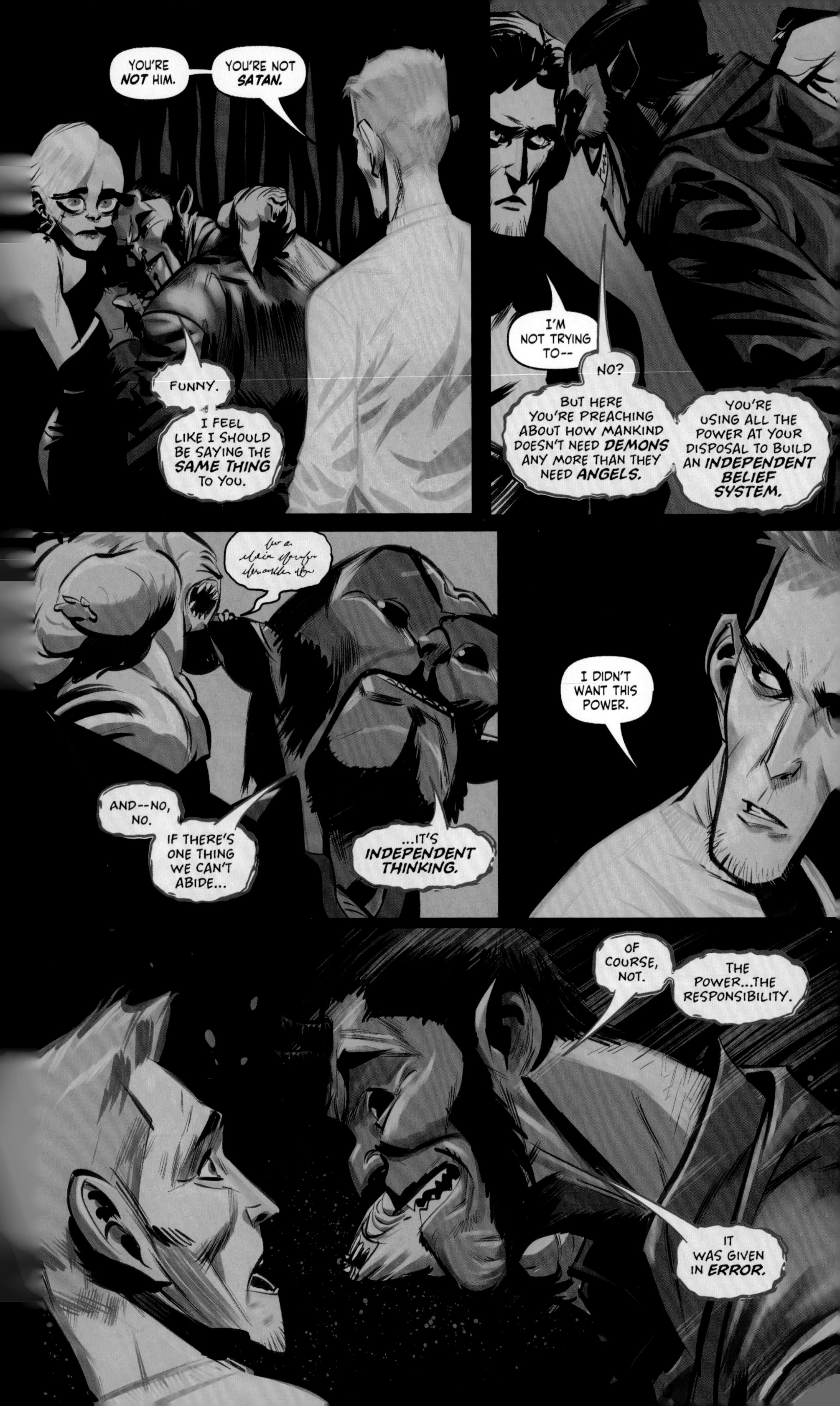
YOU'RE **NOT** HIM.
YOU'RE NOT **SATAN.**
FUNNY.
I FEEL LIKE I SHOULD BE SAYING THE **SAME THING** TO YOU.
I'M NOT TRYING TO--
NO?
BUT HERE YOU'RE PREACHING ABOUT HOW MANKIND DOESN'T NEED **DEMONS** ANY MORE THAN THEY NEED **ANGELS.**
YOU'RE USING ALL THE POWER AT YOUR DISPOSAL TO BUILD AN **INDEPENDENT BELIEF SYSTEM.**
AND--NO, NO.
IF THERE'S ONE THING WE CAN'T ABIDE...
...IT'S **INDEPENDENT THINKING.**
I DIDN'T WANT THIS POWER.
OF COURSE, NOT.
THE POWER...THE RESPONSIBILITY.
IT WAS GIVEN IN **ERROR.**

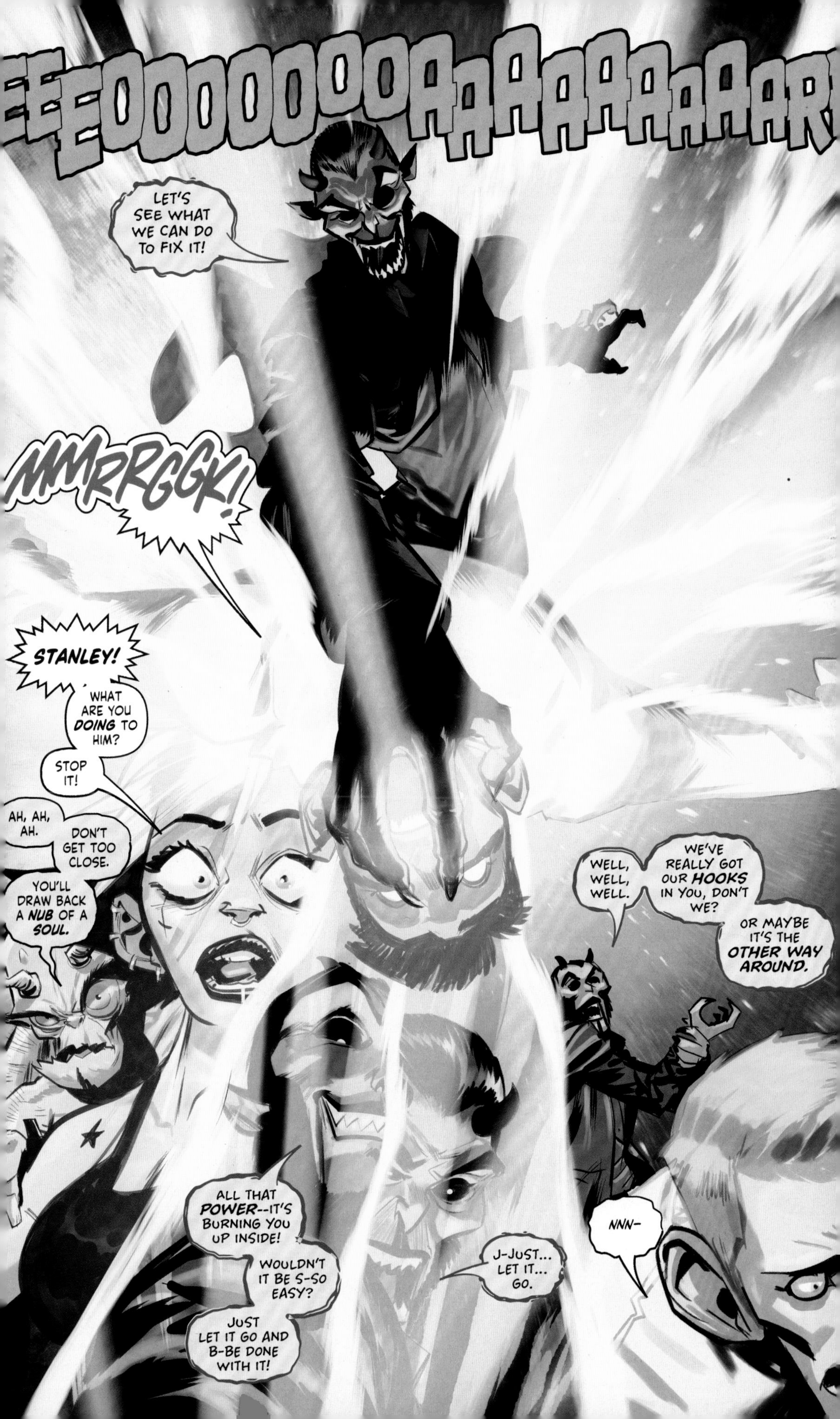
EEEOOOOOOOAAAAAAAAAAR
LET'S SEE WHAT WE CAN DO TO FIX IT!
MMRRGGK!
STANLEY!
WHAT ARE YOU *DOING* TO HIM?
STOP IT!
AH, AH, AH.
DON'T GET TOO CLOSE.
YOU'LL DRAW BACK A *NUB* OF A *SOUL.*
WELL, WELL, WELL.
WE'VE REALLY GOT OUR *HOOKS* IN YOU, DON'T WE?
OR MAYBE IT'S THE *OTHER WAY AROUND.*
ALL THAT *POWER*--IT'S BURNING YOU UP INSIDE!
WOULDN'T IT BE S-SO EASY?
JUST LET IT GO AND B-BE DONE WITH IT!
J-JUST... LET IT... GO.
NNN-

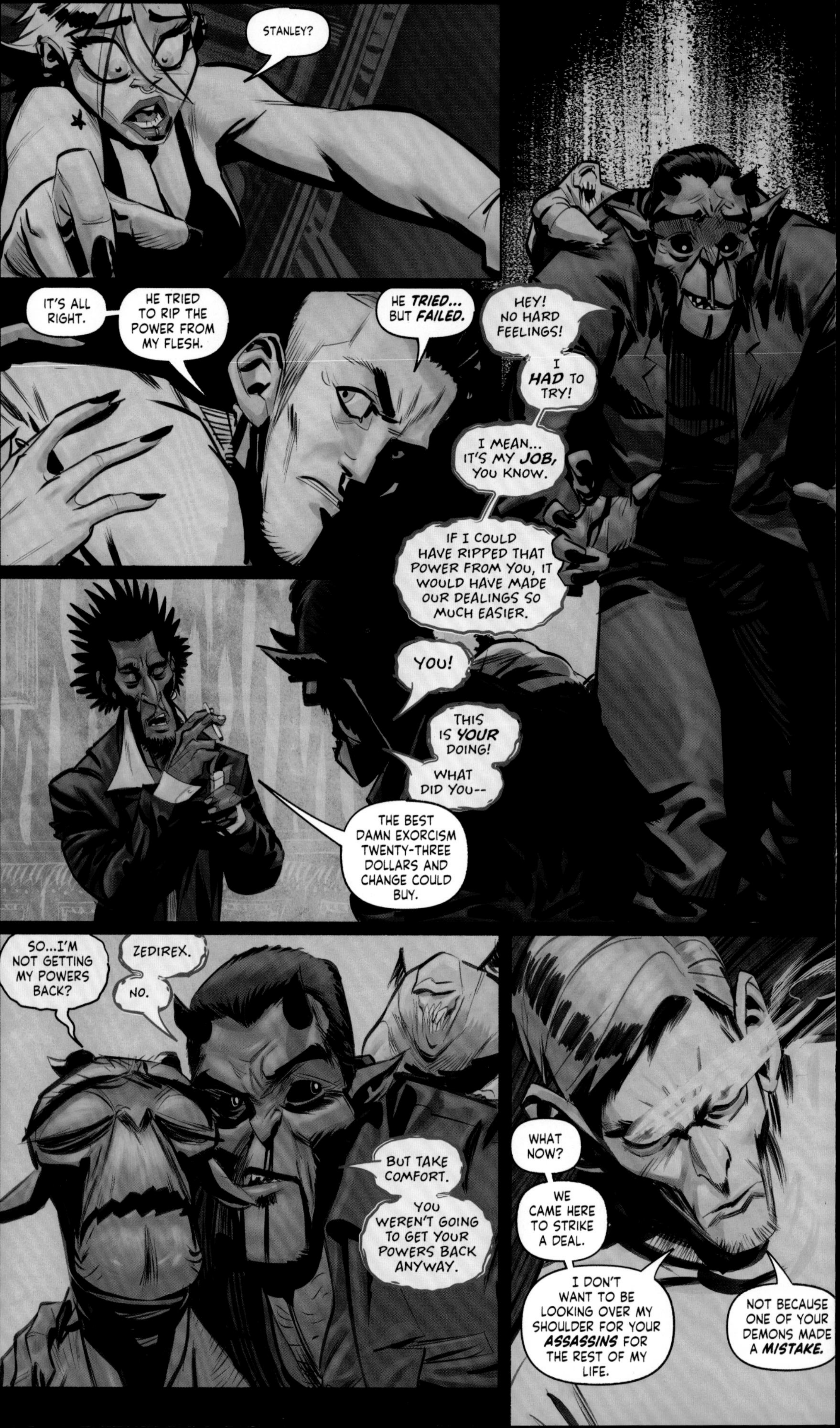
STANLEY?
IT'S ALL RIGHT.
HE TRIED TO RIP THE POWER FROM MY FLESH.
HE *TRIED...* BUT *FAILED.*
HEY! NO HARD FEELINGS!
I *HAD* TO TRY!
I MEAN... IT'S MY *JOB,* YOU KNOW.
IF I COULD HAVE RIPPED THAT POWER FROM YOU, IT WOULD HAVE MADE OUR DEALINGS SO MUCH EASIER.
YOU!
THIS IS *YOUR* DOING!
WHAT DID YOU--
THE BEST DAMN EXORCISM TWENTY-THREE DOLLARS AND CHANGE COULD BUY.
SO...I'M NOT GETTING MY POWERS BACK?
ZEDIREX.
NO.
BUT TAKE COMFORT.
YOU WEREN'T GOING TO GET YOUR POWERS BACK ANYWAY.
WHAT NOW?
WE CAME HERE TO STRIKE A DEAL.
I DON'T WANT TO BE LOOKING OVER MY SHOULDER FOR YOUR *ASSASSINS* FOR THE REST OF MY LIFE.
NOT BECAUSE ONE OF YOUR DEMONS MADE A *MISTAKE.*

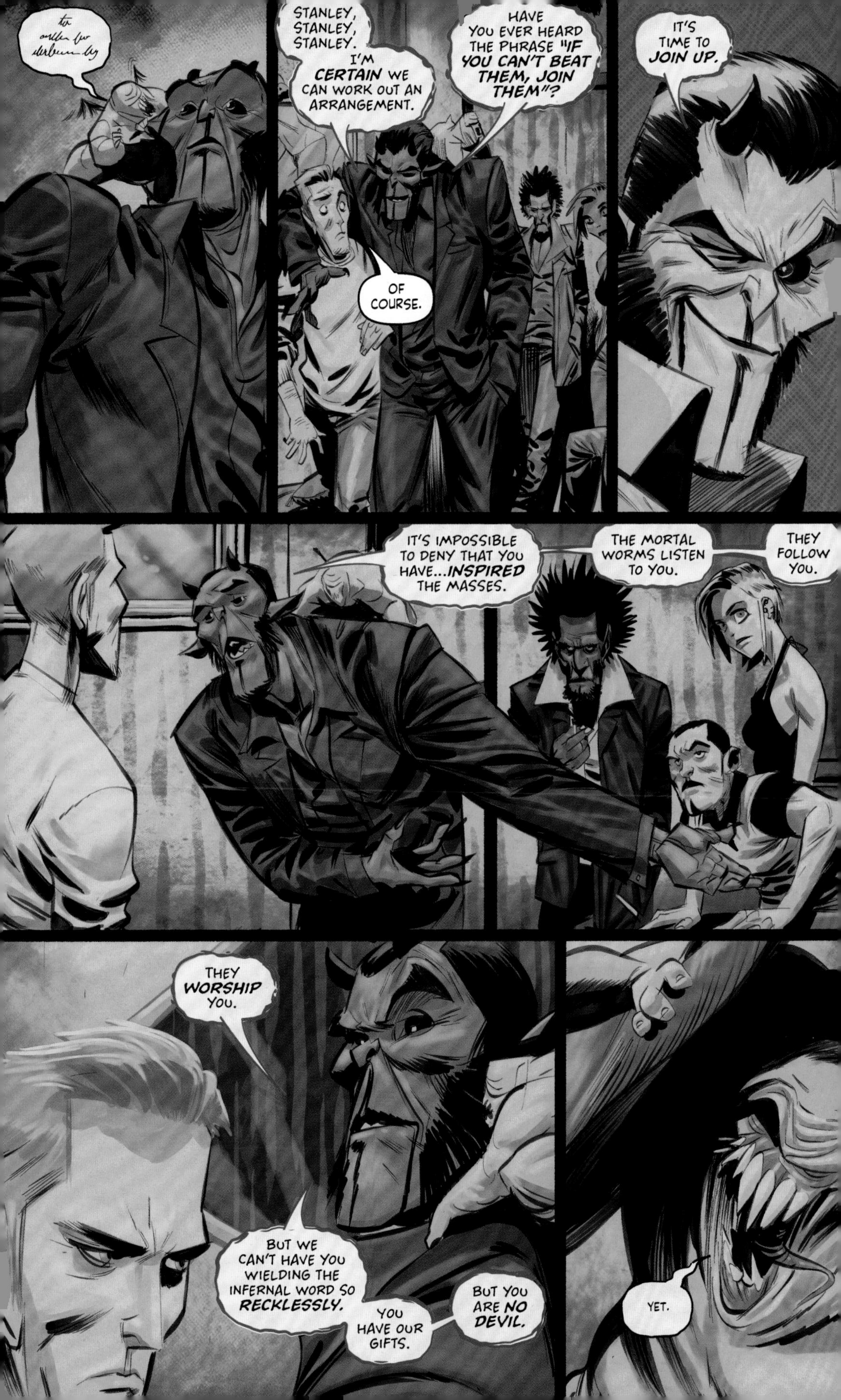
STANLEY, STANLEY, STANLEY.
I'M CERTAIN WE CAN WORK OUT AN ARRANGEMENT.
HAVE YOU EVER HEARD THE PHRASE "IF YOU CAN'T BEAT THEM, JOIN THEM"?
OF COURSE.
IT'S TIME TO JOIN UP.
IT'S IMPOSSIBLE TO DENY THAT YOU HAVE...INSPIRED THE MASSES.
THE MORTAL WORMS LISTEN TO YOU.
THEY FOLLOW YOU.
THEY WORSHIP YOU.
BUT WE CAN'T HAVE YOU WIELDING THE INFERNAL WORD SO RECKLESSLY.
YOU HAVE OUR GIFTS.
BUT YOU ARE NO DEVIL.
YET.

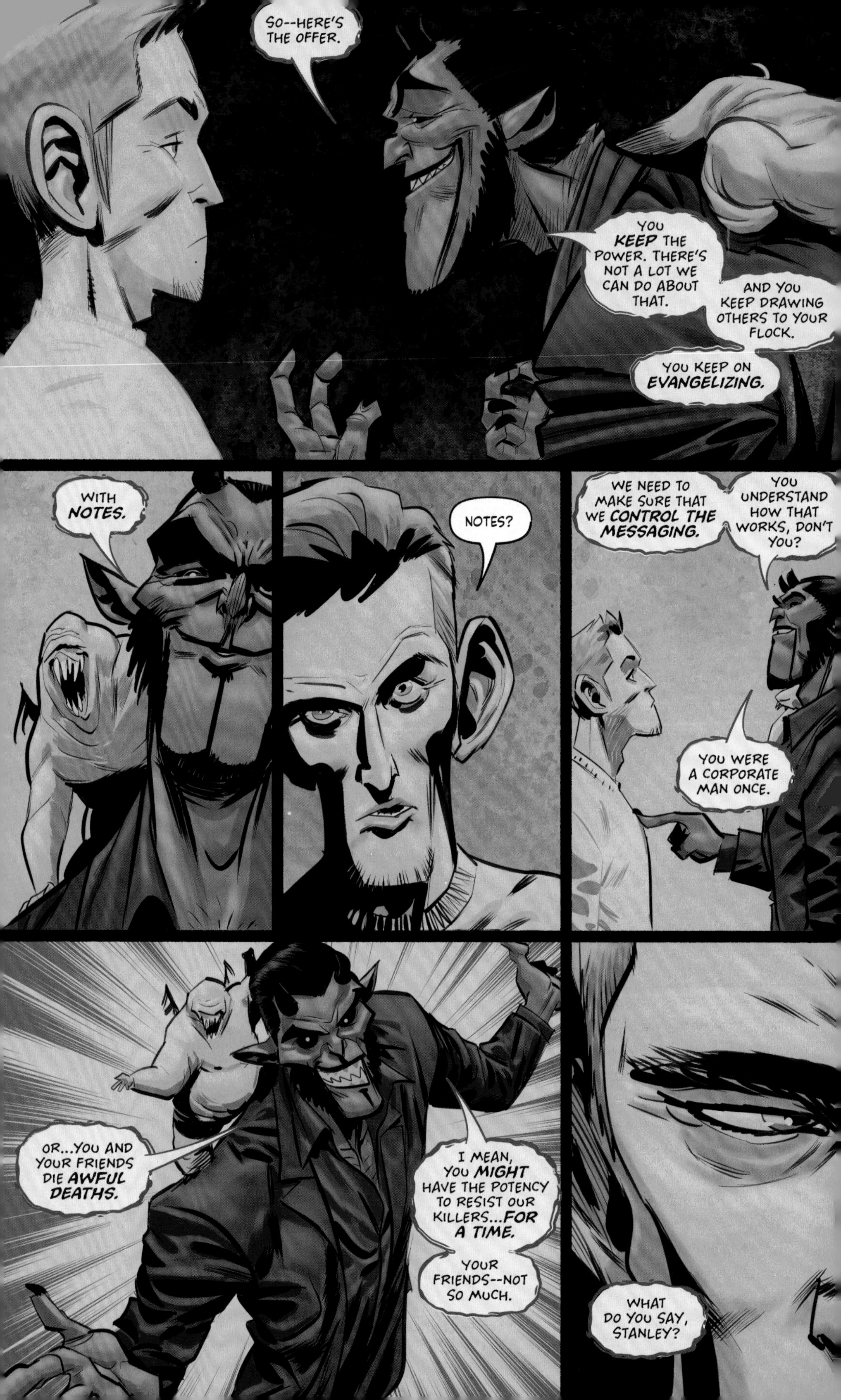

SO--HERE'S THE OFFER.
YOU **KEEP** THE POWER. THERE'S NOT A LOT WE CAN DO ABOUT THAT.
AND YOU KEEP DRAWING OTHERS TO YOUR FLOCK.
YOU KEEP ON **EVANGELIZING.**
WITH **NOTES.**
NOTES?
WE NEED TO MAKE SURE THAT WE **CONTROL THE MESSAGING.**
YOU UNDERSTAND HOW THAT WORKS, DON'T YOU?
YOU WERE A CORPORATE MAN ONCE.
OR...YOU AND YOUR FRIENDS DIE **AWFUL DEATHS.**
I MEAN, YOU **MIGHT** HAVE THE POTENCY TO RESIST OUR KILLERS...**FOR A TIME.**
YOUR FRIENDS--NOT SO MUCH.
WHAT DO YOU SAY, STANLEY?

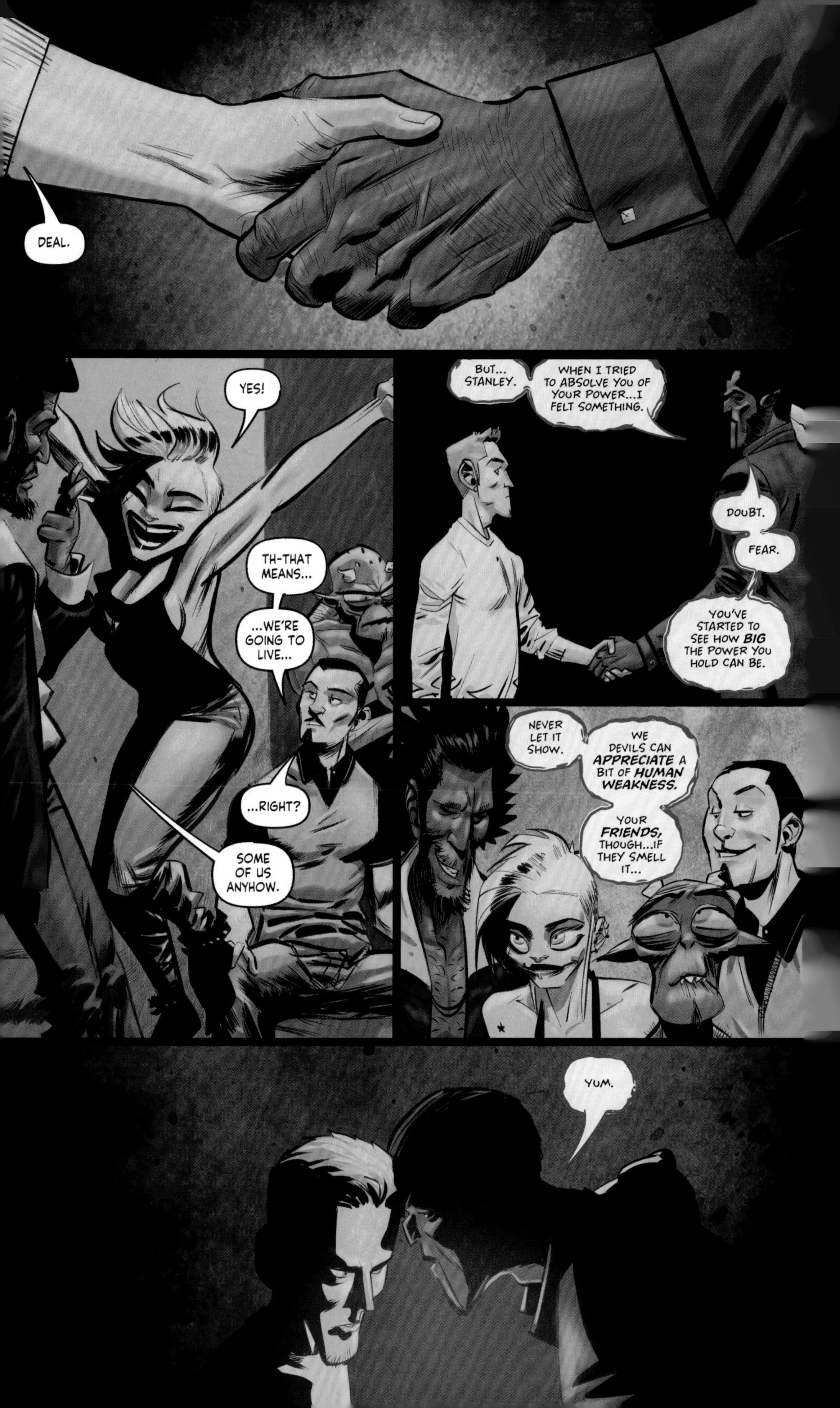
DEAL.
YES!
TH-THAT MEANS...
...WE'RE GOING TO LIVE...
...RIGHT?
SOME OF US ANYHOW.
BUT... STANLEY.
WHEN I TRIED TO ABSOLVE YOU OF YOUR POWER...I FELT SOMETHING.
DOUBT.
FEAR.
YOU'VE STARTED TO SEE HOW BIG THE POWER YOU HOLD CAN BE.
NEVER LET IT SHOW.
WE DEVILS CAN APPRECIATE A BIT OF HUMAN WEAKNESS.
YOUR FRIENDS, THOUGH...IF THEY SMELL IT...
YUM.

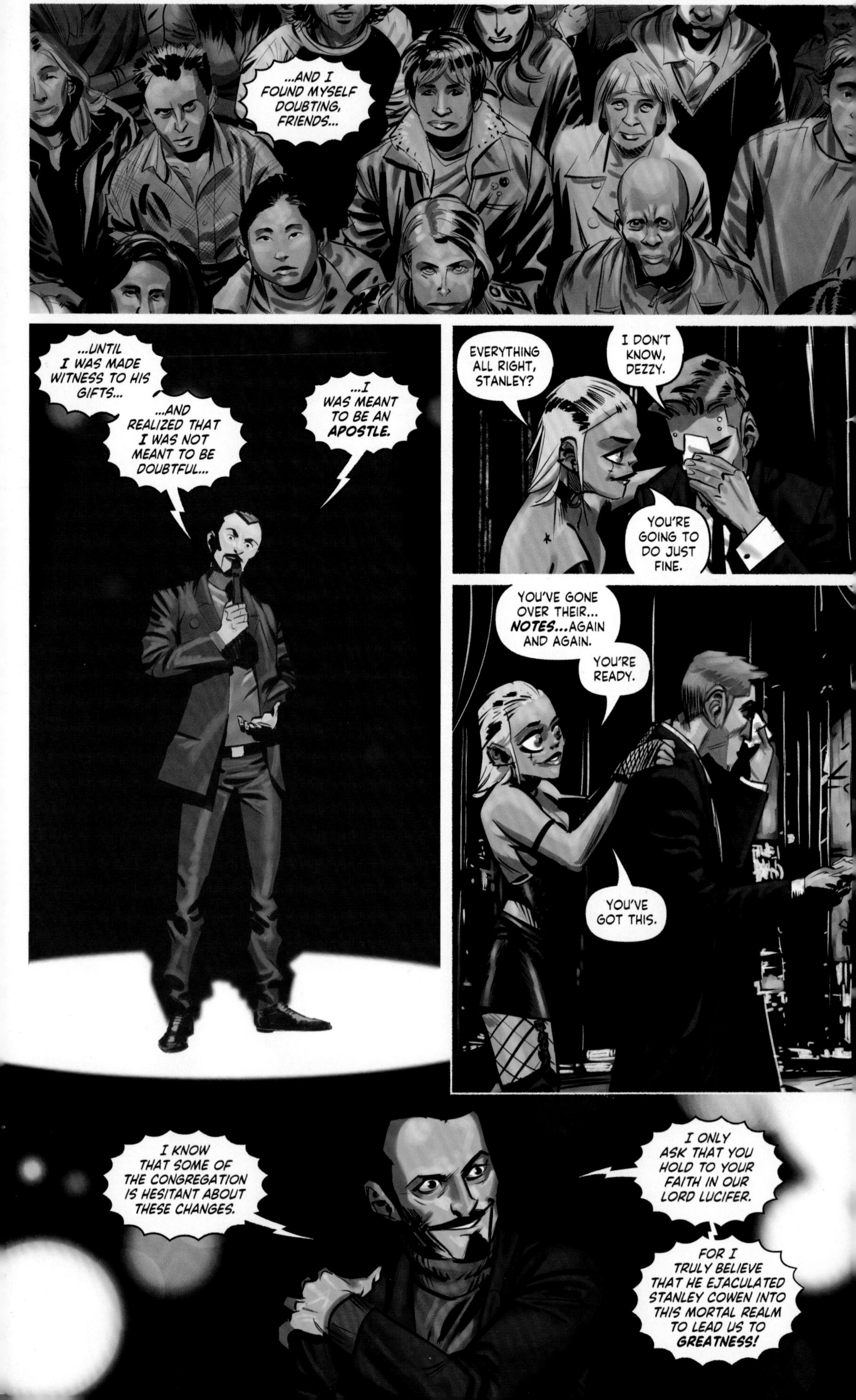

...AND I FOUND MYSELF DOUBTING, FRIENDS...
...UNTIL I WAS MADE WITNESS TO HIS GIFTS...
...AND REALIZED THAT I WAS NOT MEANT TO BE DOUBTFUL...
...I WAS MEANT TO BE AN APOSTLE.
EVERYTHING ALL RIGHT, STANLEY?
I DON'T KNOW, DEZZY.
YOU'RE GOING TO DO JUST FINE.
YOU'VE GONE OVER THEIR... NOTES...AGAIN AND AGAIN.
YOU'RE READY.
YOU'VE GOT THIS.
I KNOW THAT SOME OF THE CONGREGATION IS HESITANT ABOUT THESE CHANGES.
I ONLY ASK THAT YOU HOLD TO YOUR FAITH IN OUR LORD LUCIFER.
FOR I TRULY BELIEVE THAT HE EJACULATED STANLEY COWEN INTO THIS MORTAL REALM TO LEAD US TO GREATNESS!

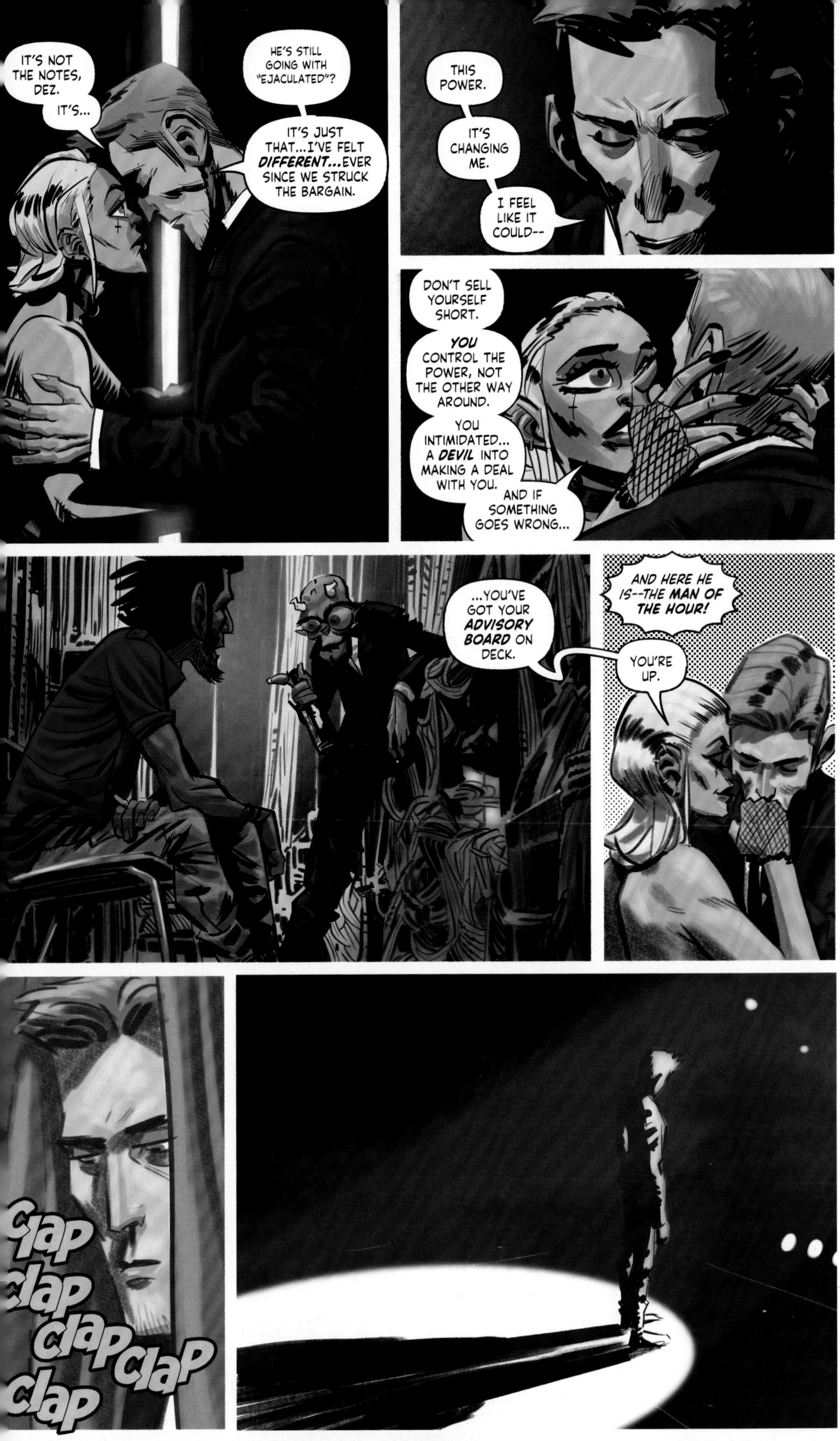
IT'S NOT THE NOTES, DEZ.
IT'S...
HE'S STILL GOING WITH "EJACULATED"?
IT'S JUST THAT...I'VE FELT DIFFERENT...EVER SINCE WE STRUCK THE BARGAIN.
THIS POWER.
IT'S CHANGING ME.
I FEEL LIKE IT COULD--
DON'T SELL YOURSELF SHORT.
YOU CONTROL THE POWER, NOT THE OTHER WAY AROUND.
YOU INTIMIDATED... A DEVIL INTO MAKING A DEAL WITH YOU.
AND IF SOMETHING GOES WRONG...
...YOU'VE GOT YOUR ADVISORY BOARD ON DECK.
AND HERE HE IS--THE MAN OF THE HOUR!
YOU'RE UP.
clap
clap
clap
clap
clap

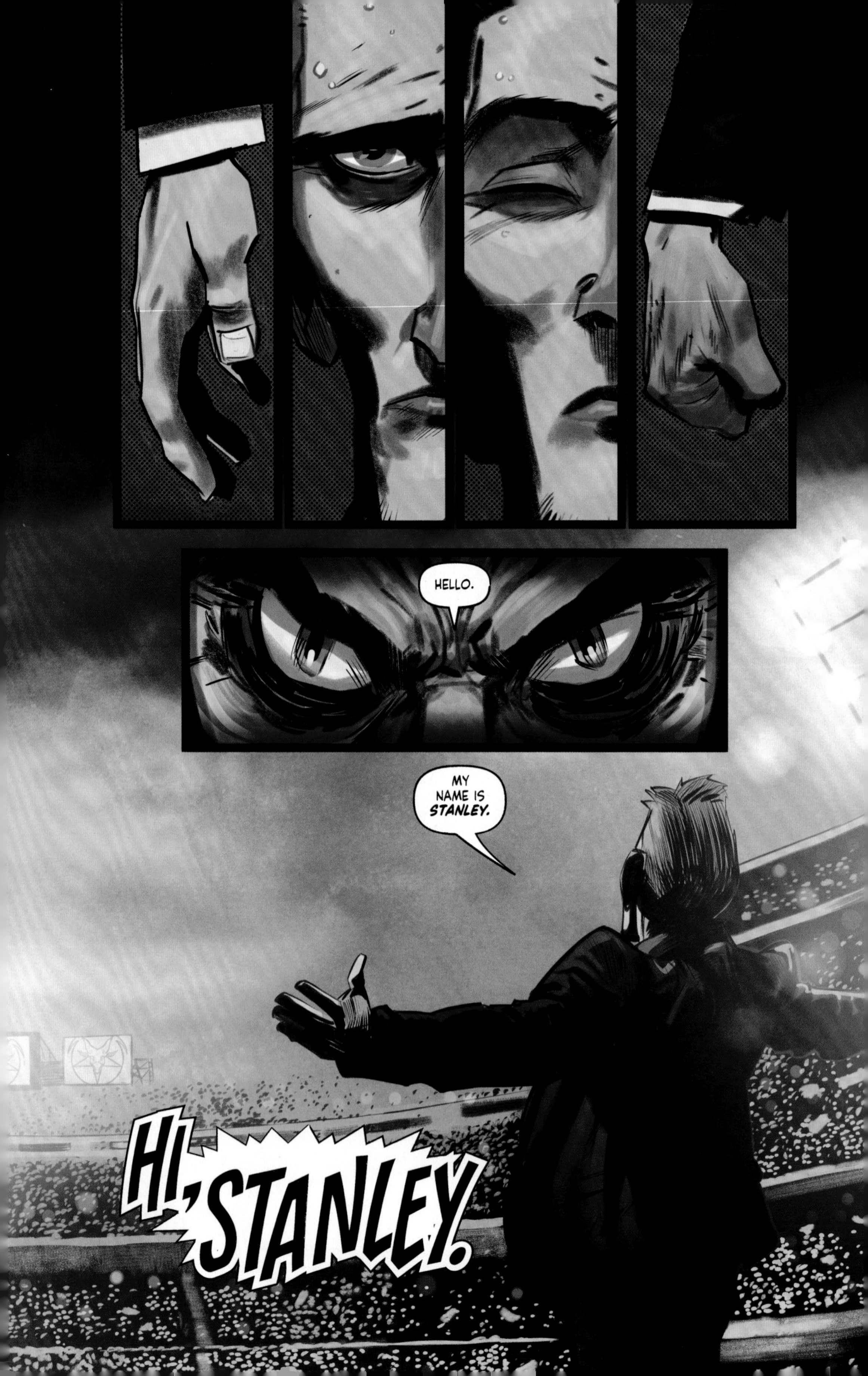
HELLO.
MY NAME IS STANLEY.
HI, STANLEY.

LUCKY DEVIL™

SKETCHBOOK

NOTES BY FRAN GALÁN

ZEDIREX

Zedirex is a peculiar type: extremely cruel but also funny. To reflect his character, I opted for some very large features that allowed me to take that personality to the extreme. Before even knowing what would happen in detail in the story, I imagined him wandering the streets, so I endowed him with a semi-human form that allowed him, in disguise, to camouflage himself among the New York crowd. This was a design that came together very quickly.

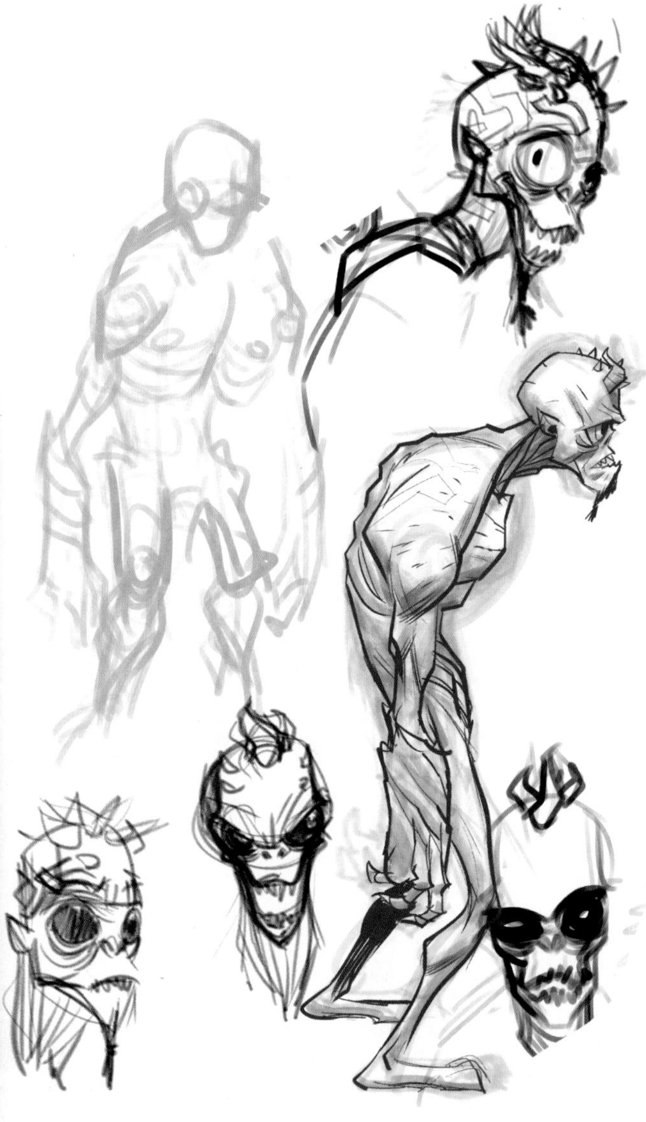

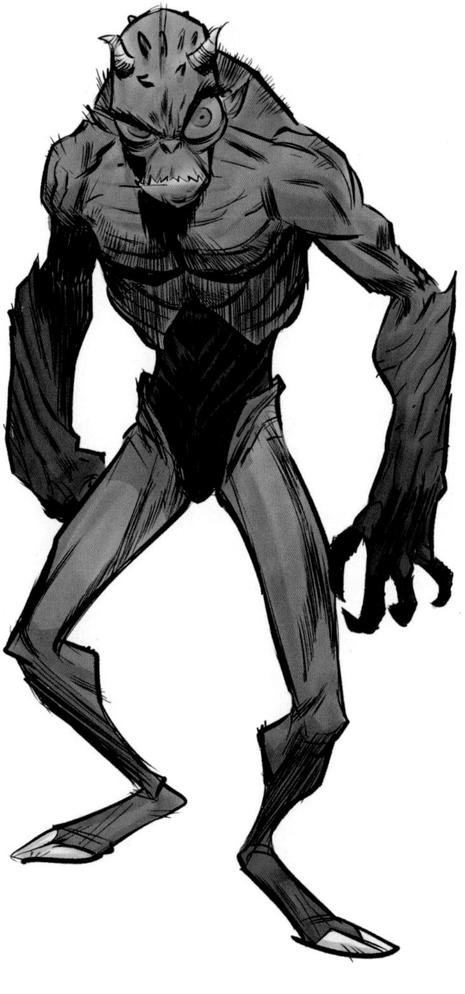

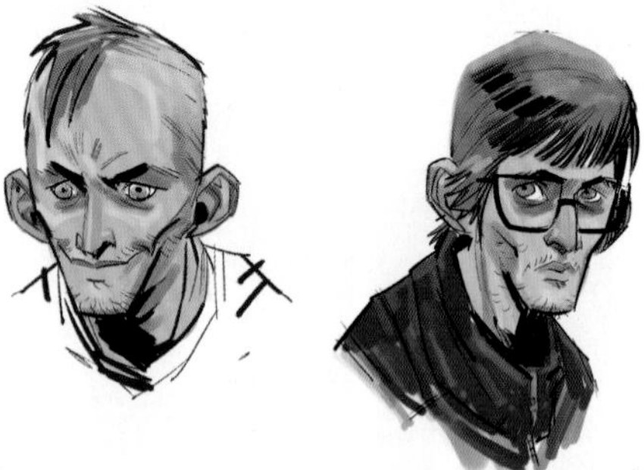

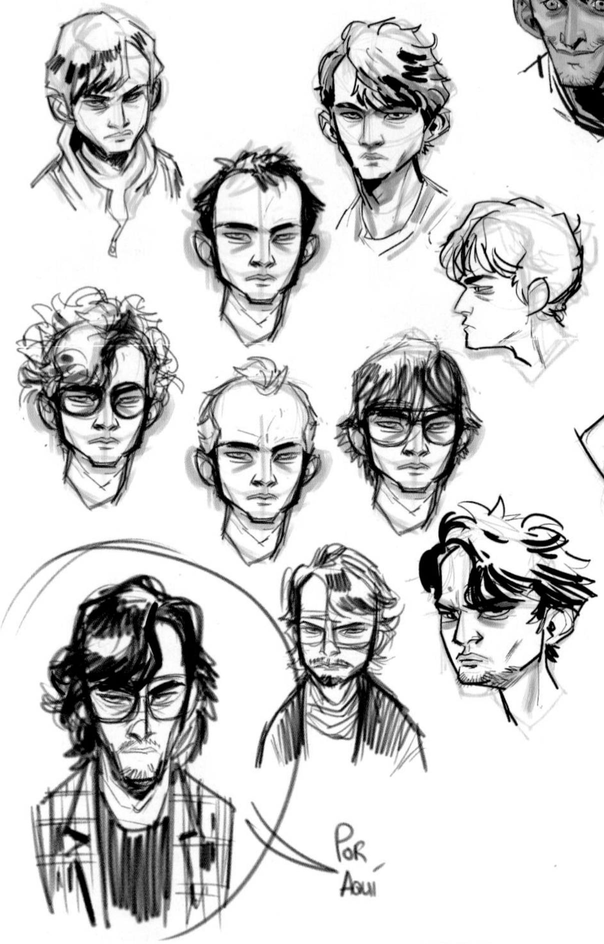
POR AQUÍ

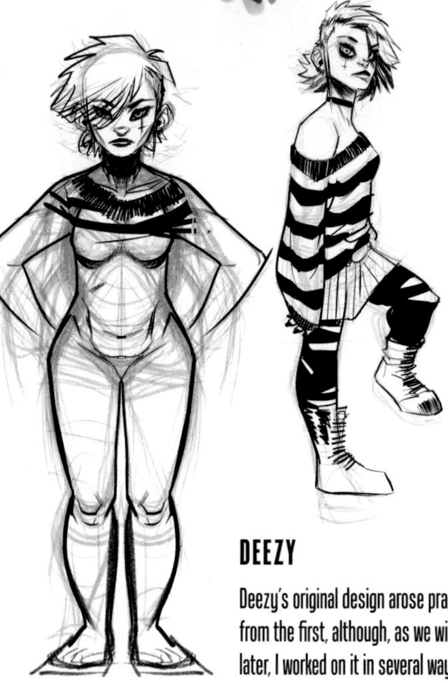

DEEZY

Deezy's original design arose practically from the first, although, as we will see later, I worked on it in several ways, finally going back to the first design, which is the one we all know.

STANLEY

Before having his final form, Stanley went through several stages in his design that were very different in appearance: blond, dark, tall, thin, obese, short . . . He had the added detail that his appearance would change as he became more confident after gaining the powers of Zedirex. I liked the idea that, even if we were seeing the new, confident Stanley, we could somehow see his old personality in the design. I decided to do it through his big ears, which are still there, although Stanley tries to camouflage them with a stylish hairstyle.

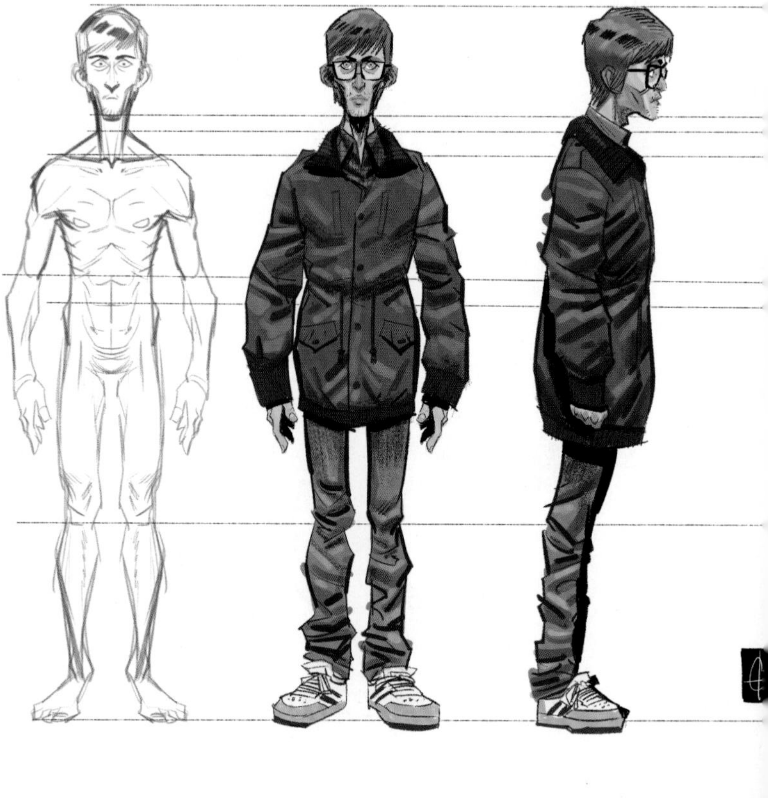

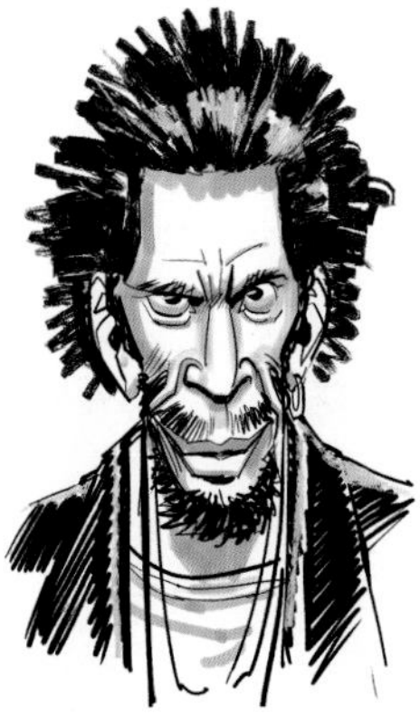

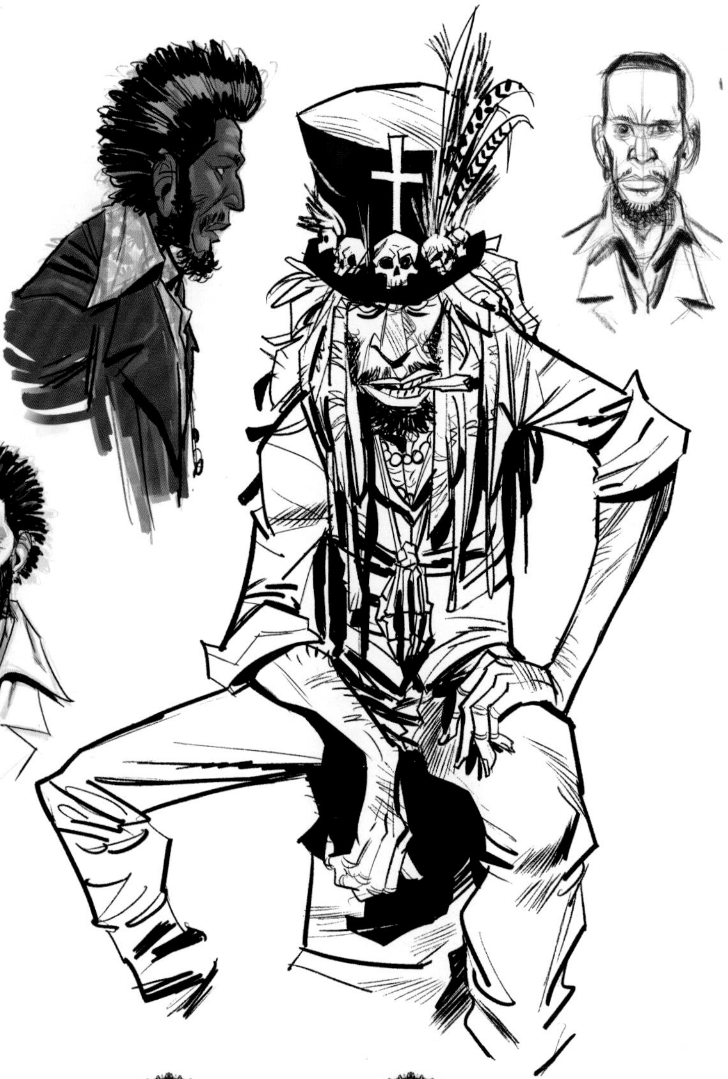

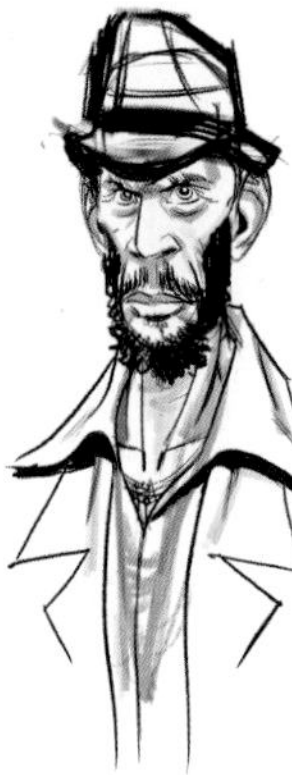

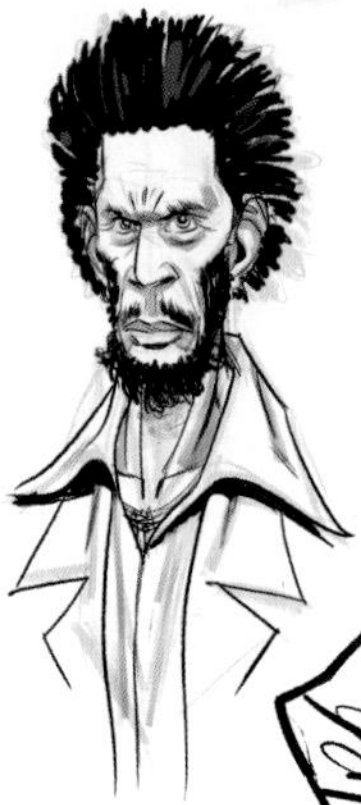

EDMOND

Although in the first draft the exorcist was described as a fortune teller, I always imagined him as a cross between a santero, a jazz man, and Bob Marley. I proposed the idea to Cullen, he liked it, and the design came out on its own. He is my favorite character and the one that I enjoy the most drawing.

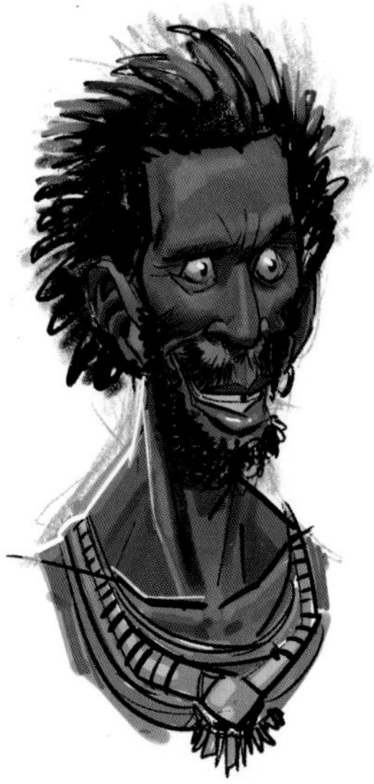

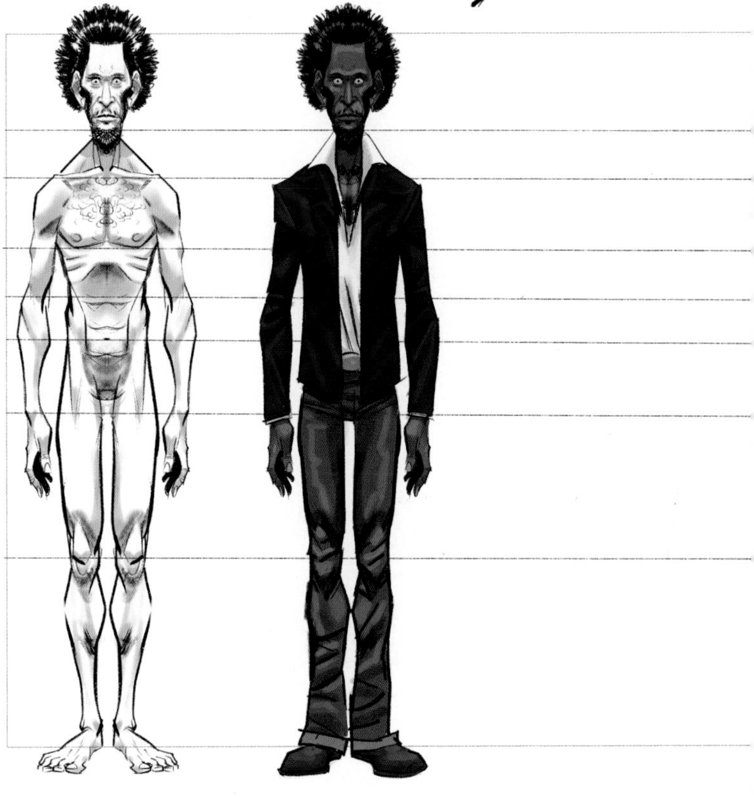

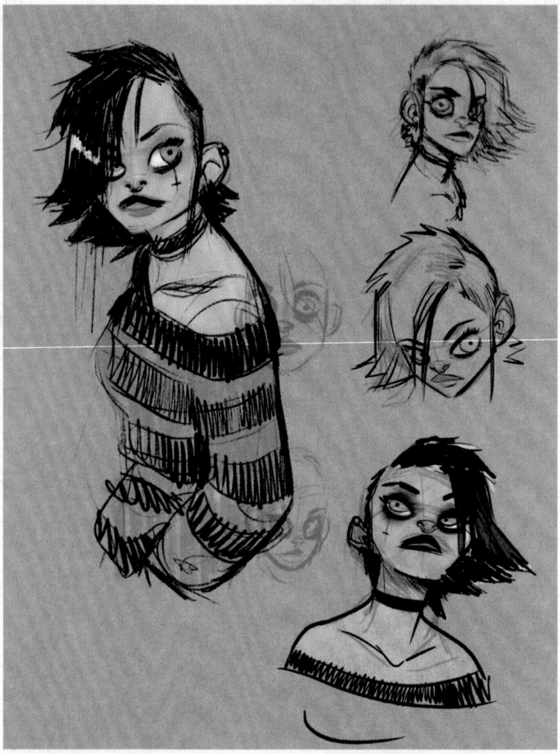

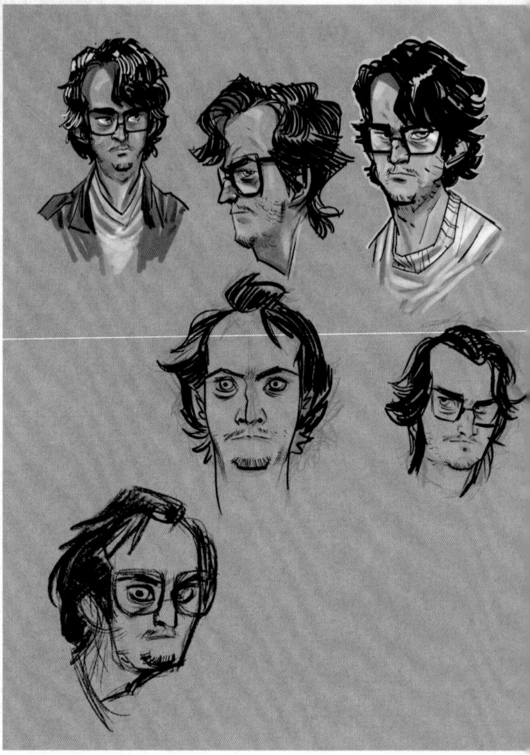

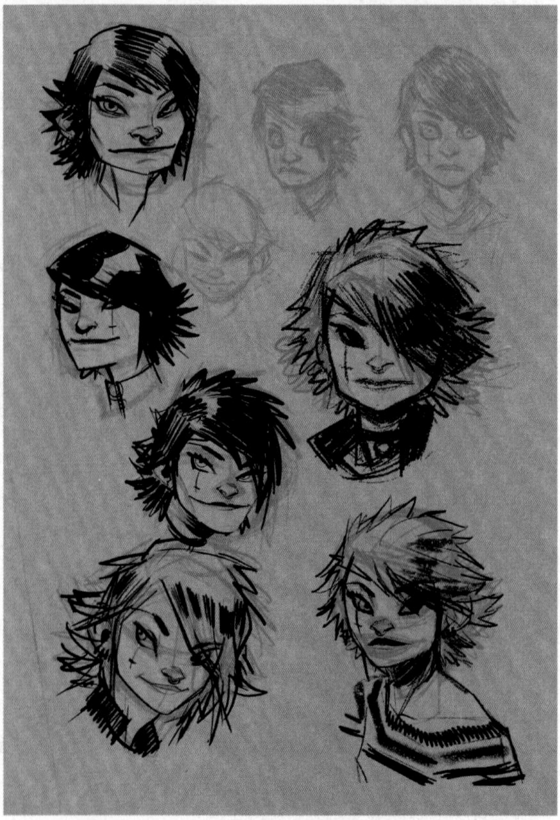

Different phases of Deezy
and Stanley's design.